The Schemer's Guide

by

Iain Ferguson

with

Edward Martin and Burt Kaufman

Foreword by Daniel P. Friedman

Schemers Inc.

This book was set by the authors in 11/14 pt Computer Modern Roman using the LaTeX document preparation system.

Publisher's Cataloguing-in-Publishing Data
Ferguson, Iain.
The Schemer's Guide/Iain Ferguson, Edward Martin, Burt Kaufman
Bibliography: p.
Includes index.
ISBN 0-9628745-7-4
1. Scheme (computer program language). 2. Functional programming. 3. Object-oriented programming. I. Martin, Edward. II. Kaufman, Burt. III. Title.
QA76.73.S34F352   1991   005.13'3   91-60023

Published by Schemers Inc.
    4250 Galt Ocean Drive, Suite 7U
    Fort Lauderdale, FL 33308
    United States of America

Contents

Foreword

I have been teaching some aspect of computer science to undergraduates since 1967. Even so I don't know much about what goes on in high school computing. I do know, however, that there are little pockets of brave souls who have opted to teach LOGO instead of BASIC or Pascal.

In the courses I teach, I always encourage my students to work in Scheme. In my undergraduate course, I don't actually require them to do so, but I assure them that they will be working on the first week's assignment long after the course is over if they choose to use imperative-style languages such as BASIC or Pascal. To grab their attention even more firmly, I tell them that in their examination during the third week of the semester they will be writing fifteen programs, in class! I once gave this test with twenty-five programs instead of fifteen, and over ten percent made perfect scores. What the students learn from this three-week introduction is that they really can acquire the ability to write fifteen programs correctly in one hour and fifteen minutes, a feat that they would not have been able to achieve in an entire semester if they were to use BASIC or Pascal.

The lesson is clear. If you want to write complicated, correct programs quickly, use Scheme. Scheme puts a premium on thinking and organizing one's thoughts. In 1972 and 1973, I taught the list processing language Lisp to graduate students in the Lyndon Baines School of Public Affairs at The University of Texas at Austin. I was curious to know if Lisp was as easy for them as it was for me. It turned out to be just that, and it was fun and different. With it they could write significant and powerful programs. Above all, it forced them to think about computation.

Then in 1975, the dialect of Scheme was developed, and my allegiance shifted. Scheme takes the clarity, elegance, and fun of Lisp, adds some technical refinements borrowed from Algol, and incorporates the flexibility of Alonzo Church's lambda calculus. So attractive are the attributes of Scheme that it is now the language used in the entry-level computer science course at many universities. There are Scheme systems for virtually every popular computer, there is an active group of researchers endeavoring to expand and improve the language, and there are now several freshman texts and other books on Scheme, with many more in preparation.

In my opinion, the reason why Scheme is becoming so popular is that it is one of the simplest languages for characterizing procedures in a clear, coherent way. This clarity is in part due to its intrinsically recursive nature and in part to its powerful abstractive facilities.

By means of data abstraction, we can write procedures without having to worry about the specific form of the procedure's arguments, thus enabling program components to survive changes in the shape of the data. Procedural abstraction frees us to solve just one problem *of a given type* rather than solving many problems. Abstraction at other levels enables us to discern and control the usually rather simple structure underlying even the most complex activity.

The power and elegance made available by Scheme's abstractive capabilities are immeasurably superior to those of the aforementioned imperative-style languages. Yet, for all its power and sophistication, Scheme is far easier to learn than any of those in common use. As a person's first encounter with computer science, Scheme is the logical choice because in addition to providing quick and easy access to raw computational power, it gives students something approaching a global appreciation of a large segment of the field of computing. Scheme is a natural and versatile language for describing algorithmic processes. It provides thinkers with the means to record systematic procedures in a succinct and organized way. It is only as an afterthought that the fruits of their labors will be run on a computer.

There are many stories that are worth telling about the economy of effort when using Scheme on a complex problem. One of my graduate students took summer employment at a research institute. During his first week on the job he went to a talk given by one of the institute's researchers. The talk was about designing and implementing a communicating, multiprocessing language, and the work was all being done in C. When asked how long it would take before he had a prototype up and running, the researcher stated that it would be at least a year. My student offered to help him develop a prototype in Scheme, and it was done in less than a week. Stories like this abound in the Scheme community. Everyone knows at least one such story. What matters is that the essence of the task and the mental effort required to produce this first prototype were held to within five days. If there was any drudgery, it was limited to just a couple of days, not a couple of years.

In imperative-style languages, programmers are bound by the language's syntax and the restrictions imposed on the semantics. They have to abide by many syntactic and semantic rules. Beginners must sit with a manual in order to get their programs right. In Scheme there is comparatively speaking almost no syntax to worry about, and what little there is can easily be changed if it doesn't happen to suit the programmer's taste. Scheme semantics is clear. This simplicity, clarity, and flexibility are what make Scheme so easy to understand. It is a very simple language.

Just about all languages have procedures, but most languages impede the writing of a large class of programs because they do not treat procedures as first-class objects that can be processed, for example, as easily as numbers. Thus high school students are, for the most part, barred from the conceptual simplification that arises from modern techniques such as object-oriented programming. Abstraction is denied to them. They spend their early years mindlessly solving lots of not-very-different, small, and uninteresting problems. They are being trained to become non-thinkers.

Until 1987 I assumed that no one at the high school level was thinking about Scheme. This meant that many students would be discouraged from entering computer science after their high school experience. However, a chance conversation with Ray Smullyan changed that. He had shown me a letter from a group of high school mathematics teachers whose students had discovered unusual solutions to combinator problems in his *To Mock a Mockingbird*. I was quite impressed and asked Ray if he thought I would be overstepping the bounds of propriety if I were to initiate a correspondence with the group. They sent me a draft of their high school computing text, based on LOGO. After reading through the draft, it was apparent that here was a group of people who were genuinely concerned with the development of good patterns of thought and the techniques of problem solving.

In the course of our correspondence they explained their ideas concerning diagramming the operation of derived functions, particularly recursive functions. They were fascinated to learn that all the features that had attracted them to LOGO were present in Scheme, and that Scheme far exceeds

LOGO in its elegance, flexibility, expressiveness, and the overwhelming sense of correctness that awaits the writer of Scheme procedures. I had the opportunity to visit them in Plantation, Florida, spend time with their amazing students, and discuss with them their dreams of changing the face of high school computing. As I left, they were talking about the possibility of designing the continuation of their computing texts so that, after spending the middle school years using LOGO, their high school students could graduate onto Scheme.

Now, two years later, they have sent me this book, the result of painstaking, informed thinking by experienced educators. All trace of LOGO has disappeared. What have survived are the methodological insights that captured my interest in those original drafts. As a result this book is a solid introduction to the power, excitement, and educational value of Scheme for the high school student.

Having become familiar with the concepts that are presented in such a carefully thought-out way, the reader will be well prepared for any college freshman course. If computer science teachers could capture the authors' vision for their subject and bring this to their students, I believe it could revolutionize the way computing is taught at the high school level and, more importantly, excite many of our best minds to a study of computer science. This book provides a convincing demonstration that Scheme removes the drudgery and the blind rule-following from the initial computing experience, restoring the sense of curiosity, fun, and wonderment, and opening the mind to much of what is exciting in computer science.

Daniel P. Friedman
Bloomington, Indiana
November, 1990

Preface

Six years ago, exasperated with the mind-numbing rule-following that characterized middle and high school computer science courses, we felt compelled to develop a course for our students which emphasized analytical thinking skills over technical wizardry. The intervening years of creation and pilot-testing have produced many pleasant surprises, not the least of which is this book.

The philosophy permeating our work in the classroom has been that programming is about solving real-world problems, and is only peripherally concerned with managing complex digital machines. In the words of the eminent computer scientist Richard W. Hamming of the Naval Postgraduate School, Monterey, CA, 'The purpose of computing is insight, not numbers.' We wanted to make students aware of the benefits of adopting a computing mode of thought without cluttering their minds with the tedious minutiae of computer control. The computing side of things was to be a means to an end, not an end in itself, so we rejected imperative-style languages such as BASIC, Pascal, and C, opting initially for LOGO.

Having chosen the vehicle, we began to explore the road ahead and we came to an unexpected realization. To our surprise, we found that it was possible to teach LOGO without resorting to the teach-by-example method that many young students find so frustrating. Prior to this we had believed that the only way to teach programming—at least at the secondary school level—was to start by having students blindly type in a program which would then form the focus of discussion, the hope being that they would eventually learn both the syntax *and* good programming practice through osmosis and pattern-recognition. Our trial classroom experience revealed to us that it was perfectly possible to follow the much more educationally desirable practice of providing students with a sound conceptual background *before* introducing new language elements.

The key to this classroom success was a remarkable pedagogical discovery. While agonizing over how to organize one of the very first introductory lessons, one of us, on the spur of the moment, suggested pressing into service some intriguing *machine* puzzles based on 'black box' problems of a kind sometimes used by high school mathematics teachers. Initially, we expected only to use such puzzles as a means to introduce certain elements of LOGO, yet their effect on our students was electrifying! So we provided more of the same, marveling at the students' appetite for such material and the speed and ease with which they were able to solve the puzzles. We soon realized that through this problem-solving activity our students were developing precisely the patterns of thinking that we had originally set out to promote. To our great delight, the students had learned in a single stride not only how to construct LOGO programs but how to construct *good* LOGO programs, correct programs with clear semantics. In the face of the mounting empirical evidence, we soon became convinced that the methodology we had hit upon could form the basis of an introductory computer science course for anyone from middle school through junior college or undergraduate school.

Since then the machine puzzles have been refined and the idiom has been extended to cover many aspects of program design. The programming language they introduce, however, is no longer LOGO but its first cousin, the Scheme dialect of the list processing language Lisp. This metamorphosis has a somewhat convoluted history. Armed with a solid conceptual framework our students were progressing more rapidly and further than we had imagined possible; they were approaching the point beyond which LOGO could not go. At the very time that we were looking for a way out of this (happy) dilemma, a series of fortunate coincidences—some of which are alluded to in the Foreword—resulted in our making contact with Professor Daniel P. Friedman of Indiana University, who is one of the independent co-discoverers of a way to represent infinite objects in Lisp and a member of the committee currently engaged in standardizing Scheme. In our developmental work we had drawn inspiration from an earlier version of his stimulating book *The Little LISPer*. Then, one action-packed day in early 1988, we were privileged to meet him in person, to witness two dynamic presentations he gave to our students, and to be bowled over by Scheme's winning combination of expressive power and elegant simplicity. Here was a language with all of LOGO's advantages and none of its restrictions. The way forward was clear!

As the book begins, we place no demands on you beyond elementary school arithmetic. The machine puzzles of which we have been speaking are introduced early in Chapter 1. You are provided with a small number of very simple-minded machines together with a means of hooking them up and challenged to construct various new machines. Then, before you know it, 300 pages have gone by, you are a more-than-competent Scheme programmer, and you have already become conversant with such advanced computer science topics as data abstraction, function abstraction, object-oriented programming, and artificial intelligence. Not only will you have familiarized yourself with Scheme, but you will have the conceptual background for more advanced work with any functional or scientific programming language.

To assist you in your studies, we have also prepared a Scheme interpreter, called *EdScheme*, with the readers of this book particularly in mind. It will enable you to implement and test all the techniques and concepts that are introduced in the pages that follow, yet it is powerful enough to support subsequent forays into more advanced scheming.

So as you start this book, arm yourself with red and black pens—the reason for the red pen will soon become apparent—and get ready for the first puzzle sequence. Somewhere in the course of studying this book you will come to understand that scheming is less a technique to be mastered and more a state of mind. At that point you may count yourself a true schemer!

$$- \, o \, O \, o \, -$$

1 The Parts List

1.1 Nuts and Bolts

Imagine that one afternoon, while sunning yourself in the back yard, you are interrupted by a passing being from outer space who asks you to explain what a sentence looks like. 'No problem,' you reply. 'A sentence is a string of words separated by spaces.'

'I see,' says the alien—who, as luck would have it, speaks English—'but what does a word look like, and what is a space?'

'Well, a word is a string of symbols, and a space is a symbol that you can't see.'

'And what is a symbol?'

The conversation seems set to go on for quite a while. Each time you try to define a term (such as 'sentence' or 'word'), you find yourself mentioning one or more new, unexplained terms. Fortunately, at this point your off-world interlocutor receives an emergency call to the other end of the galaxy and disappears in a puff of syntax.

In a sense we, the authors of this book, are faced with a problem similar to that of describing a sentence to an extraterrestrial. Our ultimate goal in this section is to explain to you how to recognize a data expression. It would be nice if we could just come right out with an explanation of the term 'data expression', but in so doing we would be hard-pressed to avoid mentioning some other new terms with which you are probably not familiar. So we begin instead by defining one primitive term in an unmistakable fashion. Then we use this term to define other terms until, eventually, we have introduced enough vocabulary to allow a description of a data expression to be given.

The primitive term with which we start the ball rolling is the word '**character**'. 'That's hardly new,' you might object. 'I already know what a character is.' Our intention, however, is to use this word in a technical sense that probably does not coincide with any other usage outside the covers of this book. So, to progress beyond this point, you must temporarily suspend your own understanding of 'character', and absorb the following declaration:

> *Each of the symbols*
>
> A B C D E F G H I J K L M N O P Q R S T U V W X Y Z
>
> a b c d e f g h i j k l m n o p q r s t u v w x y z
>
> 0 1 2 3 4 5 6 7 8 9
>
> + - * / = ? ! $ #
>
> *is a character.*

In other words, the upper-case letters 'A' through 'Z', the lower-case letters 'a' through 'z', the arabic numerals '0' through '9', and the symbols '+', '-', '*', '/', '=', '?', '!', '$', and '#' are characters. Within the context of this book, any symbol not found in the above list is *not* a character.

There is one very important point about characters that probably struck you immediately:

> *Characters are written in RED.*

So, whenever you write a symbol intending it to be a character, you should use a red pen or pencil and, of course, the symbol must be one of those listed above.

With 'character' under our belt, we move on to the term '**atom**'.

> *An atom is a string of one or more characters with no spaces between them.*[1]

For example, 'DaY' is an atom, since it is a string of three red letters (it's a red letter day—somewhat up and down, but atomic all the same), while 'an atom' is not an atom, since it includes a space, and a space is not a character (spaced-out characters aren't together enough to be atomic). 'NEEDLE', on the other hand, is not an atom since it is not printed in red—a fine point, but it serves to emphasize the requirement that atoms are made from characters and must

---

[1] For obvious practical reasons, we do not allow an atom to involve infinitely many characters; such expressions would be just too unwieldy!

therefore be entirely red. Notice that all characters are atoms, but not all atoms are characters.

Exercise 1.[2]
Which of these are atoms?

a) DNA   b) 2 + 2 = 4   c) TRUE

d) **!!*?*   e) picking nits   f) Yippee!!

We now engage in a little construction. For the moment, however, we keep you in the dark about what it is we are constructing. Our building blocks, known collectively as '**atomic elements**', are the atoms and the expression '( )' formed by a red left parenthesis followed immediately by a red right parenthesis. Our construction technique may be described as follows:

1. Draw a 'tree', a typical example of which is drawn on the right. At the top of a tree, one or more branches grow from a single branching point. The end of any branch may be considered as the top of another tree from which yet more branches grow. In our example we have drawn a  tree with three branches extending from its topmost point and a small (two-branch) 'sub-tree' extending from the leftmost branch; the tree terminates at four branch ends, called 'leaves'.

2. At each leaf, write an atomic element (in red, naturally). In the case of our example, we might obtain the diagram on the right.

3. Working from the bottom up, look at the meeting point of any branches all of whose lower ends are already labeled. At the meeting point, write the expressions from the branch ends in order, working strictly from left to right, separating them with spaces, then enclose the entire chain in red parentheses. In our example, we start with the lower left sub-tree

---

[2]Selected answers to exercises are given in the Appendix.

and write '(nuts ())' next to the point where the branches meet. The only remaining branch meeting point is at the very top of the tree. So, at that point we write the expressions '(nuts ())', 'in', and 'May' in order, separated by spaces and enclosed in red parentheses. (See the diagram on the right.)

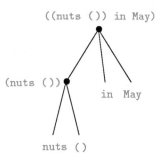

Here are three more examples of this construction technique at work. (To avoid clutter, we have omitted all 'intermediate' expressions.)

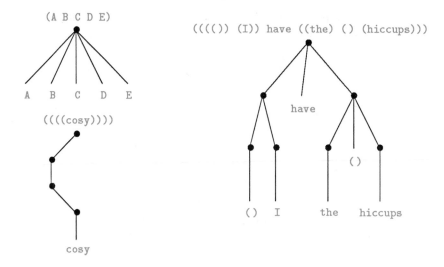

Exercise 2. Complete the following trees:

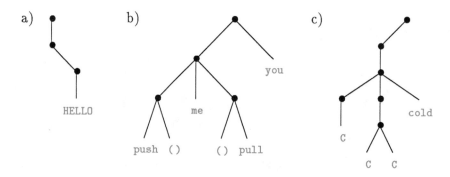

Any expression that results from this type of construction is called 'a **list**', as is the mysterious expression '()', the so-called '**null list**'. The manipulation of expressions such as these is known as 'list processing'.[3] Not only does the above technique generate lists; every list (except the null list) can be built in this way. To highlight the relationship between a list and the tree that gives rise to it we say that the tree is the **decomposition tree** of the list; it shows how the list may be decomposed into its constituent atomic elements. Thus, an expression is a list if and only if it is the null list or it has a decomposition tree.

(You have probably noticed that, as trees go, decomposition 'trees' are somewhat unusual; they grow downward. However, we prefer the term 'tree' to the perhaps more realistic 'heap' because it allows us to speak of 'branches' and 'leaves'. But inverted growth is not the only strange feature of these trees; each of their branching points is usually called the '**root**' of the sub-tree suspended from it. So the root of the whole tree is at the very top!)

To show that a given expression is a list, therefore, we have only to exhibit its decomposition tree. This may be done by reversing the three-stage construction process described above. Consider, for example, the expression '(is (this () a (list?)))'. It is obviously not the null list, so to decide if it is a list we try to decompose it. If it has a decomposition tree then the expression '(is (this () a (list?)))' itself appears at its root.

Reversing the procedure described in step 3 of the construction process, we 'strip' the outer pair of red parentheses, revealing the expressions 'is' and '(this () a (list?))'. So we draw two branches from the root, as 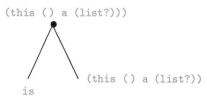 shown on the right. The left-hand branch terminates in an atomic element, namely the atom 'is'. On the other hand, '(this () a (list?))' is not an atomic element, so we must extend the right-hand branch. Stripping the outer pair of parentheses from the expression '(this () a (list?))' reveals four expressions, namely 'this', '()', 'a' and '(list?)', so we draw a branch for each one, yielding the (incomplete) tree on the left on the next page.

---

[3] As its name suggests, the programming language Lisp utilizes list processing techniques. Lists and atoms, the means of manipulating them, and Lisp itself were developed in the late 1950s and early 1960s by John McCarthy and his collaborators at the Massachusetts Institute of Technology. The dialect Scheme was invented in 1975 by Guy Lewis Steele, Jr. and Gerald Jay Sussman, also of MIT.

All the branches terminate in an atomic element except the rightmost, which ends with the expression '(list?)'. Stripping the outer pair of matching parentheses from '(list?)' reveals a single expression, 'list?', so we extend the rightmost branch as on the right below. Each branch now ends with an atomic element, so '(is (this () a (list?)))' is indeed a list.

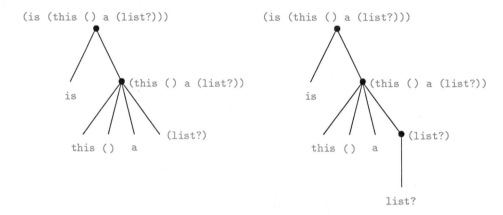

As a second example, if we were to follow a similar procedure in analyzing the expression '(to ((be) or)', then at one stage we would be faced with the expression '(be'. This contains the non-character '(', so it is not an atom. Further, it is not the null list, so it is not an atomic element. On the other hand, this expression does not involve a matching pair of red parentheses, so we cannot apply the reverse of step 3 of the construction process. We are forced to conclude that there is no way to complete the decomposition tree. Hence, our original expression has no decomposition tree, and we have shown '(to ((be) or)' not to be a list.

Exercise 3.

Which of these expressions are lists?

a) (fruit (bud) ((root)))

b) ((((on) the) way) up)

c) ((wheels) (() (within))) wheels)

d) ((no ()) moving ((parts)))

e) (two) (() pieces)

The time is now ripe for us to introduce our final item of vocabulary in this section: Atoms and lists are known collectively as **data expressions**.

Having such a collective term available allows us to simplify some of our descriptions. In particular, it makes possible a very concise description of a list. Consider, for example, the list '(() (() in) (fine) shape)'. If we were asked to demonstrate that this is a list by drawing its decomposition tree, we would first arrive at the following:

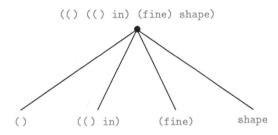

We would recognize '()' and 'shape' as atomic elements, and then go on to show that the other two expressions are the roots of sub-trees, each having leaves at which appear atomic elements. Notice that, by doing this, we would incidentally be showing that '(() in)' and '(fine)' are lists. Thus, the task of showing that '(() (() in) (fine) shape)' is a list boils down to showing that each of the four expressions '()', '(() in)', '(fine)', and 'shape' obtained at this first stage is a data expression.

This suggests the following verbal, non-pictorial description of a list:

- *The expression '()' is a list, called the* **null list.**

- *Any expression formed by a red left parenthesis, followed by one or more data expressions separated (if the number is greater than one) by spaces, followed by a red parenthesis is a list,[4] called a* **non-null list.**

- *Every list is either the null list or a non-null list.*

Despite the fact that this description defines lists in terms of data expressions, which are themselves defined in terms of lists, the above example shows that the circularity is only on the surface. If you scan back over your work with decomposition trees, you will discover that all you ever had to do was to answer a sequence of questions each of which was one of these two:

1) Is this expression an atomic element?

2) Does this red left parenthesis have a matching red right parenthesis?

---

[4] As in the case of atoms, we disallow the possibility of infinitely long lists.

The same is true when you use the above verbal description in order to check whether or not a given expression is a list.

In the spirit of the verbal description, we speak of the **number** of data expressions in a given non-null list. By that, we mean the number of branches that would be necessary *at the first stage* if we were to draw its decomposition tree. Thus, the list '(( ) (( ) in) (fine) shape)' in our earlier example contains four data expressions, namely, '( )', '(( ) in)', '(fine)', and 'shape'.

Exercise 4.

>For each of these lists, state the number of data expressions it contains and identify each one.
>
>a) (heavens (to) ((Betsy)))
>
>b) (There (are (none (left))))
>
>c) (((( ) ( ))))
>
>d) (Sorry (( ) (out) of) ((((stock)))))

So much for lists, now for processing!

1.2 The Tools of the Trade

Imagine a box. Do not concern yourself with what is in the box. Its 'insides', if indeed it contains anything at all, are hidden. We have no way of finding out what is inside and, in fact, we are not particularly interested in such matters. It is a 'black box' with no user-serviceable parts.

There are, however, two tubes protruding from the box, one (called the 'input tube') from the top, and the other (called, not surprisingly, the 'output tube') from the bottom. We temporarily represent such a box by a diagram such as the one on the right.

As you may have guessed, the input tube is designed to accept certain objects called **inputs**. Sometimes—though not always—putting an input into the input tube causes an **output** to emerge from the output tube. In a sense, the box is acting like a machine that responds to some of our actions. Since the word 'machine' is both concise and evocative, we use it to describe boxes such as the one we have just imagined. The machines in which we shall be interested are those whose inputs are data expressions.

We begin by finding out what kind of data expressions our imagined machine accepts as inputs. Since politeness costs nothing, we choose as our first input the atom 'Hello'.

The machine has not returned our pleasantry and, in fact, has indicated its displeasure in no uncertain terms. Unperturbed, we try another input, the list '(Hello)':

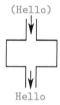

Aha! An output. Here is a record of our next three attempts. Try to figure out the relationship between the output the machine produces and the data expression that is input.

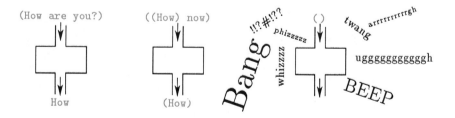

Apparently, the machine does not like atomic elements as inputs. However, for any non-null list that we input, the machine seems to output its first data expression, whether that data expression is an atom or a list. In summary, the machine accepts any non-null list, and outputs its first data expression.

Exercise 5.

What, if anything, is the output from the machine we have just described when the input is each of these?

a) (first base)   b) (((())))   c) ((snake) skin)

d) ((tiger traps) trap) (tigers))

e) ((((garbage) in) () ((garbage))) (out))

The above machine is but the first of many. Thus, to distinguish it from all the others, we give it a name. Since the machine outputs the *first* data expression in any non-null list input into it—and since, coincidentally, it is the *first* machine we have discussed—we give it the name '**first**'.[5] You will no doubt have noticed that the word '**first**' is not printed in red. Just as data expressions such as the atom 'blue' are written in red, so we insist that

The names of machines are written in BLACK.

We print everything that should be considered black using the **sans serif bold** typeface.[6] In handwriting, as you might expect, you should use a regular pencil or black pen when you wish to write in black. Incidentally, the principal typeface we use in this text (the typeface in which this parenthetical remark is written) is called 'roman',[7] and should be regarded as being colorless, not least because it makes all our explanations transparently clear!

On the right we have drawn an incomplete 'machine diagram' of **first**. A complete machine diagram consists of an input, an output, and a machine with its name written (in black) inside it. However, the diagram includes no mention of any input. What could that input be? Since **first** accepts only non-null lists, we know that it cannot be an atom or the null list. However, we know that the first data expression in the input must be the atom 'out', because that is the output. Thus the input must be

---

[5]In Scheme, as in other dialects of Lisp, this machine is often given the name used in the original versions of Lisp, namely, '**car**'. Historically, this was an abbreviation for 'contents of address register' in recognition of the fact that programmers of the first computer to run Lisp could refer to what were called the 'address' and 'decrement' parts of a memory location. We prefer the name '**first**' since it is more descriptive of the machine's action.

[6]The word 'sans' (pronounced 'sŏn') is French for 'without'. A 'serif' (pronounced 'SEH-riff') is a printer's term for the small lines used to finish off a main stroke of a letter, as at the top and bottom of the letter 'M'.

[7]Actually, the full name of the typeface is 'Computer Modern Roman'.

a non-null list whose first data expression is the atom 'out'. Here are three of the many possibilities:

(out)

(out and out lies)

(out (( ) out) ((damn) spot))

Exercise 6.

What (red) data expressions are missing from these machine diagrams? (In parts (b) and (c) there are many possible answers. Give just one for each part.)

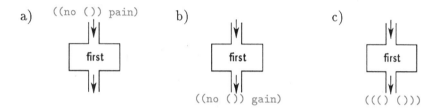

In our discussion so far we have made no mention of where the input to a **first** machine comes from; there is no reason, for example, why it could not be the output from another **first** machine. Let us see what happens when the list '((thick) skin)' is fed through *two* **first** machines one after another, that is, when the list is input to one **first** machine, and the output from that machine is immediately input to a second **first** machine. Our diagrammatic representation of this situation on the right shows a so-called **hook-up** of two **first** machines, the connection of the upper output tube to the lower input tube indicating that the input to the second machine is the output from the first.

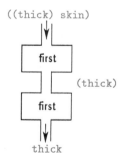

The diagram shows that, when the input to the upper machine is the list '((thick) skin)', the output is the list '(thick)'. Then, when the list '(thick)' is input to the second machine in the hook-up, the output is the atom 'thick'. Recording the intermediate step (the list '(thick)'), as in the diagram above, is not strictly necessary—it is nothing more than a 'stepping stone' to finding the final output—but including such intermediate results can often be helpful in determining the output, especially when working with more complex hook-ups.

Exercise 7.

    a) The diagram below shows that the list '(log jam)' is not a suitable input to a hook-up of two **first** machines. Why is it not suitable?

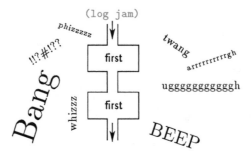

    b) One of these sentences describes *all* the suitable inputs (that is, inputs that produce an output) to a hook-up of two **first** machines. Which one?

    (i) Any non-null list containing at least one data expression.

    (ii) Any non-null list containing at least one list.

    (iii) Any non-null list whose first data expression is a list.

    (iv) Any non-null list whose first data expression is a non-null list.

    (v) Any non-null list that contains only non-null lists.

We can of course hook up more than two machines, and indeed we do so in the next exercise. Before contemplating such a possibility, however, let us simplify the task of drawing machine diagrams by stylizing them into the form on the right, where the tubes and arrows have been replaced by single arrows with centered arrowheads and the 'body' of the machine has been replaced by a circle. As you will note from the next exercise, in these stylized diagrams we write the name of a machine inside the circle.

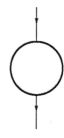

Exercise 8.

    What is missing from the machine diagrams at the top of the next page? (We are not referring here to the intermediate outputs, although you may find it helpful to determine these as you answer this question. In part (b) there are many possible answers. Give just one of them.)

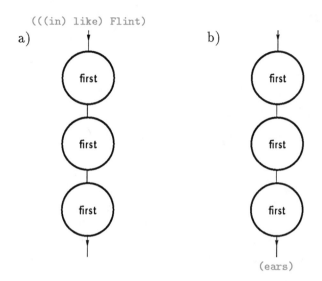

a) (((in) like) Flint)

b) (ears)

Exercise 9.

> To obtain the atom 'See' as an output of a machine hook-up, when the list '((See))' is input, we may use the double hook-up on the right.

> Draw a diagram of a machine hook-up which outputs the atom 'See' when the input is

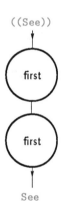

>   a) ((See) how they (run))
>   b) ((See how they) run)
>   c) (((See how) they) run)

We now introduce a new machine, which, like the **first** machine, takes one input. Here are some machine diagrams showing the new machine in operation. Try to guess what it does.

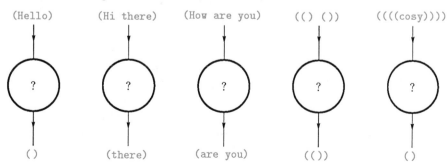

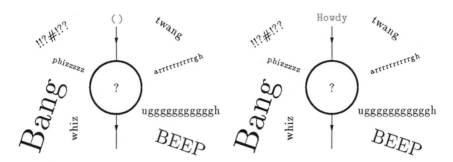

The new machine seems to agree with the **first** machine in its dislike of atomic elements. In fact, just as **first** does, this machine accepts only non-null lists as its input. When given a suitable list as an input, the machine outputs a new list that is the input list with its first data expression removed. In other words, it takes a non-null list and *erases* the first data expression, outputting the *rest* of the input list. We therefore call it the 'rest machine'.[8]

Exercise 10.

What, if anything, is the output from the **rest** machine when the input is each of these?

    a) `(sliced ham)`   b) `indigestible`

    c) `((Off with her) head)`   d) `(((Give (me))) five)`

    e) `(((( )) ((( )))))`

Exercise 11.

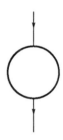

    a) Find an input and an output for the machine pictured on the right so that the diagram is correct regardless of whether the machine is labeled '**first**' or '**rest**'.

    b) Describe *all* the possible data expressions that could serve as inputs in part (a).

Exercise 12.

Is there an input that will make the **rest** machine output the atom 'ouch!'? If so, write such an input. If not, explain why not.

---

[8]Some implementations of Scheme call this machine 'cdr' (pronounced 'could-er'). Once again, this is a throwback to the early days of Lisp. It abbreviates the phrase 'contents of decrement register' (see the footnote on page 10). We prefer the more descriptive name 'rest'.

Exercise 13.

Each of these machine diagrams has one or more parts missing. Complete as many of the diagrams as possible.

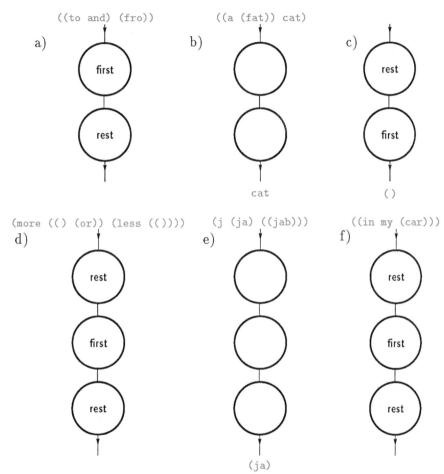

In mathematical terms, machines such as **first** and **rest** are known as **functions**. Using this vocabulary, we can speak of 'the *function* **first**' when referring to the machine whose name is '**first**' (notice that we continue to write the machine's name in black), thereby making it doubly clear that we are *not* referring to the atom '`first`'. We also remark that a hook-up of two or more functions is often itself referred to as a function. Now, it might appear that a function consisting of a hook-up of, say, a **first** machine with a **rest** machine is really two functions rather than one. However, if the hook-up were placed in a box (so that you could not see inside) then the result would be indistinguishable from a single function. Thus it is perfectly reasonable to refer to hook-ups as functions. It is indisputable, though, that there is a distinction between 'simple' functions (such as **first** and **rest**) and 'hook-up' functions. So, to preserve that distinction, we call the 'simple' functions **primitive functions**. Then the term 'function' alone will refer to functions in general, whether primitive or 'hook-up'.

Exercise 14.

> Draw a machine diagram for a function such that, when its input is the list '(tea ((for) two))', the output is

> a) the atom 'tea'   b) the list '(for)'

> c) the atom 'for'   d) the atom 'two'

As Exercise 14 suggests, the functions **first** and **rest** allow us to 'dissect' lists in the sense that, given any non-null list and any data expression from within the list, we can construct a function composed of the functions **first** and **rest** that will 'extract' the data expression in question from the list. Conversely, the function we are about to consider enables us to 'build' lists. Unlike the functions **first** and **rest**, however, the new function, called 'cons', takes two inputs. See if you can figure out what it does.

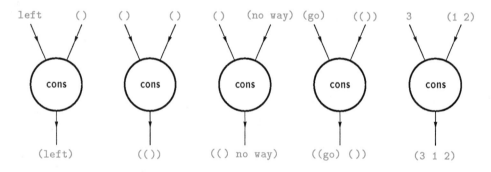

In the machine diagrams above we have carefully avoided inputs that would not be acceptable to the function **cons**. You will need to know, however, which inputs produce an output, and which do not. Since the function **cons** has two inputs and the allowable data expressions are different for each input, we must give ourselves a way to distinguish between the two. Referring to the left-hand input as the '*first* input' and the right-hand input as the '*second* input', the suitable inputs to the function **cons** are as follows: The first may be any data expression and the second may be any list. The function **cons** constructs a new list out of its two inputs by inserting the first input as the first data expression in the second input. (In fact, '**cons**' is short for 'construct'.)

Exercise 15.

Complete as many of these machine diagrams as possible.

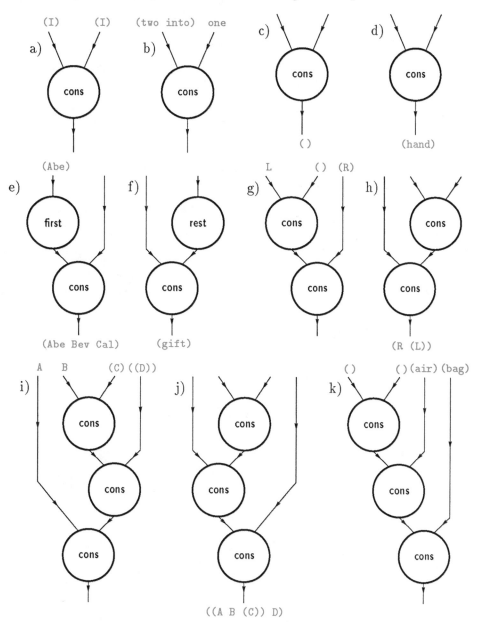

The word 'cons' is often used as a verb, as for example in 'when the atom "a" is *consed* onto the list "(b c)", the list "(a b c)" is produced', 'the function *conses* the atom "a" onto the list "(b c)"', or 'the list "(a b c)" is obtained by *consing* the atom "a" onto the list "(b c)"'.

Exercise 16.

Two machine diagrams are drawn below. For each one,

(i) say what types of data expression are suitable as the first input to **cons**.

(ii) say what types of data expression are suitable as the second input to **cons**.

(iii) experiment by entering pairs of suitable data expressions into the hook-up; then describe in words the relationship between the inputs and the output.

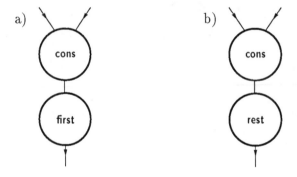

Exercise 17.

Draw a machine diagram of each of these functions. (Your diagrams should include no inputs or outputs and should perform as described no matter what acceptable inputs are used.)

a) A function that takes two inputs, the first any data expression, and the second any non-null list. The function should output a new list constructed by replacing the first data expression in the second input with the first input.

b) A function that takes two inputs, both non-null lists. The function should output a new list constructed by replacing the first data expression in the second input with the first data expression in the first input.

   c) A function that takes one input, which must be a list con-
      taining at least two data expressions. The function should
      output the second data expression in the list.

   d) A function that takes two inputs, the first a list containing
      at least two data expressions, and the second any non-null
      list. The function should output a new list constructed by
      replacing the first data expression in the second input with
      the second data expression in the first input.

With the primitive functions **first, rest** and **cons**, we can manipulate data
expressions, building and dissecting lists of any degree of complexity. We
now introduce a new type of function, called a **predicate function**,[9] which
does not so much manipulate data expressions as react to them. All that a
predicate function ever outputs, provided of course it is given suitable inputs,
is the atom '#t' or the atom '#f'. Collectively, these two data expressions are
known as **boolean objects**[10] (or **booleans**, for short).

Here is **atom?**, the first of three primitive predicate functions, in action:

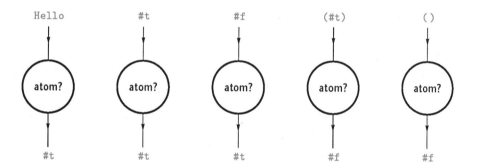

As you have probably guessed from the machine diagrams above, any data
expression is suitable as an input to this new function. It outputs the boolean
'#t' if and only if the input is an atom, otherwise it outputs the boolean '#f'.
In a sense the function **atom?** asks the yes/no question, 'Is the input data
expression an atom?' Outputting the boolean '#t' is the function's way of
saying 'Yes', and outputting the boolean '#f' is its way of saying 'No'.

---

[9] From the Latin *predicare*, 'to make known'.
[10] In honor of the English logician and mathematician George Boole (1815–1864). Boolean
objects are to computer science what truth values are to symbolic logic.

Exercise 18.

What, if anything, would the output be if the input to the function **atom?** were

a) `bomb`   b) `(nine)`   c) `31,208`

d) `(Fred's ((fleas) flipflopped))`

e) `(She (sells) (sea (shells)))`

Exercise 19. Complete the machine diagram on the left below.

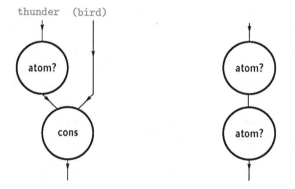

Exercise 20.

The incomplete machine diagram on the right above shows a hook-up of two machines. Explain why the output of this hook-up is always the boolean '`#t`', no matter what data expression is input.

The second predicate function we consider is called '**null?**'. As in the case of the function **atom?**, its name gives the game away. The function **null?** only accepts lists as inputs. If its input is the null list, it outputs the boolean '`#t`', but if the input list is non-null, the function outputs the boolean '`#f`'. Here are some examples:

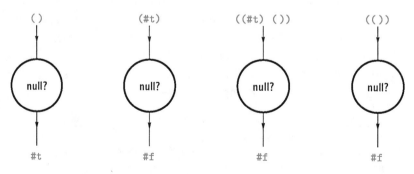

Exercise 21. Complete as many of these machine diagrams as possible.

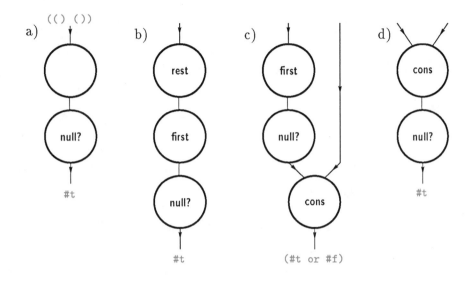

Exercise 22.

The two diagrams below show hook-ups of a **null?** and an **atom?** machine. For each one,

- describe all the data expressions, if there are any, that will cause the hook-up to produce an output.

- describe the output produced, if any.

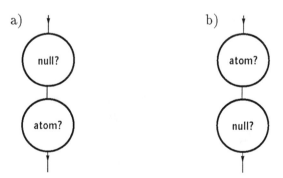

The third of our three primitive predicate functions is called 'eq?' (pronounced 'eek'). It takes two inputs, both of which must be atoms; it does not accept lists. Here are some examples that show the function **eq?** in action:

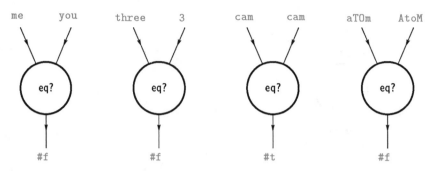

As with the function **cons**, we refer to the left-hand input of the function **eq?** as the 'first input' and the right-hand input as the 'second input'. Note that when both inputs are the same atom, the function **eq?** outputs the boolean '#t'. However, if the first and second inputs are different atoms then the function **eq?** outputs the boolean '#f'.

Exercise 23. Complete as many of these machine diagrams as possible.

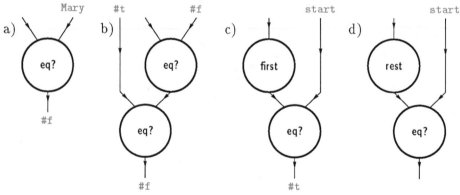

Exercise 24.

    In the machine hook-up drawn on the right, can the output ever be the boolean '#f'? Why or why not?

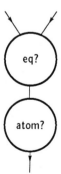

We have chosen to name predicate functions by 'blackened' atoms that terminate with a question mark so as to make them easily identifiable when, in a little while, we find ourselves in situations where the names of various kinds of functions are jumbled together. An alternative convention used by some versions of Lisp is to end each predicate function's name with a 'P'—which, as you might guess, stands for 'predicate'.

The six primitive functions **first, rest, cons, atom?, null?** and **eq?** allow us to do all sorts of interesting things with data expressions. In particular, we can construct some extremely complicated functions by hooking-up primitive functions. There remain, however, a large number of simple-looking functions we would like to build that just cannot be constructed from the primitive functions alone. Here is a description of one such function:

> The function takes any data expression as its input. The output is always the atom 'gold', regardless of the input.

Of course, given any specific list in which the atom 'gold' puts in an appearance, we could easily construct a machine diagram for a function that outputs the required atom. For example, given the list '(two gold teeth)', the machine diagram on the right pictures a function that will extract the desired 'gold'. If the input is the list '(heavy gold (bars))', then the same function does the job. But what if the input is the list '(gold and silver)'? Then, of course, the above function would output the atom 'and' instead of performing as required. Worse still, it is perfectly possible for the input not to involve the atom 'gold' at all, in which case there would be no way to construct a function using only our six primitives functions. You can't extract 'gold' if it's not there!

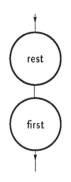

The difficulty lies in the fact that the function we have imagined, and then described above, outputs the atom 'gold' *no matter what the input*. In order to allow the construction of such machines we are forced to introduce a new type of function, called a **constant function**. Note that we say a new *type* of function; there are many constant functions, of which one is the function described above. What shall we call this function? It is very tempting to call it '**Midas**', since it turns everything into 'gold'. For each data expression, however, there is a corresponding constant function, and we would be hard-pressed to come up with a similar classical allusion for every conceivable data expression! It would be helpful if the name we chose were in some way indicative of the behavior of the function. Our next thought therefore might be to call our function 'the constant function **gold**', and to picture it in machine diagrams as shown on the right.

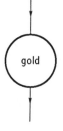

Unfortunately, it would not be long before we would run into serious difficulties if we settled on such a method of naming constant functions. Consider, for example, the function that constantly outputs the atom 'first'. If we were to call this 'the constant function **first**', then there would be ample scope for confusion, to put it mildly! The machine diagram for the *constant* function **first** would be identical to the machine diagram for the *primitive* function **first**. Would that matter? Of course it would; the two functions behave quite differently. Given the input list '(Heads or tails)', the constant function **first** outputs the atom 'first', whereas the primitive function **first** outputs the atom 'Heads'. To avoid such problems we propose the following. We will indicate that a function is a constant function by preceding its name with a little inverted triangle. Using this convention, the function that constantly outputs the atom 'first' would be given the name '▽**first**',[11] and it would be pictured as shown on the right.

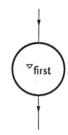

As an example of a constant function in action, consider the (incomplete) machine diagram on the right, where we must determine the identity of the lower machine. Given that the input to the hook-up is the list '(A B C)' and the upper machine is a **first** machine, its output—and therefore the input to the lower machine— will be the atom 'A'. This means that the lower machine has very little to work with in order to output the atom 'C'. Clearly, none of our six primitive functions outputs the atom 'C' when the atom 'A' is input. So we are forced to the conclusion that the lower machine must be the constant function ▽**C**.

The next exercise investigates hook-ups of constant and primitive functions. Before you tackle it, we point out that constant functions have only one input. In fact, among our six primitive functions and all the constant functions, only two take two inputs, namely, the functions **cons** and **eq?**. So the two-input function in part (c) must be one of these two.

---

[11] For the moment, we suggest that you read '▽**first**' in phrases such as 'the constant function ▽**first**' simply as 'first'. Later, once we have introduced the keyword '**quote**', an alternative reading will be suggested.

Exercise 25.

Complete as many of these machine diagrams as possible.

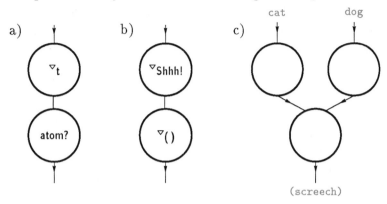

We needed the constant functions so that we could construct certain types of function that were not constructible without them. Are they enough, however? Do we now have all the necessary tools to construct any function we might need? The answer is still 'No', as the following simple example shows. Suppose we want to construct a machine which behaves like this:

Input: any data expression

Output: $\begin{cases} \texttt{atom} & \text{if the input is an atom} \\ \texttt{list} & \text{if the input is not an atom.} \end{cases}$

At first sight, it might appear that such a function could easily be constructed in terms of the primitive function **atom?** and the constant functions ▽**atom** and ▽**list**. In fact no arrangement of these or any other primitive or constant functions will produce the desired function. Try it!

In machine diagrams, we want something like the situation pictured on the right. To make sense of this diagram we need some kind of device, activated by the **atom?** machine, that will channel the input to one of the two constant machines, thereby triggering it to produce the correct output. In particular, if the output from the **atom?** machine is the boolean

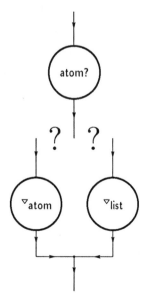

'#t' then the device should send the original input through the ∇**atom** machine; on the other hand, if the output from the **atom?** machine is the boolean '#f' then the device should send the original input through the ∇**list** machine. The device in question is called an **if-switch**, and it operates as shown below:

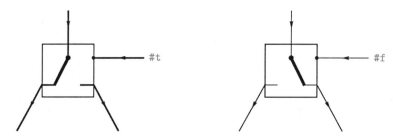

The if-switch is controlled by the right-hand input, known as the **control input**, which, since it must be either the boolean '#t' or the boolean '#f', is usually the output from a predicate function. When the control input is the boolean '#t', the arm inside the if-switch swings to the left, making a bridge between the top input and the left-hand output (see the left-hand diagram above), and when the control input is the boolean '#f', the arm swings to the right, connecting the top input to the right-hand output (see the right-hand diagram above).

It is now an easy task to construct the function we have been seeking. The following diagram not only pictures the function, but it also shows how it behaves when the input is the list '(Franz)':

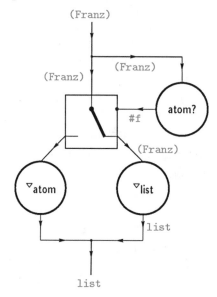

Notice that the input to our 'atom-or-list' function is 'split'. One copy of it enters the **atom?** machine, the output from which activates the if-switch; the other copy enters the if-switch itself, which diverts it either to the ▽**atom** machine or the ▽**list** machine, according to the output from the **atom?** machine. 'Split inputs' are used quite frequently in what follows.

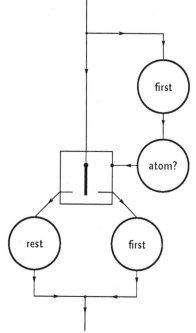

Exercise 26.

What is the output from the function whose machine diagram is shown on the right when its input is the list

a) `(() () ())`

b) `(((Fred)))`

c) `(J (F) ((K)))`

d) `((((a))) ((b)) (c) d)`

Functions whose machine diagrams involve one or more if-switches are called **conditional functions**. For simplicity's sake, in machine diagrams we reduce the if-switch to

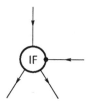

where a smaller circle is used in order to emphasize that the if-switch is not a function; as before, if the control input is the boolean '#t', then the input entering the top of the if-switch is diverted down the left-hand output, and if it is the boolean '#f', then it is diverted down the right hand output.

Exercise 27.

What is the output from the function whose machine diagram is shown on the right when its input[12] is the list

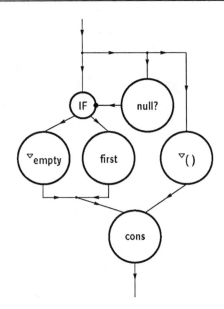

a) ( )

b) (( ))

c) ((a b) (c d))

d) (a b c d)

Exercise 28.

Draw a machine diagram for a function that behaves like this: The function takes as its only input any non-null list containing at least two data expressions, the second of which must be an atom. If the second data expression in the input list is the atom 'bingo' then the function outputs a list containing exactly one data expression, namely, the first data expression of the input list; otherwise the function outputs a list containing exactly one data expression, namely, the second data expression of the input list.

PROBLEM SET 1

1. Notice that, no matter what data expression is used as its input, the function represented by the machine diagram at the top of the next page always outputs the list '((A) B C)'. Notice also that the only primitive function involved is the function **cons**, and that all the constant functions have outputs that are atomic elements.

---

[12]This time the input is split three ways, one copy going to the if-switch, one to the **null?** machine, and one to the $^{\triangledown}$( ) machine.

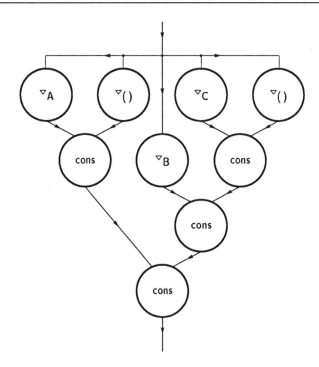

For each of these lists, design a one-input hook-up that always outputs the given list, no matter what the input is. Make each hook-up so that it involves only the function **cons** and constant functions that output atomic elements.

  a) (A (B))

  b) ((A B))

  c) ((A B) C)

2. Draw a machine diagram of a predicate function that takes one input, any non-null list, and outputs the boolean '#t' if and only if the input contains exactly one data expression. If the input contains more than one data expression, then the function should output the boolean '#f'.

3. Draw a machine diagram of a function that inputs any list containing at least three data expressions and outputs the list obtained from the input by interchanging the first and third data expressions.

4. Use if-switches to construct a function that behaves like this: The function takes one input. If the input is an atom, then the function outputs a list

containing exactly one data expression, namely, the input. If the input
is the null list then the function outputs the null list. If the input is a
non-null list then the function outputs the first data expression whenever
the first data expression is a list, or the list containing only that first data
expression otherwise.

$$- \circ \, O \, \circ -$$

1.3 Trade Talk

We are now ready to develop a notation that will allow us to describe machines
and hook-ups without having to go to the trouble of drawing machine diagrams. Ultimately, this notation will not only save us a considerable amount
of time and effort but will, in addition, allow us to explore ideas that are hard
to express in terms of machine diagrams alone.

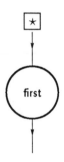

In the machine diagram on the right we have drawn
the symbol '⋆' *in black* where normally one might expect
there to be a data expression. Is this a 'complete' machine
diagram? Clearly it is not. How must it be changed so that
a complete machine diagram results? First we must replace
'⋆' by a suitable data expression and then we must indicate
the output. We discuss the output in a moment. We have
said that '⋆' must be replaced by a data expression, but
will any data expression do? For example, could we replace
it by the list '(nut)'? Yes! Could we replace it by the atom 'bolt'? No!
The function **first** only accepts non-null lists as its input. In other words, the
only suitable replacements for '⋆' are non-null lists.

To complete the machine diagram we must also indicate the output, which
in this case, since we are not dealing with a constant function, will depend on
the input. Specifically, the output will be the first data expression in the input
list. Suppose, for example, that we replace '⋆' by the list '(nut)'. Then,
of course, we must write the atom 'nut' as the output. Similarly, if '⋆' is
replaced by the list '(A B C)' then we must write the atom 'A' as the output.
In general, as we have already noted, the output is the first data expression in
the replacement for '⋆'. We can make this explicit in the machine diagram
by indicating the relationship between the input and the output as shown on
the left at the top of the next page:

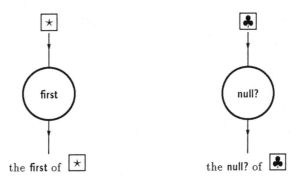

Similarly, we might indicate the general relationship between the input and output of the **null?** function as shown on the right above.

Clearly it would be to our advantage if we could simplify such machine diagrams. We have two suggestions. First, we find alternatives to symbols such as '⋆' and '♣'. Such symbols, called **variables**, serve as placeholders for data expressions and are invaluable to our discussion, but the particular symbols we have chosen are difficult to draw. Instead, therefore, we will use black bold italic letters such as '***a***', '***F***', '***y***' and '***r***'. (Of course, we do not expect *you* to write in bold italic! Instead, we suggest you write variables in lower-case cursive, using a black pencil or pen.) Here are some examples of machine diagrams whose inputs are represented by variables:

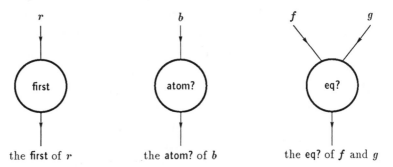

The same notation may be used in machine hook-ups. Consider, for example, the hook-up of the functions **first** and **atom?** shown on the left at the top of the next page. Suppose we replace '***y***' in this diagram by the list '(bomb)'. Then the function **first** outputs the atom 'bomb'. This is now the input to the function **atom?**, and so, since it is an atom, the output from the hook-up is the boolean '#t'. In general, if '***y***' represents the input to the function **first**, then the output of the top machine is the **first** of ***y***. The fact that this is then the input to the function **atom?** means that the output from the hook-up is the **atom?** of the **first** of y. We indicate this as shown in the machine diagram in the center below.

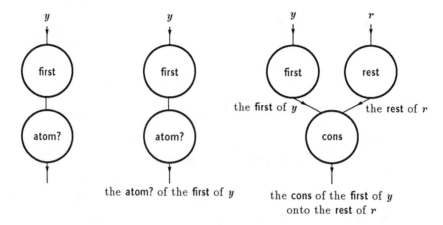

As a further example, consider the three-machine hook-up shown on the right above. Note in particular that, although the function **cons** is the last function in the hook-up, it is the first to be mentioned in the output description.

We said earlier that we had two suggestions for simplifying machine diagrams whose inputs are represented by variables. The second simplification involves abbreviating the phrases that describe the outputs of functions—for example, 'the **null?** of r' and 'the **cons** of a onto y'. These phrases contain a number of (colorless) words that do little more than link together the important (black) words and variables. In many ways they are redundant; our understanding would be impaired very little if they were not there.

Take, for example, the phrase 'the **first** of y'. The main features of this phrase are the word '**first**', which names the function we are dealing with, and the symbol 'y', which represents the input to the function. So a suitable abbreviation for the phrase 'the **first** of y' might be '**first** y'. Similarly, the phrase 'the **rest** of y' might be abbreviated to '**rest** y', and the phrase 'the **cons** of a onto y' might be abbreviated to '**cons** a y'.

As a further example, at the top of this page we presented a machine hook-up whose output is described by the phrase 'the **cons** of the **first** of y onto the **rest** of r'. Deletion of the colorless words leaves us with

cons first y **rest** r.

However, this expression is a little hard to read; in particular, it is not immediately clear what the two inputs to **cons** are. The usual way to make it evident which functions have which inputs is to enclose each function and its input(s) in parentheses. Thus, the phrase 'the **first** of *y*' is abbreviated to '(**first** *y*)'. Similarly, 'the **rest** of *r*' becomes '(**rest** *r*)' and 'the **cons** of *a* onto *y*' becomes '(**cons** *a* *y*)'.

Returning to the phrase 'the **cons** of the **first** of *y* onto the **rest** of *r*', and replacing the phrases 'the **first** of *y*' and 'the **rest** of *r*' by their abbreviated forms, we obtain

the **cons** of (**first** *y*) onto (**rest** *r*).

Then, applying the abbreviation scheme to '**cons**', we have

(**cons** (**first** *y*) (**rest** *r*)).

This expression makes it clear that the two inputs to the function **cons** are (**first** *y*) and (**rest** *r*).

Table 1.1 lists the abbreviations for each of the six primitive functions.

Phrase	*Abbreviation*
the **first** of *a*	(**first** *a*)
the **rest** of *b*	(**rest** *b*)
the **cons** of *c* onto *d*	(**cons** *c* *d*)
the **atom?** of *e*	(**atom?** *e*)
the **null?** of *f*	(**null?** *f*)
the **eq?** of *g* and *h*	(**eq?** *g* *h*)

Table 1.1: Functional Expressions

The parentheses are an essential part of each abbreviation; they must *not* be omitted. In addition, Figure 1.1 on the next page shows how these expressions may be used to describe the output from the six primitive functions. Expressions that employ the abbreviation scheme outlined in Table 1.1 are called **functional expressions**. For the sake of emphasis, we state the obvious and observe that the parentheses in functional expressions are *black*. It follows that functional expressions are entirely black.

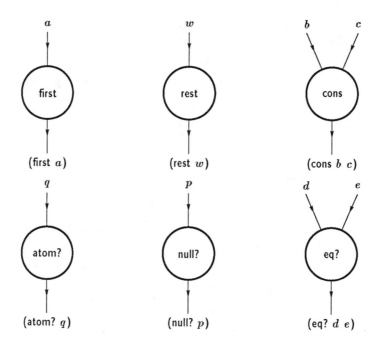

Figure 1.1: Output Descriptions of the Six Primitive Functions.

One final example: In the hook-up represented by the machine diagram on the right we note that the input is denoted by the variable '*s*'. We therefore describe the output from the **first** machine by the functional expression '(**first** *s*)'. Then, since the input to the **atom?** machine is recorded as '(**first** *s*)', we describe the output by the functional expression '(**atom?** (**first** *s*))', and we record this in the machine diagram as shown.

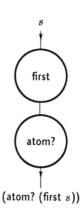

Exercise 29.

For each of the machine diagrams on the next page,

(i) write the functional expression that describes the output;

(ii) describe in general the suitable replacements for each variable that occurs in the functional expression.

(The machine in part (g) has a split input, so the variable '*m*' will occur twice in your functional expression for the output.)

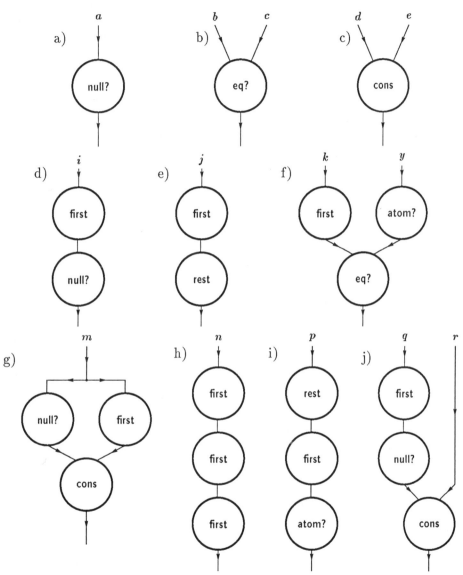

Exercise 30.

For each of these functional expressions, draw a corresponding machine diagram.

a) **(first (rest *b*))**   b) **(cons (atom? *e*) (rest *e*))**

A functional expression describes the output from a function in terms of the variable(s) representing the function's input(s). Of course, as soon as the variables that appear in a machine diagram are replaced by suitable data expressions, then we can identify a particular data expression as the output of the function. For example, consider the function whose output is described by the functional expression '(first *s*)'. (See the diagram on the left below.) What happens if we now replace each occurrence of '*s*' in this diagram by some suitable data expression (that is, one that is acceptable to the function first)? As an example, in the diagram on the right below we have replaced each occurrence of '*s*' by the non-null list '(A B C)'.

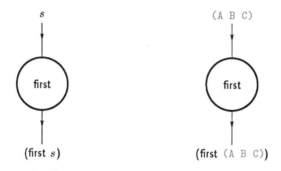

As a result of this replacement, the output is now represented by the expression '(first (A B C))', which is partly red and partly black. (Since it is neither a functional expression nor a data expression, but a little of both, we call it a **mixed expression**.) Now, when the input is the list '(A B C)', the output from the function first is the atom 'A'. We can be sure, then, that the data expression represented by the mixed expression '(first (A B C))' is the atom 'A'. In effect, we have 'changed' the black functional expression '(first *s*)' into the red data expression 'A'. The process of passing in this way from black functional expressions to red data expressions is known as **evaluation**. We record the result of this evaluation as follows:

When '*s*' is replaced by the list '(A B C)', (first *s*) ↦ A.

(The new symbol, '↦', called the **output symbol**, is read 'evaluates to' or 'outputs'. So the statement

$$(first\ s) \mapsto A$$

might be read 'The functional expression "(first *s*)" *evaluates to* the atom "A".') Similarly, if '*m*' is replaced by the list '(head (ache))', then

- (first *m*) ↦ head
- (atom? *m*) ↦ #f
- (rest *m*) ↦ ((ache))
- (null? *m*) ↦ #f

Taking a more complex example, let us evaluate the functional expression '(first (rest *s*))' when '*s*' is replaced by the list

$$\text{(sheiks (sixth sheep))}$$

We begin by replacing '*s*' in the functional expression '(first (rest *s*))' to obtain the mixed expression

$$\textbf{(first (rest }\text{(sheiks (sixth sheep))}\textbf{)).}$$

The mixed expression '(rest (sheiks (sixth sheep)))' represents the output from the function **rest** when the input is the list '(sheiks (sixth sheep))'. So it represents the list '((sixth sheep))'. Using this list in place of the mixed expression

$$\textbf{(rest }\text{(sheiks (sixth sheep))}\textbf{)}$$

in the expression '(first (rest (sheiks (sixth sheep))))', we obtain

$$\textbf{(first }\text{((sixth sheep))}\textbf{).}$$

This mixed expression represents the output from the function **first** when the input is the list '((sixth sheep))'. So it represents the list '(sixth sheep)'. We conclude that when the list '(sheiks (sixth sheep))' is the replacement for the variable '*s*',

$$\textbf{(first (rest }s\textbf{))} \mapsto \text{(sixth sheep)}$$

Similarly, if the replacement for '*a*' is the list '(shell cellar)' and the replacement for '*b*' is the atom 'sea' then

- (atom? (first *a*)) ↦ #t
- (cons *b* *a*) ↦ (sea shell cellar)
- (eq? *b* (first (rest *a*))) ↦ #f
- (first (cons *a* *b*)) cannot be evaluated. (Why not?).

Exercise 31.

Using the replacements given in this table:

Variable	Replacement
a	(A B C)
b	((Gilbert) and Sullivan)
c	((A good I))
d	(( ) ( ))
e	(polymer)

evaluate these functional expressions:

a) (rest *a*)   b) (first (rest *b*))

c) (cons (first *c*) (rest *d*))   d) (cons (atom? *e*) (rest *e*))

There are many occasions in the remainder of this book where we consider the results of replacing a certain variable by some specified data expression. It becomes very tedious having repeatedly to make statements such as 'Let the list "(A B C)" be the replacement for the variable "*r*",' so we introduce some briefer methods of passing on this information. When appropriate, we abbreviate the above statement symbolically by

$$r : (A\ B\ C).$$

In textual passages, we usually abbreviate the above statement by a phrase such as 'Let *r* be the list "(A B C)".'

Exercise 32.

Using the replacements

a : Fred   *b* : Mary

l : ( )   *m* : (( ) (( )))

r : (Jane Mary)

evaluate as many of the functional expressions at the top of the next page as possible. (If a functional expression can be evaluated, write the corresponding data expression in red. If it cannot, write 'impossible'—in colorless pencil, of course!)

a) (first *r*)   b) (rest *a*)

c) (cons *a l*)   d) (eq? *a* (first *r*))

e) (cons *l* (rest *r*))   f) (eq? *b* (first *r*))

g) (cons (first *r*) (first *m*)) h) (eq? (first (rest *r*)) *l*)

i) (null? (first *m*))   j) (atom? (first (rest *m*)))

k) (cons (rest *r*) (rest *l*))   l) (cons (rest *r*) (rest *r*))

So far in this section we have made no mention of how our new notation may be applied in the case of constant and conditional functions. The time has come to address this question, dealing first with constant functions. Consider the constant function $^\triangledown$**gold**, and suppose that the input is represented by the variable '*r*'. On the basis of our work with primitive and predicate functions, we might expect to represent the output from this function by '($^\triangledown$**gold** *r*).' Since, however, the output of this function is the same no matter what replacement is made for '*r*', the '*r*' and the parentheses in the functional expression '($^\triangledown$**gold** *r*)' are in many ways superfluous. It is therefore quite reasonable to represent the output of this function simply by '$^\triangledown$**gold**', as in the machine diagram drawn on the right.

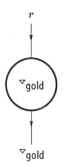

The functional expression '$^\triangledown$**gold**' gives the output of the constant function $^\triangledown$**gold** when the input is represented by '*r*' just as the functional expression '(first *r*)' describes the output of the primitive function **first** when the input is represented by the variable '*r*'. However, the functional expression '$^\triangledown$**gold**' also describes the output of the constant function $^\triangledown$**gold** when the input is represented by the variable '*j*', or '*u*', or '*s*', or by any black bold italic letter.

Obviously, the evaluation of functional expressions involving nothing but constant functions is simplicity itself, for there is no need to be concerned about variables or their replacements. Thus, no matter what the input, $^\triangledown$**busy** ↦ busy, $^\triangledown$**(( ) ( ))** ↦ (( ) ( )), and $^\triangledown$**(A B C)** ↦ (A B C).

We take this opportunity to remark that there are two constant functions which feature heavily in the remainder of this book, namely, the constant functions $^\triangledown$**#t** and $^\triangledown$**#f**. For the sake of convenience, we propose to abbreviate the functional expressions '$^\triangledown$**#t**' and '$^\triangledown$**#f**' by '**#t**' and '**#f**', respectively. Following this convention, we have that **#t** ↦ #t, **#f** ↦ #f, and

$$\text{(cons \#t (cons \#f } ^\triangledown\text{( )))) ↦ (\#t \#f) .}$$

Of course, we must also explain how to describe the
output from machine hook-ups that combine primitive and
constant functions. As a first example, we consider the
machine hook-up shown on the right. The functional expression corresponding to this hook-up is '(first $^\triangledown$(A B C)).'
So, to start our evaluation, we note that

$$^\triangledown(\text{A B C}) \mapsto (\text{A B C})$$

That is, regardless of the input, the output from the constant function $^\triangledown$(A B C) is the list '(A B C)'. When this list
is the input to the function first, the output is the atom 'A',
so this must be the output from the hook-up. Thus the functional expression
'(first $^\triangledown$(A B C))' always evaluates to the atom 'A', regardless of the initial
input. We record this information by writing

$$(\text{first } {}^\triangledown(\text{A B C})) \mapsto \text{A}.$$

We must not however leave you with the impression that every functional
expression involving constant functions always evaluates to the same data expression. For example, the functional expression '(cons *a* (first $^\triangledown$(( ))))' cannot
be evaluated until the variable '*a*' is replaced by a suitable data expression.
If we let *a* be the atom 'smasher' then

$$(\text{cons } a \text{ (first } {}^\triangledown(( )))) \mapsto (\text{smasher}).$$

On the other hand, if we let *a* be the list '(A B C)' then

$$(\text{cons } a \text{ (first } {}^\triangledown(( )))) \mapsto ((\text{A B C})).$$

Clearly, the value[13] of '(cons *a* (first $^\triangledown$(( ))))' depends on which data expression
is chosen to replace '*a*'.

Exercise 33.

    Evaluate each of the following functional expressions:

      a) (first (rest $^\triangledown$((A B) C)))

      b) (atom? $^\triangledown$A)

      c) (eq? t (null? $^\triangledown$(( ))))

      d) (cons (null? $^\triangledown$( )) (first (rest $^\triangledown$(A (B (C))))))

---

[13] By 'the value of "(cons *a* (first $^\triangledown$(( ))))"' we mean 'the data expression to which the functional
expression "(cons *a* (first $^\triangledown$(( ))))" evaluates.'

Finally in this section, we settle the question of how to describe the output from conditional functions, taking as our model the conditional function depicted on page 26, whose behavior is described as follows:

Input: Any data expression

Output: $\begin{cases} \texttt{atom} & \text{if the input is an atom} \\ \texttt{list} & \text{if the input is not an atom.} \end{cases}$

The functional expression for a conditional function begins with a black left parenthesis followed by the special black symbol '**cond**'. This is followed in turn by a black left bracket, and then the functional expression corresponding to the control input:

(cond [(atom? s) ...

Next comes the output from the function when the control input is the boolean '#t', followed by a black right bracket (to match the first left bracket):

(cond [(atom? s) ▽atom]...

The expression '[(atom? <i>s</i>) ▽atom]' is called a **clause**. There are two kinds of clauses, each of which begins and ends with black brackets. The first type—of which the above clause is an example—consists of exactly two functional expressions. (The first of these expressions is called the **predicate**, and, since it corresponds to the control input, it must evaluate either to the boolean '#t' or the boolean '#f'. The second expression is called the **consequent**.)

Following the first clause, we record what the output from our function should be when the control input is the boolean '#f'. To do this, we use the second type of clause, known as an **else-clause**. It contains the black symbol '**else**' followed by the functional expression that corresponds to the output from the function when the control input is the boolean '#f'. (This functional expression is called the **alternative**.) Finally, we close the expression with a black parenthesis to match the parenthesis preceding the symbol '**cond**'.

(cond [(atom? s) ▽atom] [else ▽list])

The entire functional expression is called a **cond-expression**; it is an example of a **special form**. (Special forms are functional expressions that have their own peculiar rules for evaluation.) Cond-expressions are distinguished from other types of functional expressions by the presence of the black symbol '**cond**', which is known as a **keyword**. In order to make their internal structure clearer to the reader, it is usual to arrange cond-expressions so that each new clause following the keyword '**cond**' is written on a separate line, and the clauses are indented and aligned vertically as shown in the following example:

$$\begin{aligned}
&\text{(cond}\\
&\quad [\,(\text{atom? } s)\ ^{\triangledown}\text{atom}\,]\\
&\quad [\,\text{else } ^{\triangledown}\text{list}\,]\,)
\end{aligned}$$

In a similar way, it follows that the output from the two-input conditional function represented by the machine diagram on the right is described by the cond-expression

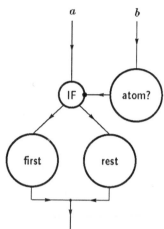

$$\begin{aligned}
&\text{(cond}\\
&\quad [\,(\text{atom? } b)\ (\text{first } a)\,]\\
&\quad [\,\text{else } (\text{rest } a)\,]\,)
\end{aligned}$$

Then, if we use these replacements

a : (contents)
b : look

the cond-expression evaluates to the atom 'contents', whereas with the replacements

a : (contents)
b : (look away)

the cond-expression evaluates to the null list.

Exercise 34.

Complete this cond-expression, which describes the output from the function depicted in Exercise 26 on page 27:

$$\begin{aligned}
&\text{(cond}\\
&\quad [\,(\underline{\quad\quad}\ (\underline{\quad\quad}\ a))\ (\underline{\quad\quad}\ a)\,]\\
&\quad [\,\text{else } (\underline{\quad\quad}\ a)\,]\,)
\end{aligned}$$

Exercise 35.

Write the cond-expression corresponding to the function depicted in Exercise 27 on page 28.

Moving on to a more complex example, let us consider the function which inputs a list a and behaves as follows:

- if a is the null list then the function outputs the null list;

- if a contains exactly one data expression then the function outputs the first data expression in a; and

- if a contains two or more data expressions then the function outputs the second data expression in a.

One way of constructing this function is shown in the following figure:

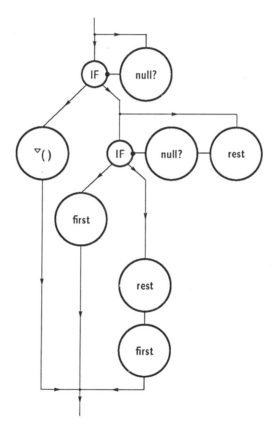

Figure 1.2: A Complex Conditional Function

To write the cond-expression corresponding to this function we proceed as follows. We note that the output depends, in the first instance, on the output

from the function **null?**. In particular, when the input is the null list, then the
function outputs the null list:

$$(\text{cond}$$
$$[(\text{null?}\ a)\ ^\triangledown()]$$
$$[\text{else} \dots])$$

On the other hand, when the input is a non-null list, the output depends on
the value of the functional expression '**(null? (rest** *a***))**'. In fact, the output in
this case is given by the cond-expression

$$(\text{cond}$$
$$[(\text{null?}\ (\text{rest}\ a))\ (\text{first}\ a)]$$
$$[\text{else}\ (\text{first}\ (\text{rest}\ a))])$$

So the complete cond-expression for this function is as follows:

$$(\text{cond}$$
$$[(\text{null?}\ a)\ ^\triangledown()]$$
$$[\text{else}\ (\text{cond}$$
$$[(\text{null?}\ (\text{rest}\ a))\ (\text{first}\ a)]$$
$$[\text{else}\ (\text{first}\ (\text{rest}\ a))])])$$

Functions, such as the one we have just been considering, whose outputs involve cond-expressions within cond-expressions, are quite common. So
much so, in fact, that a convenient abbreviation is usually adopted according
to which the clauses of the internal cond-expression(s) are incorporated as
new clauses of the external cond-expression, the order in which the clauses
are listed being determined by the order of appearance of the internal cond-
expression(s). Thus, the cond-expression above would usually be written as
follows:

$$(\text{cond}$$
$$[(\text{null?}\ a)\ ^\triangledown()]$$
$$[(\text{null?}\ (\text{rest}\ a))\ (\text{first}\ a)]$$
$$[\text{else}\ (\text{first}\ (\text{rest}\ a))])$$

Multi-clause cond-expressions like this are often referred to as **cascade
cond-expressions**. They are evaluated according to a 'trickle down' principle: We begin by evaluating the predicate of the first clause. If it evaluates
to the boolean '#t' then we evaluate the consequent of that clause, and the
resulting data expression is the value of the cond-expression. (Neither part

of any later clause in the cond-expression is evaluated.) However, if the first predicate evaluates to the boolean '#f' then, without evaluating the consequent of the first clause, we 'trickle down' to the next clause in the cond-expression. We then evaluate the predicate of this new clause and decide whether to evaluate its consequent or to 'trickle down' to the next clause. And so on. It could happen, of course, that *none* of the predicates evaluates to the boolean '#t'. In that case, we eventually 'trickle down' to the else-clause, and the value of the cond-expression is the value of the alternative. (In other words, the alternative yields the value of the cond-expression 'if all else fails'.) For example, using the replacements

$$a : \langle\text{one}\rangle \qquad b : \text{two}$$
$$c : \langle\text{three four}\rangle$$

the functional expression

(cond
  [(atom? *a*) (first *b*)]
  [(atom? *b*) ▽(a b c)]
  [else (cons *a* *c*)]]) .

evaluates as follows. We first check if *a* is an atom. It is not, so we 'trickle down' to the second clause. We check if *b* is an atom; it is, so we evaluate the consequent of this clause and conclude that the value of the cond-expression is the list '(a b c)'.

Exercise 36.
    Using the replacements

$$a : \langle\,\rangle \qquad b : \text{one}$$
$$c : \langle\text{one two three four}\rangle$$

evaluate each of these functional expressions:

a) (cond
    [(null? *a*) ▽empty]
    [(null? *b*) (cons *b* ▽(\ ))]
    [else ▽full])

b) (cond
    [(atom? *a*) (eq? *b* ▽two)]
    [(atom? *b*) (null? *a*)]
    [else (cons *b* *c*)])

c) (cond
    [(null? *c*) ▽a]
    [(atom? *a*) ▽b]
    [else (first (rest *c*))])

d) (cond
    [(atom? *a*) (cons *a* ▽(\ ))]
    [(eq? *b* (first (rest *c*))) (first *c*)]
    [(eq? *b* (first *c*)) (first (rest *c*))]
    [(null? *a*) (cons *b* *a*)]
    [else #f])

It may surprise you to learn that, as we bring this section to a close, we have dispensed with the need for machine diagrams altogether. A moment's thought should convince you that the functional expression corresponding to any given machine gives us all the information about the machine that we need. Consider, for example, the functional expression

(null? (first q)).

We observe that the expression involves the functions **null?** and **first**, that the variable q represents the input to the function **first**, and that the output from the function **first** provides the input to the function **null?**.

Since q represents the input to the function **first**, it follows that q may be replaced by any non-null list. On the other hand, since the function **null?** accepts only lists as its input, the output from the function **first** must in this case be a list. We conclude that q must be a non-null list whose first data expression is itself a list. Provided the replacement for 'q' meets these criteria, then '(null? (first q))' evaluates to the boolean '#t' if the first data expression in the list q is the null list; otherwise it evaluates to the boolean '#f'. On the other hand, the functional expression '(null? (first q))' cannot be evaluated if the replacement for 'q' does not meet these criteria. Drawing the machine diagram that corresponds to the functional expression '(null? (first q))' would not enable us to improve upon the analysis just carried out. This does not mean, however, that we will have no further use for machine diagrams. On the contrary, they will continue to provide a useful tool for thinking about list processing functions. Indeed, if you are ever uncertain about the meaning of a complex expression, or confused by a particular arrangement of functions and inputs, we strongly recommend that you draw a quick sketch of the corresponding machine diagram. Such a diagram will often help to clarify your thinking, or suggest possible solutions to your dilemma.

The functional expressions we have introduced in this section—expressions such as '(null? (first q))'—are used by programmers to control computers. (After all, it is much more convenient to type '(null? (first q))' at a computer keyboard than to input the corresponding machine diagram since, traditionally, computer systems are more adept at dealing with characters than with machine diagrams.) Indeed, these all-black expressions are part of the computer programming language **Scheme**. In the next chapter we introduce a new type of function, at which time you will have all the tools necessary to write sophisticated computer programs!

PROBLEM SET 2

1. Using the replacements

   a : Bach   *b* : Offenbach
   l : ()   *m* : (Weber)
   p : (((Mozart) Sibelius) Strauss)
   s : (Offenbach Bach Weber Strauss)

   evaluate as many of these functional expressions as possible:

   a) (first *p*)   b) (null? *s*)
   c) (cons *s* *m*)   d) (cons $^\triangledown$( ) *l*)
   e) (eq? $^\triangledown$Bach *l*)   f) (null? (rest *m*))
   g) (atom? (first (first *p*)))   h) (cons (first *s*) (first *m*))
   i) (cons (cons *a* *l*) *l*)   j) (cons $^\triangledown$(Percy Grainger) *s*)
   k) (first (rest (rest *s*)))   l) (cons (eq? (first *s*) *b*) *l*)

2. Suppose that *s* is a list containing at least two data expressions. Write a functional expression that evaluates to the second data expression in *s*. [Hint: It may help you to think about a machine whose input is represented by the variable '*s*'. When '*s*' is replaced by a list containing at least two data expressions, the machine should output the second data expression.]

3. Let *b* be a non-null list containing at least two data expressions. Write a functional expression that evaluates to a new list obtained from the list *b* by 'doubling' the second data expression in *b*. For example, if *b* is the list '(A B C)' then the functional expression should evaluate to the list '(A B B C)'; if *b* is the list '((A) (B))' then the functional expression should evaluate to the list '((A) (B) (B))'.

4. Let *w* be a list containing exactly three data expressions. Write a functional expression that evaluates to a new list obtained from *w* by interchanging the first and third data expressions.

5. Let *x* and *y* be lists. Write a functional expression that evaluates to the first data expression of the list *x* if the list *x* is non-null, or to the cons of *x* onto the list *y* otherwise.

– o O o –

2 Tool Making

In typical applications of list processing, even the simplest task may require the evaluation of functional expressions involving many hundreds of primitive and constant functions. In this chapter we explore ways to build complex functions from primitive functions, constant functions, and if-switches, while at the same time avoiding the need to draw enormous machine diagrams or write lengthy functional expressions.

2.1 New Tools for the Toolbox

In Figure 2.1 on page 50 we present a machine diagram involving eight individual primitive functions. We begin this section with a discussion that results in our being able to reduce this machine diagram to just three individual machines. If you study Figure 2.1 carefully, you will notice that there is a particular hook-up of the functions **rest** and **first** that occurs three times within the machine diagram. We show this two-machine hook-up, together with its corresponding functional expression, on the right. If this hook-up is to have an output, then its input must be a list

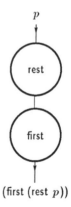

containing at least two data expressions. In other words, the suitable replacements for 'p' in the functional expression '(**first** (**rest** p))' are lists containing at least two data expressions. When provided with such an input, this functional expression evaluates to the second data expression in the list p. It

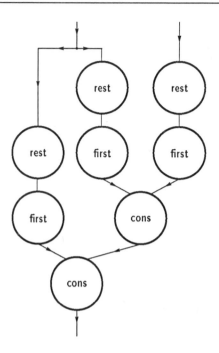

Figure 2.1: A Complex Machine Diagram

is a shame that we do not have a function that behaves like this hook-up. Having such a function would allow us to simplify the machine diagram in Figure 2.1 considerably, since each occurrence of the hook-up corresponding to the functional expression '(first (rest *p*))' could be replaced by the new function.

Since such a function would be so useful, we will build it! More accurately, we will *define* a function that behaves exactly like the hook-up on the previous page. The process of constructing this new function is very simple: We take a machine diagram showing our hook-up of the functions rest and first and we draw a 'box' around it, thereby producing the diagram on the right.

This kind of machine diagram is called a **twin-focus diagram**. To understand its significance, we must view it from two different perspectives. If we look at it from a distance, all we see is the outer function box—the inner workings are indistinct.

That is, from far away the twin-focus diagram looks like the simple diagram on the right. Viewing the diagram 'in close-up', however, we notice that our new function is really a hook-up of the functions **rest** and **first**.

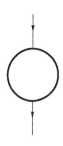

Before discussing how we can use our new function to simplify the machine diagram in Figure 2.1, let us spend a few moments engineering a functional expression that provides a written record of the construction process. We began by drawing a hook-up of the functions **rest** and **first**. If the input to this hook-up is represented by the variable 'p', then the output is described by the functional expression '(first (rest p))'. We represent this information by writing

$$(p) \ (\text{first} \ (\text{rest} \ p))$$

Next, we wrapped a 'box' around the hook-up. In terms of functional expressions, this box consists of the black word 'lambda'[1] together with two enclosing parentheses, like this:

$$(\text{lambda} \ (p) \ (\text{first} \ (\text{rest} \ p)))$$

The resulting functional expression, called a **lambda-expression**, is a written report of the information provided by the twin-focus diagram above; it describes—indeed, it defines—the new function we have built.

Every lambda-expression consists of a black left parenthesis, followed by the keyword 'lambda', followed by two sub-expressions, followed by a black right parenthesis. The first of the sub-expressions is a blackened list containing the variable(s) used to represent the input(s) to the new function. This sub-expression is called the **lambda-parameter list**, and the variables that appear in it are known as **parameters**. The second sub-expression is the functional expression that describes the output from the new function; it is called the **lambda-body**.

Exercise 37.

a) Complete this skeleton lambda-expression

$$(\text{lambda} \ (a \ b) \ _____ \ )$$

---

[1]This apparently 'off the wall' use of the name for the Greek letter 'λ' is a reference to the λ-calculus, which is a formal mathematical notation developed by the American mathematical logician Alonzo Church (1903–). Because the language Scheme incorporates many aspects of the λ-calculus, it has an ability to manipulate functions that is vastly superior to that of other programming languages.

so that it describes the function depicted by the twin-focus diagram on the left below.

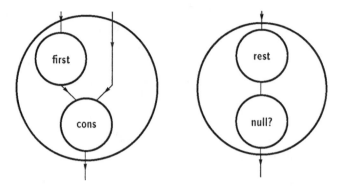

b) Write a lambda-expression that describes the function depicted by the twin-focus diagram on the right above.

c) Draw a twin-focus diagram for the function described by

(lambda (p q) (cons (first p) (rest q)))

Functions that are depicted by twin-focus diagrams are called **derived functions** to distinguish them from primitive functions and constant functions. Of course, they also need to be distinguishable from each other when viewed from a distance. We therefore introduce the possibility of giving them names. In terms of machine diagrams, we name a derived function by labeling its twin-focus diagram with an appropriate blackened atom. We may give the name 'second' to the function described by '(lambda (p) (first (rest p)))', for example, by labeling its twin-focus diagram as shown on the left below. On the right is the view of this diagram from a distance (we have taken the liberty of moving the new function's name into the function box).

Having given ourselves the ability to name derived functions, we may replace our hook-up of the functions **rest** and **first** in any machine diagram by the function **second**.

Exercise 38.

Complete each of these machine diagrams by writing a data expression (in red).

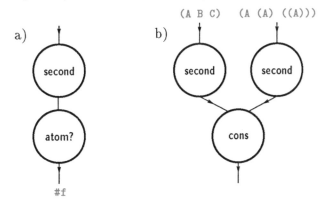

In the context of machine diagrams, we give the name 'second' to the function described by the functional expression '(lambda (p) (first (rest p)))' by writing that name next to the appropriate twin-focus diagram. The same task is performed, in terms of functional expressions, by writing

(define second (lambda (p) (first (rest p))))

This is an example of a **define-expression**; it defines and names the function **second**.[2] Every define-expression contains three components. We shall see later that define-expressions may also be used to give names to other kinds of objects besides functions, but, in the present function-defining context, these components are as follows: First, there is a black left parenthesis followed by the black keyword '**define**'. This signals that we are dealing with no ordinary expression, just as our first keyword, '**cond**', indicated the presence of a special kind of expression. Following the keyword is the (black) name we are giving

---

[2]Strictly speaking, the lambda-expression embedded within the define-expression is what actually describes which function we are talking about, and the define-expression as a whole merely assigns the name 'second' to that function. It is common practice, however, not to be so pedantic about the demarcation between these two aspects of a define-expression; rather, we usually blend them into one by using loose, but perfectly comprehensible, phrases such as 'the function **second** is defined by the above functional expression', and by referring to such a define-expression as being a 'definition' of the function it names.

to the new function, and this in turn is followed by the lambda-expression that describes its twin-focus diagram. Finally, the expression is completed with a black right parenthesis to match the black left parenthesis with which it began.

In the example above, we wrote the define-expression for the function **second** on one line. It is more usual, however, to start both the lambda-expression and the lambda-body on indented new lines, thus:

(define second
   (lambda (p)
      (first (rest p))))

Note that this definition contains all the information we need to know about the function. Specifically, it tells us that the new function's name is 'second', that it takes exactly one input and that, when the parameter is the variable 'p', the function's output is described by the functional expression '(first (rest p))'.

If the list '(one three five)' is input to the function **second**, what will the output be? From our definition of the function **second** we see that we must evaluate the expression '(first (rest p))' in the case when the parameter 'p' is replaced by the list '(one three five)'. Of course, in these circumstances, '(first (rest p))' evaluates to the atom 'three'. So, the answer to our question is that, in this case, the function **second** will output the atom 'three'.

Exercise 39.

Using the replacements

b : John m : ( )

s : (Jane Fred Mary) v : (Fred Mary John)

evaluate, where possible, each of the following functional expressions:

a) (second v)   b) (second m)

c) (second (rest v))   d) (eq? b (second (second v)))

e) (eq? (first v) (second s))

Our motivation for creating the function **second** was to simplify the machine diagram in Figure 2.1 on page 50. In Figure 2.2 on page 55 we present the same function, this time using the function **second**. If you compare this with the original diagram on page 50, we expect you will agree that it represents a significant simplification.

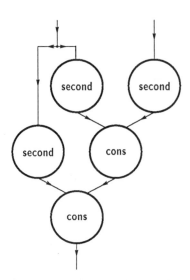

Figure 2.2: A Machine Diagram involving the Function **second**.

When we chose the name 'second' for the new function we followed the convention that the name should be a 'blackened atom', that is, it is written in black, but if it were written in red, it would be an atom. Generally speaking, when selecting function names we refrain from using certain symbols, such as '12' and '85697' that might be interpreted as being names for numbers—we indicate our preferred use for these symbols in Chapter 3—and the symbols '#t' and '#f' to which we gave special meanings in Chapter 1. In addition, we avoid naming functions with the reserved keywords of the programming language Scheme. (To find out what these are, you should consult the manual for whichever implementation of Scheme you will be using. We go into more detail about different implementations of the language in Section 2.3 below.) Finally, we take some steps aimed at our own convenience and that of anyone else reading the definition. For example, in the case of the function **second**, we took care that

- the name chosen suggests the behavior of the function—just imagine the confusion if we had instead decided, perversely, to call it 'third'!

- the name is not so long as to be unreadable—consider, for example, the equally informative but totally unmanageable alternative

this–function–outputs–the–second–data–expression–in–the–input–list.

- the name is not so short as to be ambiguous—if we had called it 'S', for example, a casual reader of the definition might wonder whether it stood for 'Stretch', 'Shorten', 'Shift', or ... In reality, no confusion is likely to arise in the present extremely simple case, but it is a very different matter when more complex 'compound' functions are involved.

Exercise 40.

a) Draw a twin-focus machine diagram depicting the derived function **third** which accepts as its only input any list containing at least three data expressions, and which outputs the third data expression from the input list.

b) Write a define-expression for the derived function **third**.

c) Using the replacements

$$a \; : \texttt{Fred}$$
$$b \; : \texttt{(apple cat Fred Pete)}$$
$$s \; : \texttt{(a (b) ((c (d)) ()) ())}$$
$$v \; : \texttt{((((()))))}$$

evaluate as many of the following functional expressions as possible:

(i) **(third b)**   (ii) **(third v)**

(iii) **(third s)**   (iv) **(third (cons a b))**

(v) **(cons (third s) (third s))**

At the beginning of this section we mentioned that the function pictured in Figure 2.1 on page 50 could be reduced to just three individual functions. However, the simplified diagram of the same function in Figure 2.2 on page 55 involves five separate machines. How then may it be simplified further? If you study Figure 2.2 carefully you will notice two occurrences of the two-machine hook-up shown on the right.

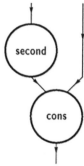

Of course, there is no reason why we cannot use the derived function **second** to define a new function, so we proceed as before. We draw a twin-focus diagram of the new function, labeling it with a suitable name—let's call it '**secons**' since it *cons*es the *second* data expression of its first input onto its second input—as shown at the top of the next page. Note that the new function has *two* inputs. Since these

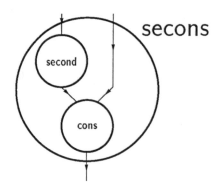

inputs may be different, we must be careful to choose different variables to represent them in the lambda-expression that describes our new twin-focus diagram.

If we choose '*r*' and '*s*' as the parameters of our new function, for example, then the corresponding lambda-expression is

(lambda (*r s*) (cons (second *r*) *s*))

So we may define the function **secons** as follows:

(define secons
(lambda (*r s*)
(cons (second *r*) *s*)))

To illustrate the behavior of this function, let us evaluate the functional expression '(secons *r s*)' using the following replacements:

r : (A B C D E)   *s* : (good)

In other words, we will evaluate the mixed expression

(secons (A B C D E) (good))

We see from the definition of the function **secons** that we must now evaluate the expression '(cons (second (A B C D E)) (good))'. But

(second (A B C D E)) ⟼ B

and (cons B (good)) ⟼ (B good), so the output from **secons** in this instance is the list '(B good)'.

Exercise 41.

  a) Rewrite the definition of the derived function **secons** so that
     the lambda-body involves only primitive functions.

  b) Draw the machine diagram that results when the derived
     function **secons** is used to simplify the machine diagram of
     Figure 2.2 on page 55.

   We are going to be defining a lot of functions in the remainder of this book,
and in every single case the relevant define-expression will involve a lambda-
expression. For brevity's sake, therefore, we intend to write the Greek letter
'λ' in place of the word 'lambda'. You may switch over to the Greek letter or
continue writing out the word, whichever you prefer.

Exercise 42.

  Complete the skeleton definition
  below of the two-input derived
  function **L** that is pictured on the
  right:

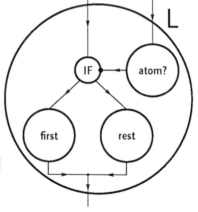

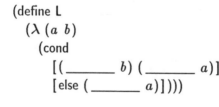

  (define L
     (λ (*a b*)
        (cond
           [(_____ *b*) (_____ *a*)]
           [else (_____ *a*)]))))

Exercise 43.

  By drawing its machine diagram and then analyzing it, or otherwise, describe the behavior of the derived function **Id**, defined as
  follows:

$$\text{(define Id}$$
$$(\lambda\ (a)$$
$$(\text{first (cons } a\ ^\triangledown(\ ))))))$$

   In the preceding exercise you probably noted that the function **Id** is a 'do
nothing' function in the sense that it accepts any data expression as an input
and, whatever data expression is used as the input, that same data expression
is the output. An easier way to construct a function that behaves in this way
is to imagine that the input and output tubes of the function are really the

same tube, as shown on the right.

To make it possible for us to write a correspond-
ingly simple define-expression, we intend from here on
to count variables as being functional expressions. Under this agreement, when the input to the above function is represented by the variable '*a*', then its output
is described by the functional expression '*a*'. The corresponding definition is therefore as follows:

(define Id

(λ (*a*) *a*))

Exercise 44.

    a) Describe the behavior of the function defined as follows:

(define Mid

(λ (*a b c*) *b*))

    b) Write a definition of a function that behaves exactly like the
function **Mid** but which involves all of the parameters '*a*', '*b*'
and '*c*' in the lambda-body.

Exercise 45.

    a) Write a definition of the derived predicate function **not** that
behaves as follows: The function takes one input, which must
be an atom. If the input is the boolean '#f', then the output
is the boolean '#t'; otherwise the output is the boolean '#f'.[3]

    b) Evaluate each of the following functional expressions:

       (i) **(not (not #t))**   (ii) **(not (not (not #f)))**

      (iii) **(not (not (not (not #f))))**

    c) Use the function **not** to write a definition of

       (i) the derived predicate function **list?** that takes as its input

---

[3]In fact, although this function accepts any atom as its input, we are really only interested
in cases when the input is either the boolean '#t' or the boolean '#f'. You will notice that,
in calling the function 'not', we have departed from our usual practice of naming predicate
functions with blackened atoms ending in the symbol '?'. We did this because the function
has a centuries-long history of use in logic, mathematics, and, more recently, computer
science, and it would be perverse of us not to use its traditional name.

any data expression and outputs the boolean '#t' if and only if the input is a list.

(ii) a derived predicate function that takes as its input any list and outputs the boolean '#t' if and only if the input list is a non-null list.

Each time we define a new derived function we add to our 'toolbox' of functions and, as the collection grows, so the complexity of the functions we define increases, since each new derived function may use any function— derived, primitive, or constant—that is already in the toolbox. To program is quite simply to use define-expressions to give names to derived functions.

We now take a short break from the mainstream of our discussion in order to look at certain predicate functions from a slightly different viewpoint. You will recall that the distinguishing feature of a predicate function is that its output is either the boolean '#t' or the boolean '#f', never anything else. While every predicate function outputs nothing but boolean objects, not all predicate functions accept boolean objects as inputs. (Consider, for example, the predicate function **null?**.) Those predicate functions that *do* accept boolean objects as inputs are often referred to as **boolean functions**, particularly when we are in a situation where all we really care about is how the function deals with boolean objects.

In the preceding exercise we met the function **not**, which you should now recognize as a one-input boolean function. Its action upon boolean objects is very easy to describe: If the input is the boolean '#f', it outputs the boolean '#t'; on the other hand, if the input is the boolean '#t', it outputs the boolean '#f'. Thus, as far as boolean objects are concerned, the behavior of the function **not** is described by the following **truth table**.

a	(not *a*)
#t	#f
#f	#t

In this truth table the left-hand column indicates the input to the function, while the right-hand column indicates the corresponding output.

There are many different functions that act upon boolean objects in this way; here are two of them:

```
(define not1              (define not2
  (λ (a)                    (λ (a)
    (eq? a #f)))              (cond
                               [a #f]
                               [else #t])))
```

(Not only do these functions have different twin-focus diagrams, in addition they really do behave differently. Since the input to the function **not2** is used as the predicate of a clause in a cond-expression, it follows that **not2** only accepts boolean objects, and nothing else. In contrast, the function **not1** accepts any atom as its input.) When discussing boolean functions, however, it is of no concern to us exactly how they are defined, that is, we have very little interest in viewing their twin-focus diagrams from close quarters. On the contrary, all we want to know about such a function is reported in its truth table. Thus, when two people are discussing the boolean function **not**, one of them may have **not1** in mind while the other is thinking about **not2**; it virtually never makes any difference, because their attention is focused so narrowly. So, despite the lack of complete certainty as to its true identity, we shall refer to 'the boolean function **not**', apply it with impunity to boolean objects, and leave you the freedom to conceive of its inner workings—if your interests lie in that direction—in any way you like.

Similar remarks are in order for all boolean functions, many of which, just like **not**, have names that have become standard through years—in some cases, centuries—of use. As we remarked when introducing the function **not**, one consequence of using these standard names (which, in all but two cases, is what we intend to do) is that these predicate functions will have names that do not end with the symbol '?'. Consider, for example, the two-input boolean function usually referred to in speech as the 'exclusive-or' function. Since this name is a little long, we shall call it '**xor**'. (It is common practice—and common sense—as much as possible to use function names that are short and to the point.) The behavior of the function **xor** is described in the truth table on the right. Any function that has this effect on boolean objects can justifiably be referred to as 'the boolean function **xor**'; we shall let the specifics of its inner workings take care of themselves.

a	b	(xor a b)
#t	#t	#f
#t	#f	#t
#f	#t	#t
#f	#f	#f

Exercise 46.

By referring to the truth table for the boolean function **xor**, evaluate each of the following functional expressions.

a) (xor (null? $^\triangledown$( )) (atom? $^\triangledown$( )))

b) (xor #t (null? $^\triangledown$( )))

c) (not (xor (xor (xor #t #t) #t) #t))

The boolean function **xor** is just one of a number of two-input boolean functions. In fact, it is a simple matter to calculate exactly how many of them there are. As you can see from the following incomplete truth table, there are just four different pairs of boolean objects that can be used as inputs to a two-input boolean function:

Input 1	Input 2	Output
#t	#t	
#t	#f	
#f	#t	
#f	#f	

For each input pair there are two possible outputs, either the boolean '#t' or the boolean '#f'. So there are $2^4 = 16$ different two-input truth tables we could construct, each of which determines a two-input boolean function. Not all of these functions have standard names, but where such names exist, they often reflect the function's behavior. For example, the two-input boolean function 'inclusive-or', to which we give the name 'inor',[4] returns the boolean '#t' if and only if one *or* other (or both) of its inputs is the boolean '#t':

---

[4]In logic, in mathematics, and in most areas of computer science this function is simply called 'or'. In Scheme, however, there is something we shall meet in Chapter 5 that is called 'an or-expression'. Such expressions involve the keyword 'or', and the behavior this keyword initiates is different in some respects from what we describe here. So, to avoid any slight possibility of confusion, we prefer to err on the side of caution and use a different name for the boolean function we are discussing.

a	b	(inor a b)
#t	#t	#t
#t	#f	#t
#f	#t	#t
#f	#f	#f

Exercise 47.

Evaluate each of the following functional expressions:

a) (inor (atom? $^\triangledown$( )) (atom? $^\triangledown$Fred))

b) (inor (not #t) (not #f))

c) (inor (xor #t #t) (inor #f #f))

d) (not (inor (not (null? (first $^\triangledown$(( ))))) (atom? $^\triangledown$(Fred))))

Exercise 48.

We give below the machine diagram and the corresponding definition for the boolean function **and2**. On the basis of this information, construct the truth table for the boolean function **and2**. Why do you think the word 'and' appears in the name of this function?[5]

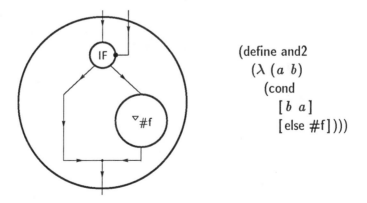

```
(define and2
  (λ (a b)
    (cond
       [b a]
       [else #f])))
```

---

[5] Outside the language we are developing, this function would be called by its traditional name, 'and'. As in the earlier case of 'or', however, 'and' is a keyword that we shall meet in Chapter 5. So we refrain from using that name here.

Exercise 49.

Evaluate each of the following functional expressions:

a) (and2 (not (inor #t #f)) #t)

b) (and2 (not #t) (not #t))

c) (not (xor (and2 #t (not #t)) #t))

d) (and2 (and2 #t #t) (not #t))

Below we provide the truth tables for the boolean functions **iff** (short for 'if and only if'; **iff** is sometimes called the 'biconditional function'), **nor** (short for 'negation of or', or 'not-or', where 'or' refers to the 'inclusive-or function'; **nor** is sometimes called 'the joint denial function'), **nand** (short for 'not-and', where 'and' refers to the function **and2**; **nand** is sometimes called the 'Sheffer stroke'[6] or the 'alternative denial function'), and **imp** (short for 'implies').

a	*b*	(iff *a* *b*)
#t	#t	#t
#t	#f	#f
#f	#t	#f
#f	#f	#t

a	*b*	(nor *a* *b*)
#t	#t	#f
#t	#f	#f
#f	#t	#f
#f	#f	#t

a	*b*	(nand *a* *b*)
#t	#t	#f
#t	#f	#t
#f	#t	#t
#f	#f	#t

a	*b*	(imp *a* *b*)
#t	#t	#t
#t	#f	#f
#f	#t	#t
#f	#f	#t

---

[6]After the American logician Henry Maurice Sheffer (1883–1964), who in 1913—and independently of similar, but unpublished, work carried out in 1880 by the American philosopher, physicist, and mathematician Charles Santiago Sanders Peirce (1839–1914)—showed that all the two-input boolean functions may be defined in terms of the Sheffer stroke. (As an exercise in elementary logic, you might like to try to show this for yourself!)

Exercise 50.

Evaluate each of the following functional expressions:

    a) (and2 (imp #t #f) #t)

    b) (iff (not (and2 #t #t)) (nor #f #f))

    c) (not (not (not (nand #t #f))))

    d) (nand (inor #t #f) (xor #t #t))

    e) (imp (inor (not #t) (not #f)) (nand #t #f))

Exercise 51.

Write a definition for a three-input boolean function that outputs the boolean '#t' if and only if *exactly two* of its inputs are the boolean '#t'.

Exercise 52.

The twin-focus machine diagram on the right depicts the conditional function **M**.

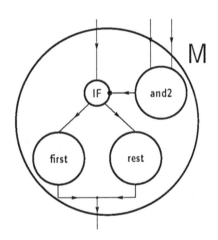

    a) Write a definition for the function **M**.

    b) Evaluate each of the following functional expressions:

        (i) (M $^\triangledown$(Fred) #f #t)

        (ii) (M $^\triangledown$(Fred) #t #t)

        (iii) (M $^\triangledown$(Fred) #t #f)

Exercise 53.

Use an appropriate boolean function to write a definition for a function that behaves as follows: The function takes three inputs. The first input may be any non-null list containing at least two data expressions. The second and third inputs must be boolean objects. If both the second and the third inputs are the boolean '#f' then the function outputs the first data expression in the first input, otherwise it outputs the second data expression in the first input.

2.2 At the Drawing Board

Armed with our six primitive functions and the if-switch and having learned how to define derived functions, we are now (at least theoretically) in a position to solve a very considerable number of programming tasks. We therefore take the opportunity to illustrate a programming technique whose usefulness you will gradually appreciate more and more as you are faced with increasingly challenging programming situations. Our first example, however, is a very simple one. Suppose we are asked to define a derived function **heads** that takes two inputs, both of which must be lists, and that behaves like this:

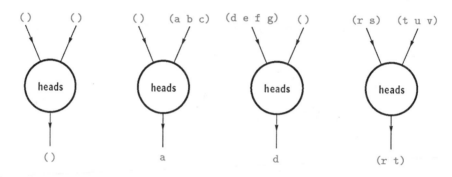

In fact, the function **heads** outputs the list formed by the first data expression in its first input followed by the first data expression in its second input, provided that such data expressions exist. If either or both of these is missing, then **heads** behaves as shown in the first three examples above.

We adopt a piecemeal approach to our programming task. Clearly, the easiest situation is when both inputs are the null list. As yet we do not have a predicate function which recognizes that both its inputs are the null list, but if we had, then it would be an easy task to say what the function **heads** should output in that case, thus leaving us with one fewer case to deal with. So we take the optimistic view that we shall later be able to define a suitable predicate function and a function that does not have to worry about the 'both null' case, and we write our definition of the function **heads** as follows:

```
(define heads
    (λ (a b)
        (cond
            [(both–null? a b) ▽()]
            [else (heads–help1 a b)])))
```

By proceeding in this manner and calling on functions we have not yet defined, we have replaced the original programming task by that of having to define *two* functions. Our only consolation is that one of them is very much easier and the other is slightly more manageable than the function **heads**. Dealing with the easier task first, we define the predicate function **both–null?**:

> (define both–null?
>   (λ (*a b*)
>   (and2 (null? *a*) (null? *b*))))

Turning our attention to the function **heads–help1**, we know for certain that at least one of its inputs is *not* the null list. It could be, of course, that *both* of them are non-null; we deal with that possibility first, again taking the optimistic approach that we shall later be able to define any additional functions for which the need arises:

> (define heads–help1
>   (λ (*a b*)
>   (cond
>   [(both–non–null? *a b*) (heads–combine *a b*)]
>   [else (heads–help2 *a b*)])))

From one point of view, things seem to be getting worse: we now have *three* functions to define. However, they are all easier to deal with than those we were faced with earlier on. Easiest things first:

> (define both–non–null?
>   (λ (*a b*)
>   (nor (null? *a*) (null? *b*))))

The function **heads–combine** is dealt with equally easily:

> (define heads–combine
>   (λ (*a b*)
>   (cons (first *a*) (cons (first *b*) ▽()))))

Finally, we must tackle the function **heads–help2**. By the time the inputs to the function **heads** reach the function **heads–help2**, we know that they have failed a 'both null' test. So at least one of them is non-null. Likewise, they have failed a 'both non-null' test. So at least one of them is the null list. It follows that, of the inputs to the function **heads–help2**, one is the null list and the other is a non-null list. This observation tells us what to do:

```
(define heads–help2
  (λ (a b)
    (cond
      [(null? a) (first b)]
      [else (first a)])))
```

We have thus arrived at the following collection of definitions which together solve our original problem of defining the function **heads:**

```
(define heads
  (λ (a b)
    (cond
      [(both–null? a b) ▽()]
      [else (heads–help1 a b)])))
```

```
(define heads–help1
  (λ (a b)
    (cond
      [(both–non–null? a b) (heads–combine a b)]
      [else (heads–help2 a b)])))
```

```
(define heads–help2
  (λ (a b)
    (cond
      [(null? a) (first b)]
      [else (first a)])))
```

```
(define heads–combine
  (λ (a b)
    (cons (first a) (cons (first b) ▽()))))
```

```
(define both–null?
  (λ (a b)
    (and2 (null? a) (null? b))))
```

```
(define both–non–null?
  (λ (a b)
    (nor (null? a) (null? b))))
```

It is likely, of course, that there are other solutions to our original problem that are more elegant and easier to follow than the one we have just presented. The foregoing development, however, serves to illustrate, in a very simple case, the power of an approach to writing function definitions that is known as **top-down programming**. A function whose behavior is quite complex has been defined by means of a collection of define-expressions each of which is extremely easy to interpret. Just how useful top-down programming really is will not become apparent until we are faced with much more complicated situations. But the secret of top-down programming remains the same, whatever the level of difficulty of the programming task. It is this: Deal with easy things first, leaving difficult things until later. Behave in the same way with the difficult things, and continue until there are no difficult things left. In particular, at each stage try to break down the task into at most three subtasks:

- the simplest case,

- the other remaining cases, and

- a test (in the form of a predicate function) to see whether you are dealing with the simplest case or not.

Exercise 54.

Use the top-down approach to write a definition for the following function: The function takes two inputs, both of which may be any data expression. If both inputs are atoms then the function should output a list containing exactly two data expressions, namely, the first input and the second input in that order. However, if one input is an atom and the other a list then the function should cons the atom onto the list. Finally, if both inputs are lists, the function should cons the second input onto the first.

2.3 Getting Your Hands Dirty

We now have at our disposal a powerful language with which to manipulate data expressions. Broadening the use of a phrase we introduced in Chapter 1, this kind of manipulation is known as **list processing**—even though some data expressions are not lists! If we so desired, we could continue to deepen our understanding of this list processing language and its applications, treating our work as a purely intellectual exercise in which all non-mental activity takes place with pencil and paper. That would hardly be fair, however, since the writing involved would often be tedious and time-consuming. The time is therefore right for us to alert you to the fact that the means are available to enable computers to engage in list processing. As we have already indicated, the list processing language we are developing is called 'Scheme'. Not only does it serve as a means of recording our list processing thoughts in writing, thereby making them communicable to other people who speak the same language, but it also enables us to exchange ideas on the subject with certain computers. More specifically, the computers with which we shall be able to communicate are those for which there exists a **Scheme interpreter** or **compiler,**[7] that is, a special program written in the computer's native language directing it to process expressions written in Scheme.

In order to take advantage of this possibility of communicating with computers (and incidentally turning over to them much of the hard labor of list processing), you will need to beg, buy, or borrow a suitable computer and either acquire a Scheme interpreter or make use of the *EdScheme* interpreter that is available with this book. Then, as you continue to work through the remaining pages, you will be able to try out what you are learning and to benefit from the immediate feedback and reinforcement that a computer provides. In this way, as we promised in the Preface, you will very shortly become a fully-fledged **schemer,** as practitioners of the art of programming in Scheme are affectionately known.

Our purpose in this short section is to alert you to some of the issues involved in communicating with computers in Scheme. The role of the computer's Scheme interpreter is to enable it to evaluate (black) functional expressions to (red) data expressions; with its help, the computer is from one point of view nothing more than a rather complicated device for changing black expressions into red. Thus, whatever the schemer types at the (monochrome) keyboard is 'understood' by the computer to be in black, and the output which in due time appears on the screen must be interpreted by the schemer to be in red. (If you are using the *EdScheme* interpreter on a system with a color monitor, the computer's output actually *is* in red.)

---

[7]Technically speaking, interpreters and compilers are different programming tools. In theory at least, interpreters are more convenient to use whereas compilers are more efficient in terms of the speed with which the output from functions is calculated. We have little or no interest in such distinctions; all we are concerned about is that they allow us to program in Scheme. From here on, therefore, we shall simply say 'interpreter' when strictly speaking we should say 'interpreter or compiler'.

There are, however, two problems to be overcome: First, while giving the user a choice of upper- or lower-case roman letters, computer keyboards typically do not provide a facility for typing directly in bold italic letters, so how are we to enter variables into the computer? The answer is that, in Scheme, variables are simply blackened atoms (just like function names).[8] Thus, for example, the functional expression '(first *s*)' should be typed as '(first s)'.

Second, what should we type instead of the symbol '$\triangledown$', which we have been using to indicate the presence of a constant function? The answer is to use a single black right-hand quote mark. Thus, the functional expression '$\triangledown$(a b c)' is typed as ''(a b c)'. Unfortunately, the black character ''' is not very visible in a typed functional expression, and matters are even worse in handwriting. So in this text we continue to use our familiar small inverted triangle, '$\triangledown$', instead of the right-hand quote mark.[9] Thus, instead of ''(quote me on this)', we shall print '$\triangledown$(quote me on this)'. We suggest that you also use the inverted triangle in handwriting. When typing such functional expressions into a computer, however, you must use the right-hand quote mark.

On the next two pages we present a colorful conversation between a schemer and a 'Scheme Machine' as it would appear on a color monitor if the *EdScheme* interpreter is being used. (In the absence of a color monitor, or if some other interpreter is being used, the conversation would be conducted in monochrome.) Let us suppose then that the schemer has turned on the computer and has instructed it to read and then run the Scheme interpreter. Somewhere on the screen a **prompt** appears. This is a symbol (or word) printed by the interpreter to indicate to the schemer that he may type a black functional expression. Often, the prompt is a punctuation mark (such as a question mark), sometimes it is a word ('Evaluate:' is quite popular), and in other cases it is some kind of compound symbol that changes with each evaluation to indicate how many expressions have been evaluated during the current conversation, starting with, say, '[1]', then '[2]', and so on. We choose to side with the *EdScheme* interpreter and use the distinctive symbol '$\Longrightarrow$'. Next to the prompt will appear some kind of **cursor**, which is a symbol (often flashing) such as an underline ('_') or a blocked-in rectangle that indicates where symbols will appear on the screen when typed by the

---

[8] In Chapter 5 we explain how the interpreter processes both function names and variables. It then becomes clear that the distinction between their roles is more apparent than real.

[9] In fact, the inverted triangle is an invention of practicing schemers that was designed specifically to make these expressions stand out more in their handwritten scheming!

schemer. In response to the prompt, the schemer types a functional expression, and presses the **return key** (sometimes marked 'enter' or 'newline') to indicate that he or she has finished typing the current line.

To open our sample conversation, the schemer types a simple functional expression, followed of course by a press of the return key:[10]

```
⟹ (first '(a b c d e))
a
⟹ _
```

The interpreter has evaluated the functional expression to the atom 'a' and printed this below the functional expression. It has then redisplayed the prompt, and placed the cursor next to it in readiness for the next evaluation. Our scheming friend now types a definition and uses the corresponding derived function:

```
⟹ (define second
        (lambda (r)
          (first (rest r))))
second
⟹ (second '(a b c d e))
b
⟹ _
```

Notice that, in recognition of the fact that normal computer keyboards include no Greek letter keys, the schemer has had to type '**lambda**' out in full. Notice also that the schemer has chosen to lay the definition out in the easy-to-read indented style we have used in the text. This happens automatically if you are using the *EdScheme* interpreter. However, if you are using some other interpreter that does not perform this service for you, the same effect may be achieved using the keyboard's **space bar** to create the desired amount of space at the beginning of the indented lines and the **return key** to begin each new line. As far as the Scheme interpreter is concerned, one space or fifteen spaces are all the same, so you should feel at liberty to use space in any way you like in order to improve the intelligibility (from a visual standpoint) of what you type into the computer.

---

[10] Note that, when displaying conversations between computer and schemer, we show variables as blackened atoms and we use the quote mark ' '. Outside such displays, however, we continue to print variables using bold italic letters and to replace the quote mark by the inverted triangle '▽'.

You will observe that the interpreter has printed the atom 'second' on the screen to indicate that it has finished processing the definition of the function **second**. In view of the possibility we have just mentioned of entering multi-line definitions, you are probably wondering why the interpreter did not print something on the screen after the first line had been typed. The answer is that each time the return key is pressed the interpreter checks to see if all the parentheses match. If they do, then it processes the expression, and if possible produces a data expression in response. If there are too many right-hand parentheses, then the interpreter simply discards the extra ones and tries to process the resulting (matched parentheses) expression. If, on the other hand, there are too many left-hand parentheses—as there are in the first line of the example above—then the interpreter 'realizes' that the functional expression is incomplete, and it waits patiently for the remainder of the expression to be typed.

The schemer who is engaged in our sample conversation now moves on to a derived function that involves a cond-expression:

```
⟹ (define atom–or–list
      (lambda (a)
        (cond
          [(atom? a) 'atom]
          [else 'list]))))
atom-or-list
⟹ (atom–or–list 'Fred)
atom
⟹ (atom–or–list '(a b
        c d e))
list
⟹ _
```

(We have—most unaesthetically—split the functional expression

$$(atom–or–list \ '(a \ b \ c \ d \ e))$$

over two lines simply to emphasize once again that the interpreter ignores such bizarre behavior on the part of the schemer; as explained above, it waits patiently until it recognizes the presence of matching right-hand parentheses for all the left-hand parentheses that have been entered.)

When it comes to typing cond-expressions into the computer, you should be warned that some Scheme interpreters do not accept brackets. If your Scheme interpreter is this fastidious, then you can overcome its sensitivities by using parentheses instead. In fact, even those Scheme interpreters that *do* accept brackets in cond-expressions will also accept parentheses in their stead. So you cannot go wrong if you use parentheses all the time. For the sake of clarity, however, we shall continue to use brackets in this book.

We hope that this brief interlude has given you some feel for the way that a typical Scheme interpreter behaves. Now would be an excellent time to become acquainted with the computer, for we are about to embark on one of the most exciting stages of our exploration into list processing, and you may find a 'real live' Scheme interpreter a useful ally.

2.4 Wheels within Wheels

We now restrict our attention for a short while to a special type of data expression called a **lat**:

> *A lat is a list that contains no lists.*

For example, '( )' and '(a list of atoms)' are lats, whereas '(a (list))' is not. As you have probably already guessed, 'lat' stands for 'list of atoms'. This represents the positive view of a lat, in contrast to the rather more negative view implicit in the above definition. Notice that the definition requires us to include the null list as a lat since it certainly contains no lists. And from the positive point of view, while it is true that you will look in vain for any atoms contained in the null list, neither does it contain any *non*-atoms. It is therefore perfectly correct to observe that the null list is a list (albeit empty) of nothing but atoms.

Having introduced the notion of a lat, we naturally would like to have at our disposal a predicate function which recognizes when one is present. We therefore begin this section by working toward the definition of the one-input predicate function '**lat?**', which inputs any list and outputs the boolean '#t' if and only if the input is a lat.

Exercise 55.

> Paula, a student of list processing, has written some lists on a sheet of paper. For her homework, she has to figure out what such a function **lat?** (behaving as we have just indicated) would

output if each list in turn were input into it. Unfortunately, on her way home from school the sheet of paper was torn, leaving Paula only with the scrap shown on the right. After some thought Paula realizes that, even after the accident, she can still do some of her homework. For which of the lists, if any, may Paula conclude that the output from the function **lat?** must be the boolean '#t'? For which lists may she conclude that the output must be the boolean '#f'?

a) ((hi)

b) (now

c) ((is)

d) (time

e) ()

f) ((for

g) (all

h) ((up)

tear

We adopt a top-down approach to writing a definition for the function **lat?**. As we proceed, bear in mind that we want the function to input a list and to output the boolean '#t' if and only if the input contains no lists. The following definition deals with the simplest case when the input is the null list (which is, of course, a lat), and it introduces the as-yet-undefined function **lat?–help1**, which is a one-input predicate function whose input we know for sure to be a non-null list.

```
(define lat?
  (λ (a)
    (cond
      [(null? a) #t]
      [else (lat?–help1 a)])))
```

We want this 'helping function', like **lat?** itself, to output the boolean '#t' if its (non-null) input is a lat, otherwise it should output the boolean '#f'.

In the exercise above, Paula's paper was torn in such a way that only the first data expression of each of the non-null lists remained. Yet she was able to conclude that lists (a), (c), (f) and (h) are *not* lats for the simple reason that no non-null list whose first data expression is a list can possibly be a lat. We deal with this easy case as we define the function **lat?–help1**:

```
(define lat?–help1
  (λ (a)
    (cond
      [(atom? (first a)) (lat?–help2 a)]
      [else #f])))
```

We have now dealt with two simple cases. We have ensured that, if the input to the function lat? is the null list, then the output is the boolean '#t', and if that input is a list whose first data expression is a list, then the output is the boolean '#f'. It remains for us to write a definition for the one-input predicate function lat?–help2, whose input we know for sure to be a non-null list whose first data expression is an atom.

Exercise 56.

Suppose that *a* is a non-null list whose first data expression is an atom.

a) Suppose that (lat? (rest *a*)) ↦ #t. What does this tell you about the presence of lists in (rest *a*)? What does this imply about *a*?

b) Suppose that (lat? (rest *a*)) ↦ #f. What does this tell you about the presence of lists in (rest *a*)? What does this imply about *a*?

Your work in this exercise should have suggested to you that the function lat?–help2 should output the boolean '#t' if the rest of its input is a lat, otherwise it should output the boolean '#f'. In other words, if the input to the function lat?–help2 is the list *a*, then it should output the value of '(lat? (rest *a*))'. Hence the definition for the function lat?–help2 is

```
(define lat?–help2
  (λ (a)
    (lat? (rest a))))
```

Bringing together the results of the above three steps, our definition for the function lat? is as follows:

```
(define lat?
  (λ (a)
    (cond
      [(null? a) #t]
      [else (lat?–help1 a)])))
```

```
(define lat?–help1
  (λ (a)
    (cond
      [(atom? (first a)) (lat?–help2 a)]
      [else #f])))
```

(define lat?–help2
(λ (*a*)
(lat? (rest *a*)))))

It will no doubt surprise you to learn that this three-part definition completely and unambiguously defines the function **lat?**! Perhaps you will object that we have still not really defined the function **lat?–help2** since its definition includes a reference to a function, namely **lat?**, that is neither primitive, constant, nor derived—or so it seems. However, we insist that no further define-expressions are necessary, and that the function **lat?** is indeed defined. On the other hand, we do not expect you to believe that this is so simply because we say that it is. We shall therefore attempt to convince you by explaining how the above definition works in practice.

Exercise 57.

Here is a twin-focus machine diagram of the function **lat?** with all the function names missing:

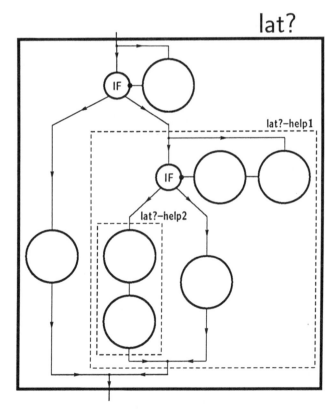

Copy this 'blank' diagram and, having referred to the above definition for the function **lat?**, write the missing function names in
the appropriate boxes. Then feed the following inputs into the
machine, and verify that it behaves correctly in each case:

a) the list '( )'.   b) the list '((b) c)'.

Exercise 58.

In Figure 2.3 on page 79 we present a new, 'exploded' version of
the twin-focus machine diagram for the function **lat?** in which the
internal occurrence of the function **lat?** has itself been drawn as a
twin-focus machine diagram. By referring to this diagram, verify
that the function **lat?** behaves correctly when its input is

a) the list '(a (b) c)'.   b) the list '(a)'.

Although the machine diagram in Figure 2.3 is one of the most complex
that we have considered, it is still inadequate for our purposes. Just as Figure 2.3 is an 'exploded' version of the diagram in Exercise 57, so we need
to 'explode' Figure 2.3, depicting each internal **lat?** machine in its twin-focus
form, if we are to cope with more complex inputs. (Try inputting the list
'(a b)', for example, into the hook-up shown in Figure 2.3; to find the output you will have to replace the innermost **lat?** machine with its twin-focus
diagram.)

An alternative way to check our definition of the function **lat?** is to **trace**
the function as it calculates its output, recording the results systematically.
We illustrate this invaluable technique by tracing the function **lat?** when its
input is the list '(a b c)'. In other words, we evaluate the mixed expression

$$\textbf{(lat?} \; (\text{a b c}))$$

in a step-by-step fashion. From the definition for **lat?** we see that when the
list '(a b c)' is the input, the function evaluates the expression

$$\textbf{(lat?--help1} \; (\text{a b c})),$$

and when the list '(a b c)' is the input to **lat?--help1**, the output is described
by the mixed expression

$$\textbf{(lat?--help2} \; (\text{a b c})).$$

The results of our trace to this point form the first three lines of a **trace
table**, as shown at the top of page 80.

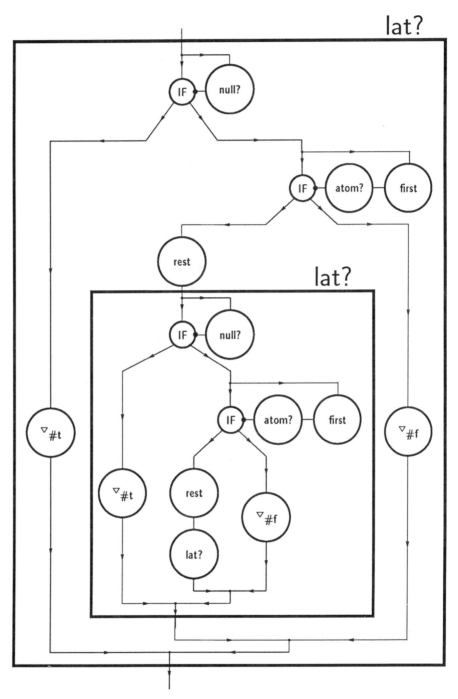

Figure 2.3: A First Expansion of the Function **lat?**.

(lat? (a b c))
(lat?–help1 (a b c))
(lat?–help2 (a b c))
⋮

Moving on, we note that when the list '(a b c)' is the input to **lat?–help2**, the output is described by

(lat? (rest (a b c))).

But the **rest** of the list '(a b c)' is the list '(b c)', so we extend our trace table accordingly:

(lat? (a b c))
(lat?–help1 (a b c))
(lat?–help2 (a b c))
(lat? (rest (a b c)))
(lat? (b c))
⋮

We continue this process of tracing the progress of the input through the function until the (totally red) output is discovered. The completed trace table is as follows:

(lat? (a b c))
(lat?–help1 (a b c))
(lat?–help2 (a b c))
(lat? (rest (a b c)))
(lat? (b c))
(lat?–help1 (b c))
(lat?–help2 (b c))
(lat? (rest (b c)))
(lat? (c))
(lat?–help1 (c))
(lat?–help2 (c))
(lat? (rest (c)))
(lat? ( ))
#t

Exercise 59.

    For each of the following mixed expressions, draw up a trace table showing how the given expression is evaluated.

    a) (lat? `(dog cat rat)`)

    b) (lat? `(squirrel (beaver) badger)`)

    c) (lat? `(do not read () this)`)

We now pause to discuss some important terminology. Functions such as lat?, whose definitions are self-referring, are called **recursive functions**. In the case of the function lat? we say that it '**recurs** on the rest of its input', since we see from the function's machine diagram that it is the rest of the input list that is 'passed' to the internal lat? machine. Functional expressions in which such a self-reference occurs—in the case of lat? the only example is the functional expression '(lat? (rest *a*))'—are called **natural recursions** of the function in question. On the other hand, when the input to the function lat? is

- the null list or

- a non-null list whose first data expression is a list,

then determining the output from the function is a simple exercise that does not involve recursion. These conditions are called the **terminating conditions** of the function lat?.

    The art of writing a definition for a recursive function involves two main steps. First, identify all the terminating conditions, and then deduce what the natural recursion(s) must be. Unfortunately, there are no hard-and-fast rules as to how you should set about doing this. It is possible, however, to offer two pointers, namely:

1. *Almost* always the first terminating condition involves the null? of (one of) the input(s). Indeed, the function null? is usually the only function involved in the first terminating condition.

2. *Almost* always, natural recursions involve the **rest** of (one or more of) the input(s).

    Now that we have written (and tested) our definition for the function lat?, it may be simplified as follows:

```
(define lat?
  (λ (a)
    (cond
      [(null? a) #t]
      [(atom? (first a)) (lat? (rest a))]
      [else #f])))
```

This last step in the development of a definition for the function **lat?** is an important one since it brings together the strands of the algorithm into a single define-expression whose structure is clear and simple. For this reason (and in the interests of conserving space) the answers provided in the Appendix to selected exercises and problems always prefer the final, simplified form to the multiple-define-expression, 'top-down' type of definition. You should feel free—certainly in these initial stages of familiarizing yourself with Scheme— to continue to present your answers in 'top-down' form. As time goes on, however, you will gradually be able to produce more and more complicated definitions in simplified form.

Exercise 60.

Suppose that the definition for the function **lat?** had been written so that the function recurs on its input rather than on the **rest** of its input. That is, suppose the function **lat?** had (erroneously) been defined like this:

```
(define lat?
  (λ (a)
    (cond
      [(null? a) #t]
      [(atom? (first a)) (lat? a)]
      [else #f])))
```

In what circumstances would this function produce an output?

Let us now turn our attention to a second recursive function. As with the function **lat?** it is a predicate function. Unlike **lat?**, however, it takes two inputs. The function is defined as follows:

```
(define member?
  (λ (a s)
    (cond
      [(null? s) #f]
      [(eq? (first s) a) #t]
      [else (member? a (rest s))])))
```

Exercise 61.

Evaluate each of the following functional expressions:

a) (member? ▽Fred ▽( ))

b) (member? ▽Fred ▽(Fred Jane Mary))

The suitable inputs to the function **member?** are somewhat difficult to describe. Since an output will always be produced if the first input is an atom and the second input is a lat, however, the following discussion deals with the situation when the inputs are of this nature. In the last exercise we saw that, when the second input is the null list, the function outputs the boolean '#f', and, when the first data expression in the second input is the atom given as the first input, the function outputs the boolean '#t'.

Suppose now that the second input is a non-null lat whose first atom is *not* the atom given as the first input. For example, suppose the first input is the atom 'and' and the second input is the lat '(war and peace)'. The following trace table illustrates the behavior of the function in this case:

(member? and (war and peace))
(member? and (rest (war and peace)))
(member? and (and peace))
#t

Exercise 62.

a) Evaluate the functional expression '(member? *a s*)' when

(i) *a* : and   (ii) *a* : and
    s : (Robin)   *s* : (Robin Hood)

(iii) *a* : and
      s : (Robin Hood and his merry men)

b) Describe carefully the behavior of the function **member?** when its first input is an atom and its second input is a lat.

Before we continue, note that the terminating conditions of the function **member?** are

- the second input is the null list, and

- the first atom in the second input is the atom given as the first input.

It is no accident that the first terminating condition of the function **member?** involves only the function **null?**, just as the first terminating condition of the function **lat?** did. Note also that the (only) natural recursion of the function **member?** is '(member? *a* (rest *s*))', so once again we have a function that recurs on the **rest** of (one of) its input(s). As you work through the problem set below, keep in mind the two 'pointers' to writing recursive functions that we listed on page 81. In other words, when writing a definition for a function you believe to be recursive, ask yourself: 'What is the output when the input (or one of the inputs) is the null list?' And, as a first guess, assume that any natural recursions will involve the **rest** of one or more of the inputs.

PROBLEM SET 3

1. The recursive predicate function **lili?** inputs any list and outputs the boolean '#t' if and only if the input contains no atoms. (The name 'lili?' is intended to make you think of the phrase 'list of lists', including of course the null list of lists.)

    a) What are the terminating conditions of the function **lili?**, and what is the output in each case?

    b) What is the natural recursion of the function **lili??**

    c) Complete the following skeleton definition for the function **lili?**:

    (define lili?
        (λ (a)
            (cond
                [(_____ a) _____]
                [(atom? (_____ a)) _____]
                [else (_____ (_____ a))]])))

    d) Check your definition for the function **lili?** by compiling trace tables showing its behavior when the input is

    (i) the list '(this should be false)'.

    (ii) the list '((this should) (be) () (true))'.

2. a) Write a definition for the function **atomic?** that outputs the boolean '#t' if and only if its input, which may be any data expression, is an atomic element.

b) Consider the following definition for the function **latel?**:

```
(define latel?
  (λ (a)
    (cond
      [(null? a) #t]
      [(atomic? (first a)) (latel? (rest a))]
      [else #f])))
```

Evaluate

(i) (latel? ▽(a ( ) c))   (ii) (latel? ▽(a (b) c))

c) Describe in words the behavior of the function **latel?**, including in your description a specification of its acceptable inputs.

3. Write a definition for a predicate function that inputs any list and outputs the boolean '#t' if and only if the input contains no atomic elements. (Think carefully about what the output should be if the input is the null list.)

4. Write a definition for a predicate function that inputs any list and outputs the boolean '#t' if and only if the input contains only null lists.

5. Write a definition for the predicate function **Lmember?** which takes two inputs, an atom **a** and a list **l**, and which outputs the boolean '#t' if and only if the list **l** contains the atom **a**.
   [Hint: You must take into account the possibility that **l** is not a lat. In consequence, you must allow for the situation when (**first l**) is a list, in which case, of course, it cannot be the atom given as the first input.]

6. Complete the skeleton definition at the top of the next page for the function **eqlat?** which takes two inputs, both of which are lats, and which outputs the boolean '#t' if and only if the inputs are the same. For example,

   * (eqlat? ▽(Fred Jane) ▽(Fred Mike)) ↦ #f
   * (eqlat? ▽(Fred Lucy) ▽(Fred Lucy)) ↦ #t
   * (eqlat? ▽(Mary Ann) ▽( )) ↦ #f
   * (eqlat? ▽( ) ▽(Fred Eric)) ↦ #f

```
(define eqlat?
  (λ (a b)
    (cond
      [(_____ a) (null? b)]
      [(_____ b) #f]
      [(eq? (_____ a) (_____ b))
       (eqlat? (_____ a) (_____ b))]
      [else _____ ])))
```

7. Write a definition for the predicate function **equal?** that takes two inputs, both of which may be any data expression, and outputs the boolean '#t' if and only if both inputs are the same data expression. (Try to write your definition before reading the following hint.)
[Hint: Check that you have taken into account all the following cases:

    1. Both inputs are atoms.

    2. One input is an atom and one is a list.

    3. Both inputs are lists. Then, perhaps,

        3.1 both inputs are the null list.

        3.2 one input is the null list and the other is a non-null list.

        3.3 both inputs are non-null lists, in which case they are the same data expression if and only if

          (a) the **first**s of the inputs are equal and

          (b) the **rest**s of the inputs are equal.]

$$- \text{o O o} -$$

All the recursive functions we have considered thus far have been predicate functions. For the sake of contrast, we now turn our attention to some recursive functions that output lists. Our first example of such a function is **rember** (short for 'remove member'). This function inputs an atom and a lat and removes the first occurrence (if there is one) of the atom from the lat. For example,

- (rember $^\nabla$Fred $^\nabla$(Fred Jane Fred)) ↦ (Jane Fred)

- (rember $^\nabla$Fred $^\nabla$()) ↦ ()

- (rember $^\nabla$Fred $^\nabla$(Jane Mike)) ↦ (Jane Mike)

- (rember $^\nabla$Jeff $^\nabla$(Fred Mary Jeff Mike)) ↦ (Fred Mary Mike)

As always we attempt to identify the terminating conditions and the natural recursion(s) of this function. The first terminating condition involves the null list, for when the second input to the function **rember** is the null list, then the output should surely be the null list. The second terminating condition deals with the situation when the first atom in the second input is the atom given as the first input; in this case, the function should output the **rest** of its second input.

We must now deal with the case when the atom given as the first input to **rember** is not the same as the first atom in the second input. Suppose that the inputs are an atom a and a non-null lat v such that the first atom in v is not the atom a. After a little thought, it becomes apparent that what we want to do in this situation is to cons the first data expression of the lat v onto the rest of the lat v with its first occurrence of the atom a removed. For example, let

$$a : \texttt{Fred}$$
$$v : \texttt{(Jane Mike Fred Paul)}.$$

Clearly, '(**first** v)' evaluates to the atom 'Jane', which is not the atom a, so we cons the atom 'Jane' onto the rest of the list '(Jane Mike Fred Paul)' with its first occurrence of the atom 'Fred' removed. Now, the rest of the list '(Jane Mike Fred Paul)' is the list '(Mike Fred Paul)', and, when we remove the first occurrence of the atom 'Fred' from this list, we obtain the list '(Mike Paul)'. So we must cons the atom 'Jane' onto the list '(Mike Paul)', thereby obtaining the list '(Jane Mike Paul)', which is the expected output.

Exercise 63.

In Figure 2.4 on page 88 we provide a twin-focus diagram for the function **rember**. By making use of this diagram, verify that when the inputs to the function **rember** are the atom 'Fred' and the list '(Fred Paul)', the output is the list '(Paul)'.

The corresponding define-expression for the function **rember** is as follows:

```
(define rember
  (λ (a s)
    (cond
      [(null? s) ▽()]
      [(eq? (first s) a) (rest s)]
      [else (cons (first s) (rember a (rest s)))])))
```

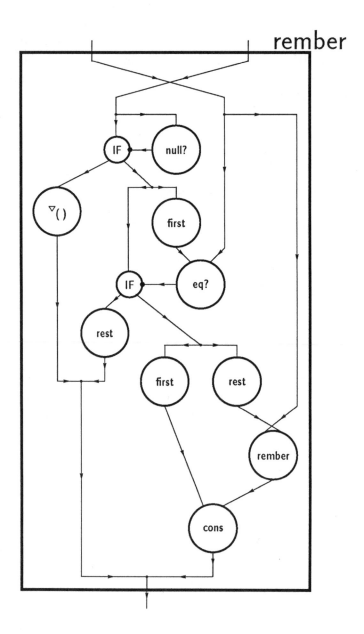

Figure 2.4: The Function **rember**.

Here is a trace table showing the behavior of the function when its inputs are the atom 'c' and the list '(a b c d)':

(rember c (a b c d))
(cons (first (a b c d)) (rember c (rest (a b c d))))
(cons a (rember c (b c d)))
(cons a (cons (first (b c d)) (rember c (rest (b c d)))))
(cons a (cons b (rember c (c d))))
(cons a (cons b (rest (c d))))
(cons a (cons b (d)))
(cons a (b d))
(a b d)

Exercise 64.

Compile a trace table showing the behavior of the function **rember** when its inputs are the atom 'd' and the list '(c d s)'.

We move on now to a second recursive function that outputs a list. The function **getfirsts** is a one-input function that requires its input to be either the null list or a list that contains only non-null lists. In the first case, it simply returns the null list, and in the second case it outputs a list made up of the first data expressions of the internal lists, in order. For example,

- (getfirsts ▽()) ↦ ()

- (getfirsts ▽((a b) (c d) (e f))) ↦ (a c e)

- (getfirsts ▽((one))) ↦ (one)

- (getfirsts ▽((off we) ((jolly)) (well go))) ↦ (off (jolly) well)

Inspired by the pointers listed on page 81, we suspect that the first terminating condition of the function **getfirsts** will involve the null list. In fact, the above description of the function's behavior makes it seem virtually certain that it will have only one terminating condition, which will check if the input to the function is the null list. According to our second pointer, the natural recursion will probably involve the **rest** of the input. So we try to use the functional expression '(getfirsts (rest *s*))' in the natural recursion. Finally, we observe that the function **getfirsts** 'builds' a list. So we can be sure that the function **cons** will be involved.

Exercise 65.

a) Complete the following skeleton definition for the function getfirsts.

```
(define getfirsts
  (λ (s)
    (cond
      [(null? s) _____ ]
      [else (_____
              (_____ (_____ s))
              (_____ (_____ s)))])))
```

b) Compile a trace table showing the behavior of the function **getfirsts** as you have defined it in part (a) when its input is

   (i) the list '((a b) (c d) (e f))';

   (ii) the list '(((a)) ((b) c))'.

PROBLEM SET 4

1. Consider carefully the following definition for the function **dupla** of a data expression and a list:

```
(define dupla
  (λ (a s)
    (cond
      [(null? s) ▽()]
      [else (cons a (dupla a (rest s)))])))
```

a) By compiling a trace table, or otherwise, evaluate each of the following functional expressions:

   (i) (dupla ▽a ▽())   (ii) (dupla ▽a ▽(one))

   (iii) (dupla ▽a ▽(one (two)))   (iv) (dupla ▽a ▽(one () (three)))

   (v) (dupla ▽() ▽(1 2 3 4 5 6 7 8 9))

b) Describe the behavior of the function **dupla**.

2. Complete the following skeleton definition for the function **double** that inputs an atom *a* and a lat *s* and 'doubles' the first occurrence of the atom *a* in the lat *s*. For example,

(double ▽cat ▽(dog cat rat)) ↦ (dog cat cat rat)

(define double
  (λ (*a s*)
    (cond
      [(_____ *s*) ▽()]
      [(eq? (_____ *s*) *a*) (_____ *a s*)]
      [else (cons (_____ *s*) (double *a* (_____ *s*)))]])))

3. Complete the following skeleton definition for the function **insertl** that takes three inputs, two atoms *a* and *b* and a lat *s* (in that order), and outputs a new lat that is the lat *s* with the atom *b* inserted to the left of the first occurrence of the atom *a*. For example,

(insertl ▽cat ▽bat ▽(sat cat mat)) ↦ (sat bat cat mat)

(define insertl
  (λ (*a b s*)
    (cond
      [(_____ *s*) ▽()]
      [(eq? (_____ *s*) *a*) (_____ *b s*)]
      [else (_____
             (_____ *s*)
             (insertl *a b* (_____ *s*)))]])))

4. Write a definition for the function **insertr** that inputs two atoms *a* and *b* and a lat *s* (in that order) and inserts the atom *b* to the *right* of the first occurrence of the atom *a* in the lat *s*. For example,

(insertr ▽c ▽g ▽(a b c d e)) ↦ (a b c g d e)

5. Write a definition for the function **subst** that inputs two atoms *a* and *b* and a lat *s* (in that order) and *replaces* the first occurrence of the atom *a* in the lat *s* with the atom *b*. For example,

(subst ▽c ▽g ▽(a b c d e)) ↦ (a b g d e)

6. Complete the following skeleton definition for the function **subst–all** that inputs two atoms *a* and *b* and a lat *s* (in that order) and replaces *every* occurrence of the atom *a* in the lat *s* with the atom *b*. For example,

(subst–all ▽c ▽g ▽(a c b c d c e)) ↦ (a g b g d g e)

```
(define subst–all
  (λ (a b s)
    (cond
      [(null? s) ▽( )]
      [(eq? (first s) a)
       (_____ b (_____ a b (_____ s)))]
      [else (_____
              (_____ s)
              (_____ a b (_____ s)))])))
```

7. Write a definition for the function **genrember** which (unlike **rember**) inputs *any* data expression *a* and *any* list *s* and removes the first occurrence of the data expression *a* from the list *s*. For example,

(genrember ▽(fo) ▽((fee fi) (fo) fum) ↦ ((fee fi) fum)

8. Write definitions for each of the following functions:

   a) The function **cons–to–end** that accepts two inputs, the first being any data expression and the second being any list, and outputs a list that is the second input with the first input inserted as the last data expression. For example,

   - (cons–to–end ▽a ▽( )) ↦ (a)
   - (cons–to–end ▽a ▽(b c d)) ↦ (b c d a)
   - (cons–to–end ▽(a (b) c) ▽(a b c)) ↦ (a b c (a (b) c))

   b) The function **burrow** that inputs any list and outputs the first atomic element that appears in the input list when the list is read literally as a string of characters. (In terms of decomposition trees, the output is the atomic element on the furthest leaf to the left.) For example,

   - (burrow ▽( )) ↦ ( )
   - (burrow ▽(a b c)) ↦ a
   - (burrow ▽((at b) c)) ↦ at

- (burrow $^\triangledown$((((hat)) b) c)) $\mapsto$ hat
- (burrow $^\triangledown$((((( )) (a)) b) c))) $\mapsto$ ( )

c) The function **make–lat** that inputs any list and 'makes a lat' by outputting a new list that is the input with *all* its internal lists removed. For example,

- (make–lat $^\triangledown$( )) $\mapsto$ ( )
- (make–lat $^\triangledown$(a b (c) (d) e)) $\mapsto$ (a b e)
- (make–lat $^\triangledown$((a b c) (d))) $\mapsto$ ( )
- (make–lat $^\triangledown$((a (b)) c (d))) $\mapsto$ (c)

d) The function **reverse** that inputs any list and outputs a new list that is obtained from the input list by reversing the order of its data expressions, if any. For example,

- (reverse $^\triangledown$( )) $\mapsto$ ( )
- (reverse $^\triangledown$(a)) $\mapsto$ (a)
- (reverse $^\triangledown$(a (b) ((c)))) $\mapsto$ (((c)) (b) a)
- (reverse $^\triangledown$(1 2 3 4 5)) $\mapsto$ (5 4 3 2 1)

e) The function **append** of lists r and s—for which a skeleton definition is provided below—that appends the contents of s to r, that is, it 'puts the two lists together', with the contents of r forming the first part of the output list. For example,

- (append $^\triangledown$(a b c) $^\triangledown$(d e f)) $\mapsto$ (a b c d e f)
- (append $^\triangledown$( )$^\triangledown$(d e f)) $\mapsto$ (d e f)
- (append $^\triangledown$(a b c) $^\triangledown$( )) $\mapsto$ (a b c)
- (append $^\triangledown$( )$^\triangledown$( )) $\mapsto$ ( )

```
(define append
  (λ (r s)
    (cond
      [(null? r) _____ ]
      [else (cons (_____ r) (_____ (_____ r) s))])))
```

f) The function **atomize**—for which a skeleton definition is provided on the next page—that inputs any list and outputs a list containing, in order of appearance, all the atoms that are involved in the list, no matter how deeply they are embedded. (In terms of decomposition trees, this function outputs, in order, the atoms that appear at the tree's leaves). For example,

- (atomize ▽( )) ↦ ( )
- (atomize ▽((a (b) ( )) ((((c d) (e ((f))))))) ↦ (a b c d e f)

```
(define atomize
  (λ (s)
    (cond
      [(null? s) ▽()]
      [(atom? (first s))
        (cons (_____ s) (_____ (_____ s)))
      [else (append (_____ (_____ s))
                    (_____ (_____ s)))])))
```

g) The function **butlast** that inputs a non-null list and outputs a list containing all the data expressions of the input list, in order, except the last.

h) The function **last** that inputs a non-null list and outputs the last data expression in the list.

$$- \text{o O o} -$$

3 Accounting Machines

We turn now to the question of how we may use lists and the techniques of list processing to work with numbers. You probably think it rather strange that we have waited until now to discuss such a topic. For, after all, the majority of computing books and courses deal with the evaluation of arithmetic expressions right from the start. Unlike 'typical' computing courses, however, the focus of our attention is not on illustrating how a computer may be used to, say, calculate the average of a sequence of integers or test whether or not an integer is a prime (although these are worthy tasks for a computer). Rather, we want to show you how a system for making such calculations may be constructed. This is not to say that we immerse ourselves in theoretical matters, paying little or no attention to questions of practical utility. Nothing could be further from the truth, as you will see.

3.1 Simple Accounting

We begin by asking the apparently simple question: How may we represent numbers in Scheme? As we search for an answer, let us restrict our attention for the moment to the **whole numbers**, that is, the integers starting at zero:

$$0, 1, 2, 3, 4, 5, 6, 7, 8, 9, 10, 11, 12, \ldots , \text{ and so on.}$$

Your first thought is probably to use atoms built from the red numerals '0', '1', '2', '3', '4', '5', '6', '7', '8', and '9'. Perhaps, for example, we could use the atom '0' to represent the number 0, the atom '1' to represent the number 1, the atom '125739' to represent the number 125739, and so on. Unfortunately, straightforward though it may seem, such a representation runs into difficulty when we try to define even the simplest of operations on whole numbers. For example, let us try to define the function **add1** which inputs a representation of a whole number[1] n and returns the representation of $n + 1$. Here is one attempt:

```
(define add1
  (λ (n)
    (cond
      [(eq? n ▽0) ▽1]
      [(eq? n ▽1) ▽2]
      [(eq? n ▽2) ▽3]
         ⋮
      [(eq? n ▽13195) ▽13196]
      [(eq? n ▽13196) ▽13197]
         ⋮
)))
```

Such an indefinite and endless define-expression is acceptable neither to us nor to the computer. In fact, as we shall see shortly, if we wish to manipulate numbers named by their red arabic numerals, then we require some additional primitive functions. Before introducing you to these new functions, however, we discuss some ingenious methods of manipulating numbers using only the list processing techniques we have developed to this point.

Ideally, what we need is a representation of whole numbers, using only data expressions, that allows us to define functions such as **add1** *recursively*. As it happens, there are many such representations for us to choose from, one of which may be described as follows:

REPRESENTATION W1.

Each whole number n is represented by the list built by writing $n + 1$ red left parentheses followed by $n + 1$ red right parentheses.

---

[1] We adopt the usual mathematical convention of using *italic letters* for variables that may be replaced by the names of numbers. Thus, we now have two types of variable, those in the bold italic typeface, such as 'a' and 'r', which are used in functional expressions and whose replacements are data expressions, and those in the regular italic typeface, such as 'n' and 'p', which are used in the text and whose replacements are names of numbers.

For each whole number n, if n is represented by the list l under Representation W1, then we say that 'l is the W1-representation of n'. Under Representation W1, 0 is represented by the null list and 1 is represented by the list written as two red left parentheses followed immediately by two red right parentheses, that is, the list '$(\,(\,)\,)$'. Similarly, the W1-representation of 5 is the list '$(\,(\,(\,(\,(\,(\,)\,)\,)\,)\,)\,)$' written as six red left parentheses followed immediately by six red right parentheses.

Exercise 66. Write the W1-representation of the whole number 3.

Exercise 67.
        Which whole number is represented by this list?

$$(\,(\,(\,(\,(\,(\,(\,(\,(\,(\,(\,(\,)\,)\,)\,)\,)\,)\,)\,)\,)\,)\,)\,)$$

Having identified a suitable way to represent numbers, we would obviously like to write some functions that input and output W1-representations of whole numbers.

Exercise 68.
        Write a definition for

a) the predicate function **zero?** of the W1-representation of a whole number n that returns the boolean '#t' if and only if $n = 0$.

b) the function **add1** of the W1-representation of a whole number n that returns the W1-representation of $n + 1$.

c) the function **sub1** of the W1-representation of a natural number[2] n that returns the W1-representation of $n - 1$.

d) the predicate function **number?** of a data expression a that returns the boolean '#t' if and only if a is a W1-representation of a whole number.

Judging by their definitions, the functions **zero?**, **add1**, and **sub1** seem to have little to do with numbers. Nevertheless, it *is* possible to use them to perform simple calculations. For example, the functional expression

$$(\text{sub1 } {}^{\triangledown}(\,(\,(\,(\,(\,(\,(\,)\,)\,)\,)\,)\,)\,)\,))$$

evaluates to the list '$(\,(\,(\,(\,(\,(\,)\,)\,)\,)\,)\,)$'. So, after laboriously counting parentheses, we can conclude that $7 - 1 = 6$. Furthermore, the functions **zero?**, **add1**, and **sub1** may be used to construct other more complicated functions

---

[2] Here, and throughout this book, by 'natural number' we mean 'non-zero whole number'.

that operate on W1-representations of whole numbers. Here, for example, is a definition for the function + of W1-representations of whole numbers m and n that returns the W1-representation of $m + n$:

```
(define +
  (λ (m n)
    (cond
      [(zero? n) m]
      [else (add1 (+ m (sub1 n)))])))) 
```

To convince you that this function behaves as we claim, we now trace its operation when the inputs are '(((((( )))))) ' and '(((( ))))' —that is, the W1-representations of 5 and 3—in that order. Of course, with these inputs we expect the function + to return the W1-representation of 8. The trace table begins with the mixed expression

$$(+\ (((((( )))))) \ (((( ))))).$$

Working through the define-expression for the function +, we note that the second input, the list '(((( ))))', is not the W1-representation of 0, and so, since (sub1 (((( ))))) ↦ ((( ))), we must evaluate

$$(add1\ (+\ (((((( )))))) \ ((( )))))$$

Moving on to the sub-expression '(+ (((((( )))))) ((( ))))', we note that the second input to the function + is again a non-null list, so the next step in the trace is to evaluate the mixed expression

$$(add1\ (add1\ (+\ (((((( )))))) \ (( ))))).$$

Since the list '(( ))' is not the W1-representation of 0, the next expression to be evaluated is

$$(add1\ (add1\ (add1\ (+\ (((((( )))))) \ ( ))))).$$

Summarizing our work so far, we have the following incomplete trace table:

```
(+ ((((( ( )))))) (((( ))))) 
(add1 (+ ((((( ( )))))) ((( ))))) 
(add1 (add1 (+ ((((( ( )))))) (( ))))) 
(add1 (add1 (add1 (+ ((((( ( )))))) ( )))))
        ⋮
```

At this stage, however, the second input to the function + is (finally) the W1-representation of 0. So (+ (((((( )))))) ( )) ↦ (((((( )))))), and the next line of the trace table is (add1 (add1 (add1 ((((((( ))))))))))).

It is then an easy matter to complete the trace table, as follows:

(+ ((((((( ))))))) ((((( )))))
(add1 (+ ((((((( ))))))) ((((( ))))))
(add1 (add1 (+ ((((((( ))))))) ((( ))))))
(add1 (add1 (add1 (+ ((((((( ))))))) (( )))))))
(add1 (add1 (add1 ((((((( )))))))))))
(add1 (add1 ((((((( )))))))))))
(add1 ((((((( ))))))))))))
((((((((( )))))))))))

As expected, the function **+** has returned the W1-representation of 8.

We mentioned earlier that Representation W1 is but one of several possible representations of whole numbers. Here is an alternative:

REPRESENTATION W2.

> *Each whole number n is represented by the list containing exactly*
> *n data expressions, each of which is the null list.*

Under Representation W2, 0 is represented by the list '( )', 1 by the list '(( ))', 2 by the list '(( ) ( ))', and so on.

When you answered Exercise 68, you wrote definitions for the functions **zero?**, **add1**, **sub1**, and **number?** on the assumption that their inputs were W1-representations of whole numbers. It is to be expected, therefore, that these definitions will have to be adjusted or totally rewritten so as to conform to the new representation.

Exercise 69.

Write a definition for

a) the predicate function **zero?** of the W2-representation of a whole number n that returns the boolean '#t' if and only if $n = 0$.

b) the function **add1** of the W2-representation of a whole number n that returns the W2-representation of $n + 1$.

c) the function **sub1** of the W2-representation of a natural number n that returns the W2-representation of $n - 1$.

d) the predicate function **number?** of a data expression *a* that returns the boolean '#t' if and only if *a* is a W2-representation of a whole number.

Exercise 70.

Write a definition for the function **+** that inputs W2-representations of whole numbers *m* and *n* and returns the W2-representation of $m + n$.

[Hint: Use the definition for the function **+** on page 98 as a model. What expressions in the definition (if any) need to be changed in light of the new representation?]

It may have surprised you to discover that the definition for the function **+** seems not to depend on which representation of whole numbers is in use. We verify that this is so by presenting a trace of the function **+** (as defined on page 98) when the inputs are the W2-representations of 5 and 3 (compare this trace table with the one on page 99):

```
(+ (() () () () ()) (() () ()))
(add1 (+ (() () () () ()) (() () ())))
(add1 (add1 (+ (() () () () ()) (() ()))))
(add1 (add1 (add1 (+ (() () () () ()) (())))))
(add1 (add1 (add1 (() () () () ()))))
(add1 (add1 (() () () () () ())))
(add1 (() () () () () () ()))
(() () () () () () () ())
```

The reason the function **+** works on both Representations W1 and W2 is that we have written its definition in such a way that it does not refer directly to the current representation, but instead uses the functions **add1**, **sub1**, and **zero?** to do its work. Of course, the definitions for the functions **add1**, **sub1**, and **zero?** depend very much on the particular representation chosen. In fact, these functions—which are known as **data abstractor functions**—serve the very important purpose of *hiding* the actual representation of whole numbers from the function **+**.

It so happens that the data abstractor functions **zero?**, **add1**, and **sub1** are all that we need in order to perform many quite sophisticated operations on whole numbers. At the top of the next page, for example, is a definition for the function **−** of representations of whole numbers *m* and *n*, with *m* not less than *n*, that returns the representation of $m - n$:

```
(define −
  (λ (m n)
    (cond
      [(zero? n) m]
      [else (sub1 (− m (sub1 n)))])))
```

In this definition, we have totally ignored the question as to which representation of whole numbers is currently in use because, by using only data abstractor functions to manipulate the inputs, we are assured that the function behaves correctly provided that the data abstractor functions are defined appropriately. In a moment we compile a trace table showing the behavior of the function −, but the time has come to introduce a more convenient representation for whole numbers.

It has certainly not escaped your attention that the lists we have been using to represent whole numbers are, to put it mildly, rather unwieldy. True, we could use the functions we have developed as the basis for a simple calculator, but in the time it takes to figure out which number is represented by the output of a numeric function we could probably calculate the result by hand. Fortunately, we shall not have to work with such inconvenient and cumbersome representations any longer, for Scheme recognizes a much more natural method to represent whole numbers and goes so far as to provide the functions **zero?**, **add1**, **sub1**, and **number?** as primitives that process these more natural representations. As we hinted earlier, the representation to which we refer is the one you first thought of:

REPRESENTATION W.

   Each whole number is represented by its red arabic numeral.

Under Representation W, zero is represented by the atom '0', the number 1 by the atom '1', the number 9986 by the atom '9986', and so on. The primitive predicate function **number?** returns the boolean '#t' if and only if its input is a W-representation of a whole number, and the functions **zero?**, **add1** and **sub1** behave exactly as you would expect. For example,

- (zero? $^\triangledown$99) ↦ #f
- (add1 $^\triangledown$1425795) ↦ 1425796
- (zero? $^\triangledown$0) ↦ #t
- (sub1 $^\triangledown$5) ↦ 4

There is an additional special service provided by Scheme that further cuts down the amount of typing required when working with W-representations of numbers. Consider the constant function $^\nabla$**97** that returns the W-representation of the number 97. Under normal circumstances, we would expect to record the output from this function by means of the functional expression '$^\nabla$**97**'. However, just as Scheme accepts the abbreviations '**#t**' and '**#f**' for the functional expressions '$^\nabla$**#t**' and '$^\nabla$**#f**', respectively, so it accepts '**97**' as an abbreviation for '$^\nabla$**97**', and similarly for all other numerical constant functions. Using these abbreviations, the examples given above become:

- (zero? 99) $\mapsto$ #f
- (zero? 0) $\mapsto$ #t

- (add1 1425795) $\mapsto$ 1425796
- (sub1 5) $\mapsto$ 4

Following up on our earlier promise, we now provide a trace table showing how the function − behaves when its inputs are the W-representations of the numbers 5 and 3 (in that order):

(− 5 3)
(sub1 (− 5 2))
(sub1 (sub1 (− 5 1)))
(sub1 (sub1 (sub1 (− 5 0))))
(sub1 (sub1 (sub1 5)))
(sub1 (sub1 4))
(sub1 3)
2

From this point on, in the interests of brevity we often speak as if the functions we define manipulate whole numbers. In reality, of course, it is the *representations* of whole numbers that are involved. Using this kind of elliptical language, we make statements such as 'The function **+** inputs whole numbers m and n and returns $m + n$.' At face value, such a statement is nonsense! The only functions we consider in this book are those that input and output data expressions—and whole numbers are not data expressions. Of course, the intention is that the statement should be understood as meaning:

The function **+** inputs *the representations of* whole numbers m and n and outputs *the representation of* $m + n$.

Rest assured, however, that in situations where confusion would otherwise arise we shall include explicit reference to representations.

Exercise 71.

Use the function **+** in completing the following skeleton definition for the function ***** of whole numbers m and n that returns the product $m \cdot n$ (the convention in computing circles is that '*****' denotes multiplication):

(define *
 (λ (m n)
  (cond
   [(_____ n) 0]
   [else (_____ m (_____ m (sub1 n)))]])))

We are about to launch into a fairly extensive problem set in which a large collection of numeric functions are developed. Each such function is built on the foundations of the data abstractor functions **zero?**, **add1**, and **sub1** (the role played by the data abstractor function **number?** becomes apparent later in this chapter). In some cases, it is not at all clear how a given function depends on the underlying data abstractor functions. This is because we have organized our development in a hierarchical fashion, each level in the hierarchy containing functions that are at the same time more sophisticated than and supported by lower level functions.

To be honest, it must be admitted that some of the high level functions we ask you to define in the problem set—the functions **=**, **quotient**, and **remainder**, for example—are provided by most implementations of Scheme as primitive functions which, in most cases, accept a broader range of inputs than we specify here. If, however, we just let matters rest at that, there would be little left to discuss in this chapter. Were we simply to announce the existence of these primitives and to move on from there, we would be depriving you of a golden opportunity. For in asking you to define these functions we are giving you the chance to develop your ability to create definitions and to experience the immense personal satisfaction that is to be gained from devising elegant algorithms. (It is also virtually certain that at least *some* of the functions we discuss are not primitive in your Scheme interpreter.[3])

Unhappily, elegance and efficiency are not often easy bedfellows. To show you what we mean, let us suppose that the Scheme interpreter takes one-

---

[3] If you attempt to check your work in the problem set by entering your definitions of **length**, **quotient**, and so on, with a view to making sure they work as you expect, most Scheme interpreters will object that the function you are attempting to define is primitive. In such circumstances, simply invent another name for the function you are defining and enter your definition under the new name.

thousandth of a second to do whatever is necessary in order to calculate the output from each of the data abstractor functions **zero?**, **add1**, and **sub1**. And suppose further, for the sake of argument, that it processes all other functions instantaneously. Then, for example, the function **+** as we have defined it would take about thirty seconds to calculate '10 000 + 10 000', a task that you could do in your head in the time that it takes to say 'twenty thousand'. Worse still, using the definition for the function ***** developed in the exercise above, the interpreter would take approximately twenty-eight hours to calculate '10 000 · 10 000'. Such an utterly abysmal level of performance is unacceptable in a programming language, and it is for this reason that Scheme provides many of the higher level arithmetic functions (such as **+**, **–**, and *****) as primitives. Over the years, mathematicians have gradually developed ever more sophisticated and efficient algorithms for performing numeric operations, and professionally written interpreters typically incorporate the most efficient algorithms available. (For example, the three higher level primitives we have just mentioned use algorithms that take advantage of the positional nature of W-representations.) Needless to say, many such algorithms involve clever mathematical 'tricks' aimed at saving time, but in consequence they often lack the simple elegance of the definitions we have been writing in this chapter. For practical reasons, however, it is usually advisable to use the 'built-in' arithmetic primitives provided by your Scheme interpreter. Note, though, that it is good style to prefer '(**add1** n)' to '(**+** n 1)', and similarly for **sub1**.

PROBLEM SET 5

1. Using the functions **zero?** and **sub1**, write a definition for the predicate function **one?** of a natural number n that returns the boolean '#t' if and only if $n = 1$.

2. Write a definition for the function **square** of a whole number n that returns the square, n^2, of the number. (For example, $4^2 = 4 \cdot 4 = 16$.)

3.   a) Evaluate the functional expression '(**length** $^\triangledown$(a b c))', where the function **length** is defined as shown at the top of the next page.

     b) Describe the behavior of the function **length**. (Remember to include a description of its suitable inputs.)

```
(define length
  (λ (d)
    (cond
      [(null? d) 0]
      [else (add1 (length (rest d)))])))
```

4. Complete the following skeleton definition for the function **occur** of a data expression **a** and a list **r** that returns the number of times that the data expression **a** appears in the list **r**:

```
(define occur
  (λ (a r)
    (cond
      [(_____ r) _____ ]
      [(_____ a (_____ r))
       (_____ (occur a (_____ r)))]
      [else (_____ a (_____ r))])))
```

5. Write a definition for the function **duplicate** of a whole number n and a data expression **r** that returns a list containing exactly n data expressions, each of which is the data expression **r**.

6. Complete the skeleton definition on the right for the function **nth** of a natural number k and a list l containing at least k data expressions that returns the kth data expression in l.

```
(define nth
  (λ (k l)
    (cond
      [(one? k) (_____ l)]
      [else (_____
             (_____ k)
             (_____ l))])))
```

7. Write a definition for the function **position** of a data expression **a** and a list **r**, one of whose data expressions is **a**, that returns the position of the first occurrence of **a** in **r**. For example,

- (position ▽A ▽(A B B A)) ↦ 1
- (position ▽B ▽(A B B A)) ↦ 2

8. Write a definition for the function **replace–nth** of a natural number k, a data expression **a**, and a list **r** containing at least k data expressions that returns the list **r** with its kth data expression replaced by **a**. For example,

$$\text{(replace–nth 4 } {}^{\triangledown}\text{W } {}^{\triangledown}\text{(B R A I N))} \mapsto \text{(B R A W N)}$$

9. Complete this skeleton definition for the predicate function = of whole numbers m and n that returns the boolean '#t' if and only if $m = n$.[4]

      (define =
        (λ (m n)
          (cond
            [(zero? m) (_____ n)]
            [(_____ n) #f]
            [else (_____ (_____ m) (_____ n))]])))

10. Write a definition for the predicate function **less?** of whole numbers m and n that returns the boolean '#t' if and only if $m < n$. (By '$m < n$' we mean that m is *strictly less than* n. Indeed, the related standard Scheme function—whose inputs are not restricted simply to whole numbers—is denoted by '<'.) Note that, if $m = n$, then the function should return the boolean '#f'.)

11. In this question we consider the division of whole numbers. Our discussion is based on the following result (known as the 'Division Theorem') from elementary number theory:

> *If a and b are whole numbers and $b \neq 0$, then there is exactly one pair of whole numbers q and r satisfying the conditions*
>
> $$(\star) \qquad a = bq + r \text{ and } 0 \leq r < b.$$

The number q is called the **quotient**, r the **remainder**, b the **divisor** and a the **dividend** (this terminology is applicable only when *both* conditions $(\star)$ are satisfied). As an example, let us take 19 to be the dividend and 5 to be the divisor. The theorem states that there exists one (and only one) pair of whole numbers q and r such that

$$19 = (5 \cdot q) + r \text{ and } 0 \leq r < 5.$$

A moment's reflection reveals that $q = 3$ and $r = 4$. Thus, when 19 is divided by 5, the quotient is 3 and the remainder is 4.

---

[4]Since W-representations of whole numbers are atoms it is possible to use the predicate function **eq?** to test whether two representations are the same. As a matter of style, however, we prefer to use the function = when comparing representations of whole numbers.

a) Complete this table:

dividend	divisor	quotient	remainder
19	5	3	4
5	7		
11	22		
22	9		
40	5		
0	34		

b) Complete the following skeleton definition for the function **quotient** of whole numbers a and b such that $b \neq 0$ that returns the quotient when a is divided by b:

(define quotient
  (λ (*a b*)
    (cond
      [(less? *a b*) _____]
      [else (_____ (_____ (– *a b*) *b*))]))))

c) Complete the following skeleton definition for the function **remainder** of whole numbers a and b such that $b \neq 0$ that returns the remainder when a is divided by b:

(define remainder
  (λ (*a b*)
    (cond
      [(_____ *a b*) _____]
      [else (_____ (_____ *a b*) *b*))]))))

d) Solving the equation '$a = bq + r$' for 'r' yields '$r = a - bq$', and this transformed equation may be used to help us calculate the remainder when the dividend, divisor, and quotient are known. For example, suppose that the dividend is 19, the divisor is 5 and the quotient (as calculated, perhaps, by the function **quotient**) is 3. Substituting in the formula '$r = a - bq$', we find that $r = 19 - (5 \cdot 3) = 19 - 15 = 4$. That is, the remainder is 4. Use this method to write an (apparently) non-recursive[5] definition for the function **remainder**.

12. A whole number a is said to **divide** a whole number b if and only if there is a whole number x such that $b = a \cdot x$. In symbols, we write '$a \mid b$' to mean 'a divides b' and '$a \nmid b$' to mean 'a does *not* divide b'. For example,

   - $2 \mid 6$ since $6 = 2 \cdot 3$;
   - $6 \nmid 2$ since there is no whole number x such that $2 = 6 \cdot x$;
   - $6 \mid 0$ since $0 = 6 \cdot 0$;
   - $0 \nmid 6$ since there is no whole number x such that $6 = 0 \cdot x$;
   - $0 \mid 0$ since $0 = 0 \cdot 1776$.

   a) Use the function **remainder** to write a definition for the predicate function **divides?** of whole numbers a and b that returns the boolean '#t' if and only if $a \mid b$. (Make sure that your function deals correctly with the cases when one or both of the inputs are zero.)

   b) Use the function **divides?** to write a definition for the predicate function **even?** of a whole number a that returns the boolean '#t' if and only if a is an even number.

13. The **greatest common divisor**[6] of natural numbers a and b is the largest natural number d such that both $d \mid a$ and $d \mid b$. We denote the greatest common divisor of a and b by '$a \sqcap b$'.

   The following method for finding the greatest common divisor of two natural numbers a and b is based on what is known as Euclid's Algorithm:[7]

   Calculate the remainder r when a is divided by b:

   1. if $r = 0$, then the result is b;

   2. if $r \neq 0$, then the result is the greatest common divisor of b and r.

---

[5] While your definition will not be recursive in an explicit sense, it will call on the function **quotient** whose definition is, of course, recursive.

[6] When the whole number p divides the whole number q, we say that p is a **divisor** of q or, equivalently, that q is a **multiple** of p (see the next problem).

[7] This algorithm appears in Euclid's *Elements* (circa 300 B.C.) and it has been said that it is the oldest known nontrivial algorithm to have been presented as a general procedure rather than as a set of illustrative examples.

a) Complete the following skeleton definition for the function **gcd** of natural numbers *a* and *b* that returns *a* ⊓ *b*.

```
(define gcd
   (λ (a b)
      (cond
         [(divides? b a) _____ ]
         [else (_____ b (_____ a b))]))))
```

b) Trace the function **gcd** and hence find its output when its inputs are (in order)

(i) 15 and 69.   (ii) 6643 and 2273.

14. The **least common multiple** of natural numbers *a* and *b* is the smallest natural number *c* such that both *a* | *c* and *b* | *c*. We denote the least common multiple of *a* and *b* by '*a* ⊔ *b*'.

a) Complete the following table:

x	y	$x \sqcap y$	$x \sqcup y$
6	4	2	12
4	5	1	
8	3	1	
12	8	4	
9	6	3	

b) Use the function **gcd** to write a definition for the function **lcm** of natural numbers *a* and *b* that returns *a* ⊔ *b*.

15. The **factorial** of a whole number *n*, which we denote by '*n*!', may be defined as follows:

$$n! = \begin{cases} 1 & \text{if } n = 0 \\ n \cdot (n - 1)! & \text{if } n \neq 0. \end{cases}$$

In words: For each whole number *n*, *n*! (read '*n*-factorial') is 1 if *n* is zero, or *n* times $(n - 1)!$ otherwise. For example, the value of 5! may be calculated as follows:

$$
\begin{aligned}
5! \;&=\; 5\cdot 4! \\
&=\; 5\cdot(4\cdot 3!) \\
&=\; 5\cdot(4\cdot(3\cdot 2!)) \\
&=\; 5\cdot(4\cdot(3\cdot(2\cdot 1!))) \\
&=\; 5\cdot(4\cdot(3\cdot(2\cdot(1\cdot 0!)))) \\
&=\; 5\cdot(4\cdot(3\cdot(2\cdot(1\cdot 1)))) \\
&=\; 120.
\end{aligned}
$$

Write a definition for the function **factorial** of a whole number n that returns $n!$.

16. One of the prime movers in introducing our current, very efficient, positional system of writing numbers into Western culture was the medieval Italian mathematician Leonardo of Pisa (c. 1170–c. 1230), who is generally known by his nickname, Fibonacci—which is pronounced 'Fee-bon-ATCH-ee' and means 'son of Bonacci'. The book, *Liber Abaci*, in which he popularized the positional system also includes a mention of an interesting sequence of numbers, which have become known as 'the Fibonacci numbers'. These may be defined for each natural number n as follows:

$$
fib(n) = \begin{cases} 1 & \text{if } n = 1 \text{ or } n = 2 \\ fib(n-1) + fib(n-2) & \text{if } n > 2, \end{cases}
$$

where, of course, for each natural number k, '$fib(k)$' denotes the kth Fibonacci number. Thus $fib(4) = 3$, as the following calculation reveals:

$$
\begin{aligned}
fib(4) \;&=\; fib(3) + fib(2) \\
&=\; [fib(2) + fib(1)] + fib(2) \\
&=\; [1 + 1] + 1 \\
&=\; 2 + 1 = 3.
\end{aligned}
$$

a) Complete the recursive definition at the top of the next page for the function **fib** of a natural number n that returns $fib(n)$.

b) The definition in part (a) is said to employ **full** recursion. Fully recursive definitions may be recognized from the related machine diagrams as follows: If the machine(s) corresponding to the recursive

```
(define fib
  (λ (n)
    (cond
      [ (inor (one? n) (one? (sub1 n)))  _____ ]
      [ else ( _____
               ( _____ ( _____ n))
               ( _____ (sub1 (sub1 n))))]))))
```

call(s) is (are) *not* at the very bottom of the machine diagram, then the definition is fully recursive. (Check, for example, that the definition for the function **rember** depicted by the machine diagram in Figure 2.4 on page 88 is fully recursive.)

There is a second type of recursion, known as **tail** recursion. Tail-recursive definitions may also be recognized from the related machine diagrams. If the machine(s) corresponding to the recursive call(s) *is* (*are*) at the very bottom of the machine diagram, then the definition is tail-recursive.[8] (Check, for example, that the definition for the function **lat?** depicted by the machine diagram that you completed when you answered Exercise 57 on page 77 is tail-recursive.)

Write a tail-recursive definition for the function **fib**.

[Hint: This is quite a challenging task. One way of tackling it is to define **fib** so that, after taking care of the trivial cases, it calls a 'helping' function, **fib–help**, say. This helping function is the one that will be tail-recursive. It should take three inputs, the first being the representation of a number (which, as the recursion proceeds, will work its way down to zero), and the others being the two 'most recent' Fibonacci numbers.]

$$- \circ \, O \, \circ \, -$$

3.2 Creative Accounting

Mathematicians often use an abbreviative device called **exponential notation**, whereby instead of writing, say, '3 · 3 · 3 · 3 · 3' they write '3^5' and read

---

[8] Functions with tail-recursive definitions correspond to processes that are said to be iterative.

this as 'three to the fifth power' or 'three to the power five'. In general, if x and y are natural numbers then

$$x^y = \underbrace{x \cdot x \cdot x \cdot \ldots \cdot x}_{y \text{ factors}}.$$

In the expression 'x^y', 'x' is called the **base** of the power and 'y' is called the **exponent** (or the **index**).

We focus our attention in this short section on two alternative definitions for a function of natural numbers x and y that returns x^y. We also take the opportunity to add some remarks to the elegance/efficiency debate we began in the last section. In designing our first definition, we take the elementary approach that, since x^y is the product of y factors, each being the number x, then our function—let us call it '**power**'—should keep on multiplying x by itself until y factors have been multiplied. This sounds as if our definition will be recursive, and indeed the mechanics of a suitable recursion become apparent from the observations that

$$\text{when } y = 1, \quad x^y = x,$$
$$\text{and when } y > 1, \quad x^y = x \cdot x^{y-1}.$$

Consider, for example, the following calculation of 2^5:

$$
\begin{aligned}
2^5 &= 2 \cdot 2^4 \\
&= 2 \cdot (2 \cdot 2^3) \\
&= 2 \cdot (2 \cdot (2 \cdot 2^2)) \\
&= 2 \cdot (2 \cdot (2 \cdot (2 \cdot 2^1))) \\
&= 2 \cdot (2 \cdot (2 \cdot (2 \cdot 2))) \quad \text{since } 2^1 = 2 \\
&= 32.
\end{aligned}
$$

Exercise 72.

Complete the following skeleton definition for the function **power** of the natural numbers x and y that returns x^y:

```
(define power
  (λ (x y)
    (cond
      [(one? y) _____ ]
      [else (_____ x (_____ x (_____ y)))])))
```

The definition for the function **power** developed in this exercise is perhaps the most intuitive and obvious, but is it the most efficient in terms of speed of operation? Consider, for example, the calculation of 3^{10} using the function **power** as defined above. We note that the function $*$ will be invoked nine times—as might be expected from the fact that there are nine multiplication symbols in the expression '$3 \cdot 3 \cdot 3 \cdot 3 \cdot 3 \cdot 3 \cdot 3 \cdot 3 \cdot 3 \cdot 3$'. Now the function $*$ is surely the most complicated of the functions involved in our definition for the function **power**. So, if we wish to improve the function's performance, then it seems reasonable that we should try to reduce the number of times that the function $*$ is called as the power is being calculated. Is such a reduction possible?

An algorithm that requires fewer multiplications was reported by the French mathematician Adrien-Marie Legendre (1752–1833) in his book *Théorie des Nombres*, published in 1798. Note that for all natural numbers x and y, if y is even then

(1) $$x^y = (x \cdot x)^{y/2}.$$

For example, $3^{10} = (3 \cdot 3)^{10/2} = 9^5$:

$$
\begin{aligned}
3^{10} &= 3 \cdot 3 \cdot 3 \cdot 3 \cdot 3 \cdot 3 \cdot 3 \cdot 3 \cdot 3 \cdot 3 \\
&= (3 \cdot 3) \cdot (3 \cdot 3) \cdot (3 \cdot 3) \cdot (3 \cdot 3) \cdot (3 \cdot 3) \\
&= (3 \cdot 3)^5 \\
&= 9^5.
\end{aligned}
$$

Moreover, as we have already observed, for all natural numbers x and y, if $y > 1$, then

(2) $$x^y = x \cdot x^{y-1},$$

and if $y = 1$, then

(3) $$x^y = x.$$

Legendre remarked that a power may be calculated by applying formula (1) when the exponent is even, formula (2) when the exponent is odd (but greater than 1) and formula (3) when the exponent is 1.

Using Legendre's method to calculate 3^{10}, we proceed as follows: Since 10 is even, we apply formula (1):

$$3^{10} = (3 \cdot 3)^{10/2} = 9^5.$$

We now have an odd exponent (namely, 5) which is greater than 1, so we apply formula (2):

$$9^5 = 9 \cdot 9^{5-1} = 9 \cdot 9^4.$$

Since 4 is even, we apply formula (1) again:

$$9 \cdot 9^4 = 9 \cdot (9 \cdot 9)^{4/2} = 9 \cdot 81^2.$$

The exponent, 2, is again even, so we call on formula (1) once more:

$$9 \cdot 81^2 = 9 \cdot (81 \cdot 81)^{2/2} = 9 \cdot 6561^1.$$

This time the exponent is 1, so we apply formula (3):

$$9 \cdot 6561^1 = 9 \cdot 6561 = 59049.$$

At first sight, it might appear that Legendre's method of calculating 3^{10} is overly complex. In actual fact, however, it saves a considerable amount of time for the simple reason that it usually involves fewer multiplications than the algorithm underlying the definition for the function **power** given in Exercise 72. Analyzing our above calculation of 3^{10}, we see that it involves only four multiplications:

$$
\begin{aligned}
3^{10} &= (3 \cdot 3)^5 = 9^5 & \textit{multiplication \#1} \\
&= 9 \cdot 9^4 & \\
&= 9 \cdot (9 \cdot 9)^2 = 9 \cdot 81^2 & \textit{multiplication \#2} \\
&= 9 \cdot (81 \cdot 81)^1 = 9 \cdot 6561^1 & \textit{multiplication \#3} \\
&= 59049 & \textit{multiplication \#4.}
\end{aligned}
$$

Exercise 73.

a) Show that the calculation of 2^{15} involves just six multiplications when Legendre's algorithm is used.

b) How many multiplications are involved in calculating 2^{16} using Legendre's algorithm?

Exercise 74.

Complete the following skeleton definition (based on Legendre's algorithm) for the function **superpower** that inputs natural numbers x and y and returns x^y:

```
(define superpower
  (λ (x y)
    (cond
      [(one? y) _____ ]
      [(even? y) ( _____ ( _____ x) ( _____ y 2))]
      [else ( _____ x ( _____ x ( _____ y)))])))
```

Once again, efficiency has been improved thanks to a clever trick, but at the expense—in our view—of the simple elegance of the original definition for the function **power**.

3.3 Accounting for Small Amounts

We began this chapter by raising the question as to how lists and the techniques of list processing could be used if we want to work with numbers. We then very quickly narrowed our focus from numbers in general to *whole* numbers in particular. Our purpose in this section is to indicate how other kinds of numbers may be dealt with using techniques similar to those we have already discussed. Specifically, we look at ways to work with the non-negative rational numbers, that is, the numbers, such as $\frac{1}{2}$, 5 $(= \frac{5}{1})$, and $\frac{22}{7}$, that may be expressed in fractional form as a whole number over a natural number.

First of all, we shall need a way to represent such numbers. In view of the description we have just given of the non-negative rationals, it is natural to look for a representation that is based in some way on our representation of whole numbers. The following suggestion is inspired by the possibility of expressing any non-negative rational 'in its lowest terms', that is, in such a way that the numerator and denominator have no common whole number divisor other than 1.

REPRESENTATION Q.

   i) *The rational number 0 is represented by the list* '(0 1)'.

   ii) *Each positive rational number x is represented by the list containing exactly two data expressions, namely, the W-representations of the natural numbers m and n, in that order, where m and n are such that $m \sqcap n = 1$ and $x = \frac{m}{n}$.*

Here are some examples:

- The Q-representation of the rational number $\frac{1}{2}$ is the list '(1 2)', since 1 and 2 are natural numbers, $1 \sqcap 2 = 1$, and $\frac{1}{2} = \frac{1}{2}$.

- The Q-representation of the rational number $\frac{3}{12}$ is the list '(1 4)', since 1 and 4 are natural numbers, $1 \sqcap 4 = 1$, and $\frac{3}{12} = \frac{1}{4}$. The list '(3 12)' is *not* the Q-representation of $\frac{3}{12}$, for, although 3 and 12 are obviously natural numbers such that $\frac{3}{12} = \frac{3}{12}$, it is *not* the case that $3 \sqcap 12 = 1$.

- The Q-representation of the rational number 12 is the list '(12 1)'.

Notice that certain numbers (such as 12) are represented differently according to whether they are being viewed as rational numbers (in which case the Q-representation is appropriate) or as whole numbers (in which case the W-representation is suitable).

Exercise 75.

Write the Q-representation of

a) 1.   b) 30.   c) $\frac{9}{10}$.   d) $\frac{14}{63}$.

To help us in our discussion, and inspired by the usual terminology that is employed when working with fractions, we shall refer to the first data expression in the Q-representation of a non-negative rational number x as the **Q-numerator** of x, and to the second data expression in its Q-representation as the **Q-denominator** of x. Thus, for example,

- the Q-numerator of $\frac{2}{3}$ is the W-representation of 2, that is, the atom '2', and its Q-denominator is the atom '3';

- the Q-numerator of $\frac{20}{28}$ is the atom '5' and its Q-denominator is the atom '7', since the Q-representation of $\frac{20}{28}$ is '(5 7)'.

Before embarking on the problem set, we would like to point out that, although we do not do so here, it is a simple matter to use W-representations of whole numbers to develop a representation for the integers.[9] (How do you think this might be done?) Of course, once we can represent negative integers, then very minor modifications of Representation Q will yield a representation that is appropriate for *all* rational numbers, both non-negative and negative.

---

[9]That is, the whole numbers and their additive inverses, -1, -2, and so on.

PROBLEM SET 6

1.   a) Write a definition for the data abstractor function **num** of the Q-representation of a non-negative rational number x that returns the Q-numerator of x.

   b) Write a definition for the data abstractor function **den** of the Q-representation of a non-negative rational number x that returns the Q-denominator of x.

   c) Write a definition for the function **pair** of data expressions a and b that returns the list containing just two data expressions, namely, a and b, in that order.

   d) Complete the following skeleton definition for the constructor function **make–rational** of the W-representations of whole numbers m and n such that $n \neq 0$ that returns the Q-representation of $\frac{m}{n}$:

> (define make–rational
>   (λ (m n)
>   (cond
>   [(zero? m) $^\triangledown$(0 1)]
>   [else (make–rational–help m n (_____ m n))])))

> (define make–rational–help
>   (λ (m n g)
>   (pair
>   (_____ m g)
>   (_____ n g))))

   [Hint: Think about 'reducing a fraction to its lowest terms'.]

2. Write a definition for

   a) the function **+Q** of Q-representations of non-negative rational numbers r and s that returns the Q-representation of $r + s$.

   b) the function **–Q** of Q-representations of non-negative rational numbers r and s such that r is not less than s that returns the Q-representation of $r - s$.

   c) the function ***Q** of Q-representations of non-negative rational numbers r and s that returns the Q-representation of the product $r \cdot s$.

d) the function **/Q** of Q-representations of non-negative rational numbers r and s such that $s \neq 0$ that returns the Q-representation of the quotient $r \div s$.

3. It is possible to determine which of two distinct non-negative rational numbers is the greater by making use of the fact that for all whole numbers a, b, c, and d such that $b \neq 0$ and $d \neq 0$,

$$\tfrac{a}{b} < \tfrac{c}{d} \; \text{if and only if } a \cdot d < b \cdot c,$$

where the right-hand inequality, of course, involves a comparison of two *whole* numbers. Suppose, for example, we wish to know which of $\tfrac{2}{5}$ and $\tfrac{3}{7}$ is the greater. Making the substitutions

$$a : 2 \qquad b : 5 \qquad c : 3 \qquad d : 7$$

in the formula above, we conclude that $\tfrac{2}{5} < \tfrac{3}{7}$ if and only if $2 \cdot 7 < 5 \cdot 3$. Since $2 \cdot 7 = 14$, $5 \cdot 3 = 15$, and $14 < 15$, we deduce that $\tfrac{2}{5} < \tfrac{3}{7}$, that is, $\tfrac{3}{7}$ is the greater of the two. (Check: $\tfrac{2}{5} = \tfrac{14}{35}$ and $\tfrac{3}{7} = \tfrac{15}{35}$ and, clearly, $\tfrac{14}{35} < \tfrac{15}{35}$.) As a further example, let us discover which is the greater of the rational numbers $\tfrac{5}{6}$ and $\tfrac{8}{11}$. Substituting in the formula above, we have that $\tfrac{5}{6} < \tfrac{8}{11}$ if and only if $5 \cdot 11 < 6 \cdot 8$. But, $5 \cdot 11 = 55$ and $6 \cdot 8 = 48$, and 55 is *not* strictly less than 48. On the contrary, $48 < 55$, so we deduce that $\tfrac{8}{11} < \tfrac{5}{6}$, that is, $\tfrac{5}{6}$ is the greater of the two numbers.

Write a definition for the function **lessQ?** of Q-representations of non-negative rational numbers p and q that returns the boolean '#t' if and only if $p < q$.

4. Write a definition for the function **sumQ** of a list r, each of whose data expressions is a Q-representation of a non-negative rational number, that returns the Q-representation of the sum of the numbers in r.

5. Write a definition for the function **meanQ** of a non-null list r, each of whose data expressions is a Q-representation of a non-negative rational number, that returns the Q-representation of the arithmetic mean[10] of the numbers in r. [Hint: Use the function **/Q**, but take care that both its inputs are Q-representations.]

$$-\text{o}\,\text{O}\,\text{o}-$$

---

[10]The arithmetic mean of a non-null list of numbers is the sum of those numbers divided by the number of numbers in the list.

3.4 Calculating Machines

With the help of a Scheme interpreter, we could use the functions defined earlier in this chapter to calculate the value of arithmetic expressions such as '35 − (25 + 3)' in much the same way as we might use a calculator. We could, for example, use the computer to evaluate the functional expression '(+ 25 3)', obtaining an answer of 28, and then use it to evaluate '(− 35 28)', arriving at the final answer, 7. Alternatively, we could devour the problem in one gulp by evaluating the functional expression '(− 35 (+ 25 3))'. Whichever method we choose, the path to success relies on our being able to apply our knowledge of arithmetic expressions and the functions we have defined in Scheme in order to identify which functional expressions need to be evaluated. Consider how much easier it would be, however, if we could somehow 'feed' the expression '35 − (25 + 3)' directly to a single function that would output the correct answer without further ado. We develop such a function in this section.

Our first job is to specify exactly what kinds of arithmetic expression we want to deal with. You will certainly have seen and worked with many types of arithmetic expressions during the course of your educational career, including in all likelihood expressions such as

$$10 + 5 \qquad [(1 + 2) + (3 + 4)] \qquad \tfrac{9}{8} + (\tfrac{3}{4} - 2)$$
$$(10 + 5) \qquad (1 + [3 - 1]) \cdot 2 \qquad 12 - (\tfrac{3}{2} + \tfrac{13}{5})/4$$
$$[10 + 5] \qquad 1 + 3 \cdot 2 + 5 - 4 \qquad [10 \cdot (\tfrac{2}{3} - \tfrac{1}{5})^2 - (\tfrac{4}{9} + \tfrac{1}{7})^3]^5.$$

Ideally, we would like our function to be capable of interpreting all of these expressions, but we are limited to a certain extent by the fact that any function we define will be a list processing function, and therefore it will only be able to accept data expressions as inputs. So neither of the expressions '3 + (4 + 5)' and '(3 + (4 + 5))' will be acceptable inputs because they are not data expressions. On the other hand, the list '(3 + (4 + 5))' is a data expression that we might reasonably expect our function to accept. Just to get a feel for how this kind of function may be defined, let us construct a function that handles only those data expressions that represent arithmetic expressions in the following way:

REPRESENTATION A1.

> *A data expression is an A1-representation of an arithmetic expression if and only if one of the following holds:*

i) *It is the W-representation of a whole number.*

ii) *It is the list*[11] *'(**a** + **b**)', where **a** and **b** are A1-representations of arithmetic expressions.*

Let us familiarize ourselves with Representation A1 by building some data expressions that represent arithmetic expressions in this way. From part (i) we see that W-representations of whole numbers are to be regarded as A1-representations of arithmetic expressions. So, for example, '0', '2', and '9342' are A1-representations. Then part (ii) implies that the list '(2 + 9342)' is an A1-representation since both '2' and '9342' are A1-representations. Similarly, the list '(34 + 42)' is also an A1-representation of an arithmetic expression. But then, by part (ii) again, the list '((2 + 9342) + (34 + 42))' is an A1-representation of an arithmetic expression.

Turning from construction to destruction, let us choose an expression and try to decide whether it is an A1-representation of an arithmetic expression. Consider the list '(3 + (4 + 5))', for example. It is clearly not a W-representation of a whole number, so if it is an A1-representation at all it must be one by part (ii) of Representation A1. This is perhaps an opportune moment to point out that part (ii) may be restated in the following way: A list is an A1-representation of an arithmetic expression if it contains exactly three data expressions, the second of which is the atom '+' and the first and third of which are A1-representations of arithmetic expressions. We observe that the list '(3 + (4 + 5))' does indeed contain exactly three data expressions, and the second data expression is the atom '+', so we have only to check that its first and third data expressions are A1-representations. The first data expression is the W-representation of the whole number 3 and is therefore an A1-representation by part (i). The third data expression, the list '(4 + 5)', is an A1-representation by part (ii), since it is a list containing exactly three data expressions, the second of which is the atom '+' and the first and third of which are both W-representations of whole numbers and therefore A1-representations by part (i). We conclude that the list '(3 + (4 + 5))' is an A1-representation of an arithmetic expression.

Exercise 76.

Which of the following expressions are A1-representations of arithmetic expressions?

---

[11]Technically speaking, '(*a* + *b*)' is not a list; it becomes one, however, as soon as '*a*' and '*b*' are replaced by actual A1-representations of arithmetic expressions. We frequently abuse the technical language in this way throughout this section.

a) 32   b) -12   c) (3 + 32)

d) (9 + (4 + 1))   e) (3 + 5 + 4 + 2)

f) (((3 + 5) + 7) + 9)   g) ((3 + 5) + (7 + 9))

h) (9)   i) (9 - 4)

j) ((1 + (1 + 2)) + ((1 + (2 + 3)) + 4))

We now move on to the task of defining a function—let us call it '**A1–value**'—that inputs A1-representations of arithmetic expressions and outputs the W-representations of their numerical values. In view of the above description of Representation A1, we know that any input to the function **A1–value** will be either a W-representation of a whole number, or a list containing three data expressions such that the first and third data expressions are A1-representations of arithmetic expressions and the second data expression is the atom '+'. What should the output be if the input is a W-representation? Common sense tells us that, in this case, the function **A1–value** should simply output its input.[12] So we may begin our definition for the function **A1–value** like this:

```
(define A1–value
  (λ (aexp)
    (cond
      [(number? aexp) aexp)
        ⋮
      )))
```

If the input is not a whole number then it must be a list of the form ' (a + b)' where a and b are A1-representations of arithmetic expressions. We have not explicitly said so thus far, but we are interpreting such an A1-representation as denoting the sum of the arithmetic expressions represented by the first and third data expressions of the list. It would therefore be very convenient if we had data abstractor functions that would enable us to extract these two data expressions from the input to the function **A1–value**. Such functions are extremely easy to define, so we do so without further ado.[13]

---

[12]In this definition, we use the black symbol '*aexp*' as a parameter. Scheme allows such compound symbols to be used in this way, and we encourage their use where it aids readability. In this case, we use '*aexp*' since its replacement must be (an A1-representation of) an Arithmetic EXPression.

[13]Operands are what an operation (in this case, +) operates upon.

(define operand1
    (λ (*m*)
        (first *m*)))

(define operand2
    (λ (*m*)
        (third *m*)))

In the case we are considering, we want our function **A1–value** to output the sum of the numerical values of the first and third data expressions of the input. Since each of these data expressions is an A1-representation of an arithmetic expression, their numerical values must themselves in turn be determined by calling on the function **A1–value**. Thus our completed definition for the function **A1–value** is as follows:

(define A1–value
    (λ (*aexp*)
        (cond
            [(number? *aexp*) *aexp*]
            [else (+
                    (A1–value (operand1 *aexp*))
                    (A1–value (operand2 *aexp*)))])))

Here is a trace table showing how the function **A1–value** evaluates the A1-representation '(3 + (4 + 5))':

(**A1–value** (3 + (4 + 5)))
(+ (**A1–value** 3) (**A1–value** (4 + 5)))
(+ 3 (**A1–value** (4 + 5)))
(+ 3 (+ (**A1–value** 4) (**A1–value** 5)))
(+ 3 (+ 4 5))
(+ 3 9)
12

Exercise 77.

> Write a definition for the predicate data abstractor function **A1–rep?** of a data expression *m* that returns the boolean '#t' if and only if *m* is an A1-representation of an arithmetic expression.

Now that we have a function that successfully evaluates (representations of) 'additive' arithmetic expressions, let us extend the range of expressions that can be handled to include multiplication.

REPRESENTATION A2.

A data expression is an A2-representation of an arithmetic expression if and only if one of the following holds:

i) It is the W-representation of a whole number.

ii) It is the list '(a + b)', where a and b are A2-representations of arithmetic expressions.

iii) It is the list '(a * b)', where a and b are A2-representations of arithmetic expressions.

Exercise 78.

Which of the following are A2-representations of arithmetic expressions?

a) 5   b) (3 * 5)

c) (5 + (a * 3))   d) (5 * 3 + 3 * 5)

e) (((5 * 4) * 3) + (2 * 1))

Obviously, every A1-representation of an arithmetic expression is also an A2-representation of an arithmetic expression, but there are A2-representations of arithmetic expressions (namely, those involving the atom '*') that are not A1-representations of arithmetic expressions. Since we are now in a situation where the second data expression in a three-data-expression representation of an arithmetic expression is no longer always the same, it will be convenient to define another data abstraction function that will extract this data expression from such a representation. Here is a suitable candidate, defined in the obvious way:

```
(define operation
    (λ (m)
       (second m)))
```

It is now a simple matter to define a function (called, naturally enough, 'A2–value') that evaluates A2-representations of arithmetic expressions:

```
(define A2–value
  (λ (aexp)
    (cond
      [(number? aexp) aexp]
      [(eq? (operation aexp) ▽+) (+
                              (A2–value (operand1 aexp))
                              (A2–value (operand2 aexp)))]
      [else (*
              (A2–value (operand1 aexp))
              (A2–value (operand2 aexp)))])))
```

Exercise 79.

Write a definition for the predicate data abstractor function **A2–rep?** of a data expression *m* that returns the boolean '#t' if and only if *m* is an A2-representation of an arithmetic expression.

It should now be clear that the foregoing development can be extended to include representations of just about any conceivable type of arithmetic expression. Let us therefore go straight to the bottom line and describe the kind of representation we shall be asking you to work with in the next problem set.

REPRESENTATION A3.

A data expression is an A3-representation of an arithmetic expression if and only if one of the following holds:

   i) It is the W-representation of a whole number.

   ii) It is the list '(a + b)', where a and b are A3-representations of arithmetic expressions.

   iii) It is the list '(a - b)', where a and b are A3-representations of arithmetic expressions.

   *iv) It is the list '(a * b)', where a and b are A3-representations of arithmetic expressions.*

   v) It is the list '(a / b)', where a and b are A3-representations of arithmetic expressions.

   vi) It is the list '(a power b)', where a and b are A3-representations of arithmetic expressions.

*vii) It is the list '(**a** `rem` **b**)', where **a** and **b** are A3-representations of arithmetic expressions.*

*viii) It is the list '(**a** `gcd` **b**)', where **a** and **b** are A3-representations of arithmetic expressions.*

*ix) It is the list '(`factorial` **a**)', where **a** is the A3-representation of an arithmetic expression.*

*x) It is the list '(`fib` **a**)', where **a** is the A3-representation of an arithmetic expression.*

So as to remove any possible confusion, let us also explain precisely how these A3-representations of arithmetic expressions are to be interpreted in terms of the notation and vocabulary we have encountered in this chapter:

(**a** + **b**) $a + b$, where a and b are whole numbers.

(**a** - **b**) $a - b$, where a and b are whole numbers such that a is not less than b.

(**a** * **b**) $a \cdot b$, where a and b are whole numbers.

(**a** / **b**)   The quotient when a is divided by b, where a and b are whole numbers such that $b \neq 0$.

(**a** `power` **b**) a^b, where a and b are natural numbers.

(**a** `rem` **b**)   The remainder when a is divided by b, where a and b are whole numbers such that $b \neq 0$.

(**a** `gcd` **b**) $a \sqcap b$, where a and b are natural numbers.

(`factorial` **a**) $a!$, where a is a whole number.

(`fib` **a**)   The ath Fibonacci number, where a is a natural number.

PROBLEM SET 7

1. Write an A3-representation for the arithmetic expression

$$[(13+75)^4 - (863 \sqcap 14!)] \cdot (fib\,(28) + 977)^{\frac{25!}{17!}}.$$

2. Write a definition for the function **A3–value** of an A3-representation of an arithmetic expression that calculates its numerical value.

3. Type the function **A3–value** into a computer equipped with a Scheme interpreter, and use it to calculate the value of the following arithmetic expressions. (Note: In these expressions, we use the symbols '$\frac{a}{b}$' and 'a/b' to mean the *quotient* when a is divided by b and the symbol '$[a]_b$' to mean the *remainder* when a is divided by b.)

   a) $(92\,513\,745 - 1\,252\,413) + (499\,975\,441 - 9\,999) + 396\,427\,547$

   b) $(3 \cdot 1087 \cdot 1723 \cdot 29 \cdot 6) + 9\,999\,999$

   c) $9\,999 \cdot \dfrac{\left(\dfrac{782\,717\,564/3}{9\,834/2}\right)}{\left(\dfrac{350}{16/2}\right)} - 11\,104\,199$

   d) $4^{(3^{(2^1)})}$

   e) $fib\left(\dfrac{fib\,(fib\,(7))}{6}\right) - [532\,516]_{88\,888}$

   f) $477\,879 + \left(\dfrac{19\,365\,771 \sqcap 510\,510}{4}\right)!$

– o O o –

4 Warehousing

It has been said, and with good reason, that the art of computer programming lies in the successful design of the two fundamental components of computer programs—algorithms and data structures. Our study of list processing and recursion has already touched on the first of these, for we have seen how complex derived functions may be built from simple primitive functions. In this chapter, we turn our attention to the second component.

From one point of view, you are already a data structure expert for you have mastered the list, which is one of the most sophisticated and complicated of data structures. In many ways, the list is an all-purpose data structure, since many other data structures—a few of which we discuss a little later in this chapter—can be implemented using lists. We begin, however, by introducing a technique that allows us to 'store' the long and complex lists that we shall be using as we explore data structures.

4.1 Storage Facilities

Consider the following trivial problem:

Let **s** : (Hi there). Then evaluate

a) **(first s)**   b) **(rest s)**

c) **(cons (first s) (rest (rest s)))**

Of course, these functional expressions evaluate, respectively, to the atom 'Hi', the list '(there)', and the list '(Hi)'. Although it is hardly necessary in this

instance, we could use a computer to evaluate these functional expressions.
A typical conversation between a schemer and the Scheme interpreter might
be as follows:[1]

```
⟹ (first '(Hi there))
Hi
⟹ (rest '(Hi there))
(there)
⟹ (cons (first '(Hi there)) (rest (rest '(Hi there))))
(Hi)
⟹ _
```

Notice that the schemer has painstakingly replaced each occurrence of the
variable '**s**' in the functional expressions by ''(**Hi there**)', that is, the functional
expression for the output from the constant function ▽(**Hi there**). We now
increase the level of complexity somewhat.

> Let **s** : ((T ((i) ()) a) (v) ((c) ((a)) v) (((t))))
> Then evaluate
>
> a) (first **s**)   b) (rest **s**)
> c) (cons (first **s**) (rest (rest **s**)))

This time the functional expressions are not so easy to evaluate 'by eye',
so you might be more inclined to use a computer. Unfortunately, the list
that is to replace each occurrence of the variable '**s**' is so long and complex
that typing the result of all such replacements will require a great deal of
concentration and be very prone to error. A very careful, detail-oriented
schemer, however, could achieve the exchange with the Scheme interpreter
that is recorded at the top of the next page.

It would certainly be of enormous benefit if we could tell the interpreter
something to the effect, "From now on, in every functional expression that
I type, let the replacement for the variable '**s**' be the list '(...)'." Happily,
there is a way to do this using a define-expression. The general form of a
define-expression is as follows: It has three components, namely,

---

[1]We continue our practice of 'color coding' these conversations so as to highlight the fact
that a schemer types (black) functional expressions at the keyboard and the computer
responds with (red) data expressions. If you are not using the *EdScheme* interpreter, of
course, only a monochrome 'echo' of all this colorful activity will actually show up on the
computer screen.

⟹ (first '((T ((i) ()) a) (v) ((c) ((a)) v) (((t)))))
(T ((i) ()) a)
⟹ (rest '((T ((i) ()) a) (v) ((c) ((a)) v) (((t)))))
((v) ((c) ((a)) v) (((t))))
⟹ (cons (first '((T ((i) ()) a) (v) ((c) ((a)) v) (((t)))))
        (rest (rest '((T ((i) ()) a) (v) ((c) ((a)) v) (((t))))))))
((T ((i) ()) a) ((c) ((a)) v) (((t))))
⟹ _

Figure 4.1: A Complicated Conversation.

- the keyword '**define**', followed in order by

- a blackened atom (which, as we explained on page 55, should neither be
  a blackened numeral, nor a reserved keyword of Scheme, nor a blackened
  boolean object) and

- a functional expression,

the whole expression being enclosed in black parentheses. In all the in-
stances we have met so far, the third of these components has been a lambda-
expression. This is because all the define-expressions up to this point have
been used to define derived functions. At the stage when they were introduced, however, we mentioned that define-expressions may be used to give
names to other kinds of objects besides functions. In fact, a define-expression
tells the interpreter that, until further notice, the blackened atom (its second
component) is to have as its replacement the data expression to which the
functional expression (its third component) evaluates. That is, it lets the
intepreter know that the blackened atom is a name for the value of the functional expression.[2] For this reason, define-expressions are often referred to as
assignments.

In Scheme, any blackened atom that is acceptable as the second component in a define-expression is known as an **identifier**. We follow the convention that the identifier in a function-defining define-expression is thought of

---

[2]It is perhaps rather difficult to appreciate in what sense this statement holds true in the
case of a function-defining define-expression. All will be revealed, however, in Chapter 5
where we explain how lambda-expressions are evaluated.

as a function name and is therefore printed in the same sans serif bold type-face as the names of primitive functions such as **first**. On the other hand, the identifier in a define-expression that does not define a function is thought of as a variable[3] and is therefore printed in the bold italic typeface. It is impor-tant to realize, however, that this convention does not reflect any significant, underlying distinction; in a very real sense all identifiers have equal status. And of course, in practice, when entering define-expressions into a computer, everything is typed using the same typeface.

Returning to the problem that led to the foregoing discussion, we remark that the expression

$$\text{(define } s \ ^\triangledown\text{(Hi there))}$$

assigns the name '*s*' to the list '(Hi there)'. (In computer jargon, the as-signment is said to 'create a **binding**' for the variable '*s*'.[4] Following the assignment, we say that '*s*' is **bound** to the list '(Hi there)'.) In fact, this assignment has exactly the same effect as that intended when, in the shorthand notation introduced on page 38, we write

$$s : \text{(Hi there)}$$

Being able to establish bindings in this way makes a computer-aided solu-tion to our last problem much more of a viable proposition, as the following conversation shows:

```
⟹ (define s '((T ((i) ()) a) (v) ((c) ((a)) v) (((t)))))
s
⟹ (first s)
(T ((i) ()) a)
⟹ (rest s)
((v) ((c) ((a)) v) (((t))))
⟹ (cons (first s) (rest (rest s)))
((T ((i) ()) a) ((c) ((a)) v) (((t))))
⟹ _
```

---

[3]As we noted on page 121, Scheme accepts (and we encourage the thoughtful use of) compound symbols as variable names. We re-emphasize, however, that such compound symbols have to be blackened atoms of the type described above.

[4]In the next problem set we provide a little more information about what bindings are, and we elaborate a good deal further in Chapter 5.

We see here a further example of the general behavior of the interpreter when a define-expression is entered. We noted in Chapter 2 that it responds to a function-defining define-expression by printing in red the name being given to the derived function. In exactly the same way, the interpreter responds to an assignment of the above type by printing in red the name being assigned.

Bindings that are established by assignments remain in effect until they are changed by subsequent assignments or until the computer is switched off. The following example shows just such a binding change taking place.

```
⟹  (define a '(Hi there))
a
⟹  a
(Hi there)
⟹  (define a '(Good bye))
a
⟹  (first (rest a))
bye
⟹  _
```

The interpreter will signal an error if an attempt is made to evaluate a functional expression containing a variable for which no binding exists. Of course, such behavior is just common sense, for obviously the interpreter cannot evaluate '(first b)', say, unless it knows what to replace 'b' by.

Variables whose bindings are created by an assignment are called **global variables** and their bindings are called **global bindings**. We remark that it is perfectly legitimate for a global variable to appear in the third component (that is, the functional expression) of an assignment. For example, if these two assignments:

$$(\text{define } a \; {}^{\triangledown}(\text{there}))$$
$$(\text{define } b \; (\text{cons } {}^{\triangledown}\text{Hi } a))$$

are typed into the computer in the above order, then the net effect will be to create these global bindings:

$$a : (\text{there})$$
$$b : (\text{Hi there})$$

However, if the second assignment is typed first, then the interpreter will signal an error. (Why?)

In fact, it is often useful to include a global variable in an assignment that changes the binding for that variable. For example, suppose we were to enter

$$\text{(define } s \ ^{\triangledown}(\ ))$$

thereby creating the global binding '*s* : ( )'. What would then be the result of typing

$$\text{(define } s \ (\text{cons } ^{\triangledown}\text{A } s))?$$

Since *s* : ( ),

$$(\text{cons } ^{\triangledown}\text{A } s) \mapsto (\text{A}),$$

so the second assignment would create the new global binding '*s* : (A)'. Suppose we were then to continue by typing

$$\text{(define } s \ (\text{cons } ^{\triangledown}\text{A } s))$$

for a second time. Since, prior to this latest assignment, '*s*' is bound to the list '(A)', it follows that this time

$$(\text{cons } ^{\triangledown}\text{A } s) \mapsto (\text{A A}).$$

That is, the global binding '*s* : (A A)' has been created.

One final example: The net result of typing the expressions

$$\text{(define } q \ ^{\triangledown}(\ ))$$
$$\text{(define } q \ (\text{cons } ^{\triangledown}(\text{A}) \ q))$$
$$\text{(define } q \ (\text{cons } q \ ^{\triangledown}(\text{B})))$$

in order is to create the global binding '*q* : (((A)) B)'.

Exercise 80.

What is the global binding that is created as a result of each of these assignments?

a) (define *a* $^{\triangledown}$Fred)   b) (define *b* $^{\triangledown}$(A B C))

c) (define *c* (first (rest $^{\triangledown}$(A B C))))

d) (define *longname* $^{\triangledown}$(an even longer list))

Exercise 81.

    a) What is the final binding for the global variable '*r*' after the following assignments are typed into the computer in order?

        (define *r* ▽(A B C))

        (define *r* (cons ▽D *r*))

        (define *r* (cons ▽(E F) (rest *r*)))

    b) What are the final bindings for the global variables '*i*', '*j*' and '*k*' after the following assignments are typed into the computer in order?

        (define *i* ▽(Fred Jane))

        (define *j* (first *i*))

        (define *k* (cons *j* ▽()))

        (define *i* (cons *k* *k*))

4.2 Keeping Stock

Widget World claims to stock the world's largest collection of widgets, which, needless to say, come in a variety of handy sizes and in a selection of contemporary colors that according to Ms. Thingamijig, the store manager, stands second to none. The weighty task of ensuring that the store never runs short of widgets of whatever size or color falls on the shoulders of Mr. Doodad, the warehouse supervisor, who has been in widgetry for longer than he cares to remember. Indeed, Mr. Doodad is often heard to reminisce, fondly recalling the good old days when all widgets were medium-sized and bright red. These days he has to keep track of widgets in six colors and five sizes, no small task. When the stock of a certain type of widget falls below an acceptable level, Mr. Doodad is required to restock his shelves by ordering the widget in question from the manufacturer. Unfortunately for Mr. Doodad, however, the manufacturer does not refer to widgets by color and size but by code numbers each constructed by juxtaposing a color code and a size code. These codes are given in Table 4.1. So, for example, if Mr. Doodad wishes to order a gross of Extra Large Caustic Crimson widgets he must refer to them on the order form as type 'CR2 X'.

    Mr. Doodad finds it difficult to remember the code for each type of widget, a problem compounded by the fact that widget specifications change

Color	Awful Azure	Baleful Blue	Caustic Crimson	Dreadful Drab	Edacious Ebony	Fearsome Fawn
Code	AZ5	BL5	CR2	DR1	EB6	FA5

Size	Small	Medium	Large	XLarge	Mammoth
Code	S	M	L	X	T

Table 4.1: The Manufacturer's Widget Codes.

frequently in response to fluctuations in the widget market. So, being an amateur schemer, he decides to design a function to help him keep abreast of widget codes. It crosses his mind to write a couple of function definitions, one of the form

```
(define lookup–color–code
  (λ (color)
    (cond
      [(eq? color ▽azure) ▽AZ5]
      [(eq? color ▽blue) ▽BL5]
        ⋮
      [else ▽FA5])))
```

and a similar definition for size codes, but he dismisses this on practical grounds, for any change in the codes would require him to redefine the functions. Instead, he decides to develop a function called 'lookup', which takes two inputs, the first being a data expression and the second being a special type of list called an **association list**:

> An association list is a list that contains nothing but pairs.

(In this description, a **pair** is a list containing exactly two data expressions, possibly the same; it is the kind of list that is output by the function **pair**, which you defined in Problem 1(c) of Problem Set 6.) Thus, for example, the list '`((is an) ((association) (list)))`' is an association list since each of its data expressions is a pair. Furthermore, the null list is an association list since it contains nothing at all, and therefore nothing that is *not* a pair. The first input to the function **lookup** must be such that it occurs as the first data expression of one or more of the pairs in the second input, and the data expression returned is the second data expression of the first such pair:

```
(define lookup
  (λ (s alist)
    (cond
      [(equal? s (first (first alist))) (second (first alist))]
      [else (lookup s (rest alist))])))
```

Exercise 82.

Evaluate these functional expressions:

a) (lookup ▽three ▽((one 1) (two 2) (three 3) (four 4)))

b) (lookup ▽three ▽((one plus) (three is) (three plus) (one wow)))

The function **lookup** is designed so that Mr. Doodad will never have to change its definition in response to changes in widget specifications. He keeps track of everything that is subject to change by means of suitable association lists. Since the properties of widgets that interest him most are color and size, Mr. Doodad uses an assignment to bind the variable *colors* to an association list reflecting the current palette of available colors:

```
(define colors
  ▽((azure AZ5)
    (blue BL5)
    (crimson CR2)
    (drab DR1)
    (ebony EB6)
    (fawn FA5)))
```

and, by a similar assignment, he binds the variable *sizes* to the following association list:

```
((small S) (medium M) (large L) (xlarge X) (mammoth T))
```

Then to find the color code of, say, Awful Azure, Mr. Doodad has only to evaluate the functional expression '(lookup ▽azure *colors*)' to obtain the code 'AZ5'. Similarly, to find the manufacturer's code for Extra Large widgets he can evaluate the functional expression '(lookup ▽xlarge *sizes*)', whereupon he will obtain the atom 'X'.

Since association lists tend to be rather long and complicated, Mr. Doodad writes some additional function definitions aimed at making it easier and more convenient to manipulate them. For example, the function **make–alist**—Mr. Doodad's definition for which is given below—builds an association list from two lists of the same length.

```
(define make–alist
  (λ (r s)
    (cond
      [(null? r) ▽()]
      [else (cons
              (pair (first r) (first s))
              (make–alist (rest r) (rest s)))])))
```

A second of the functions Mr. Doodad defines is the function **remove** of a data expression and an association list:

```
(define remove
  (λ (s alist)
    (genrember (pair s (lookup s alist)) alist)))
```

(Notice that he has made use of the function **genrember**, which was introduced in Problem 7 of Problem Set 4.)

Exercise 83.

    a) Evaluate

      (i) **(make–alist** ▽(keeping stock) ▽(a car)**)**

      (ii) **(remove** ▽ebony *colors***)**

    b) Describe the behavior of the function **remove** in words.

Exercise 84.

    Write a definition for the function **switch** of an association list *alist* that returns the association list obtained by reversing each pair in *alist*.

As part of his job as warehouse supervisor, Mr. Doodad keeps track of his widget stock by means of a daily inventory. The company provides him with a ledger in which are printed nicely laid out blank tables which, when completed, look like the sample shown in Table 4.2. Of course, as he is walking through the warehouse taking stock, Mr. Doodad does not take the time to

July 10	Azure	Blue	Crimson	Drab	Ebony	Fawn
Small	30	27	9	3	57	25
Medium	23	54	84	61	60	54
Large	18	24	17	25	11	79
XLarge	39	57	29	18	27	74
Mammoth	47	93	75	43	2	54

Table 4.2: An Excerpt from Mr Doodad's Daily Ledger.

write out on his notepad all the column and row headings that appear in the pre-printed tables in his ledger. On July 10, for example, this is what he wrote on his notepad, before transferring the information to the ledger:

$$
\begin{array}{cccccc}
(30 & 27 & 9 & 3 & 57 & 25) \\
(23 & 54 & 84 & 61 & 60 & 54) \\
(18 & 24 & 17 & 25 & 11 & 79) \\
(39 & 57 & 29 & 18 & 27 & 74) \\
(47 & 93 & 75 & 43 & 2 & 54)
\end{array}
$$

Naturally, Mr. Doodad cannot resist computerizing his ledger. He realizes that a simple way of preparing for this is to think of what he writes each day on his notepad as being (red) data expressions. Thought of in this way, each line of what Mr. Doodad writes on his notepad is what is known as a **vector**.[5]

> *A vector is a list that contains nothing but W-representations of whole numbers.*

Thus, for example, the list '(30 27 9 3 57 25)', corresponding to the number of small widgets of each color in stock on July 10, is a vector, and so is the

---

[5] Technically speaking, we ought really to say 'a representation (or a name) of a vector', since what Mr. Doodad has written involves numerals—that is, names (or representations) of numbers—rather than actual numbers themselves. In fact, vectors are mathematical objects whose study forms part of the subject of Linear Algebra and which are widely used throughout mathematics and physics. No confusion will arise, however, as a result of our intention throughout this book to gloss over the object/representation distinction in this case and always say 'vector' instead of the strictly correct 'representation of a vector'.

null list. Thinking ahead, Mr. Doodad chooses appropriate global variables to which, each day, will be bound the vectors corresponding to that day's holdings of widgets of the various sizes. Thus, for example, if his computerized system had been in operation on July 10, he would have bound the vector '(30 27 9 3 57 25)' to the variable '*small*'.

There are a number of routine tasks that Mr. Doodad has to perform on the raw data of his daily inventory. One such task is the calculation of the subtotals giving the numbers of widgets of each size that are in stock on any given day. For this purpose, Mr. Doodad writes the following definition for the function **sum** of a vector that returns the sum of the numbers in the vector:[6]

```
(define sum
  (λ (vec)
    (cond
      [(null? vec) 0]
      [else (+ (first vec) (sum (rest vec)))])))
```

Check that, when *small* : (30 27 9 3 57 25), (sum *small*) ↦ 151

Exercise 85.

Complete the following tail-recursive version of the function **sum**:

```
(define sum
  (λ (vec)
    (sum–help vec 0)))
```

```
(define sum–help
  (λ (vec acc)
    (cond
      [(_____ vec) acc]
      [else (_____
              (_____ vec)
              (_____ acc (_____ vec)))])))
```

[The 'helping' function **sum–help** uses what is known as an **accumulator**, denoted by the variable '*acc*', which in this case is such that, at any given moment, its value is a (W-representation of a) whole number giving the 'running total' of the sum so far.

---

[6]You should notice a marked similarity between this definition and the one you wrote for the function **sumQ** in Problem 4 of Problem Set 6 on page 118.

Notice that the first effect of a call to the function **sum** is to call the function **sum–help** of the input to **sum** together with a second input, namely, the atom '0'. Thus, during that initial call, the accumulator '*acc*' is replaced by the atom '0'. In computer jargon, we say that the accumulator is '**initialized** to zero'.]

Many other functional expressions involving the vector *small* yield useful results. For example, the functional expression '(nth 4 *small*)' evaluates to the number of Small Dreadful Drab widgets in stock, and the functional expression '(quotient (sum *small*) (length *small*))' evaluates to the arithmetic mean number (rounded down to the nearest whole number) of small widgets of each color in stock.

Although vectors are of immense help to Mr. Doodad, his thirst for generality remains unquenched, for any technique he wants to apply to the vector corresponding to his stock of small widgets will usually also have to be repeated for each of the other four vectors. He begins to think that perhaps it was not such a good idea after all to use variables for these vectors that are so closely related to English words that suggest how to interpret the contents of the vectors. What is needed is a more systematic way of referring to the vectors.

It so happens that Mary Beth Oojitz, the warehouse fork-lift operator, has been taking night school mathematics classes at the local community college, and she recognizes Mr. Doodad's 'stack' of five vectors as being very much like a **matrix**.[7] 'Actually,' she informs him helpfully, 'it would be an honest-to-goodness matrix if you wrote it like this.' And she scribbles down the following array corresponding to the July 10 inventory:

$$\begin{pmatrix} 30 & 27 & 9 & 3 & 57 & 25 \\ 23 & 54 & 84 & 61 & 60 & 54 \\ 18 & 24 & 17 & 25 & 11 & 79 \\ 39 & 57 & 29 & 18 & 27 & 74 \\ 47 & 93 & 75 & 43 & 2 & 54 \end{pmatrix}$$

Adopting Mr. Doodad's 'seeing red' method of translating his notepad scribbles into computing terms, we obtain the following general description of matrices:

---

[7]Once again, because of the involvement of numerals, we should say 'representation of a matrix'. As in the case of 'vector', we choose not to tie ourselves in knots with such technicalities in what follows. (For your information, the plural of 'matrix' is 'matrices', which is pronounced 'MAY-tri-sees'.)

A matrix is a list that contains nothing but vectors and has the property that any vectors it contains are all the same length as each other.

Thus the null list is a matrix, and so is the list

```
((30 27  9  3 57 25)
 (23 54 84 61 60 54)
 (18 24 17 25 11 79)
 (39 57 29 18 27 74)
 (47 93 75 43  2 54))
```

Having decided to use a matrix to record his daily inventory, Mr. Doodad realizes that he now only needs one variable, and he settles (not surprisingly) on the variable '*widgets*'. One of the advantages of using the vector/matrix terminology is that there is an established vocabulary that comes with it. For example, each vector in a matrix is called a **row** of the matrix, and the vector formed by writing in order the numbers that are in a given position in the each row of a matrix is called a **column** of the matrix. So, for example, if the variable '*widgets*' is bound to the above matrix (corresponding to the July 10 inventory), then the vector '(39 57 29 18 27 74)' is the fourth row of the matrix *widgets*, and the vector '(27 54 24 57 93)' is its second column.

Exercise 86.

Write a definition for the function **sum–nth–row** of a natural number k and a matrix containing at least k rows that returns the sum of the kth row of the matrix. For example, when '*widgets*' is bound to the matrix for the July 10 inventory, the function **sum–nth–row** should behave like this:

(**sum–nth–row** 3 *widgets*) ↦ 174.

While familiarizing himself with the techniques of 'processing' matrices, Mr. Doodad writes a definition (given at the top of the next page) for the function **nth–column** of a natural number k and a matrix containing at least k columns that returns the kth column of the matrix. For example, with '*widgets*' bound to the matrix for the July 10 inventory, the functional expression (**nth–column** 2 *widgets*) evaluates to the vector '(27 54 24 57 93)' that gives the numbers of Baleful Blue widgets of each size.

```
(define nth–column
  (λ (k mat)
    (cond
      [(null? mat) ▽()]
      [else (cons
              (nth k (first mat))
              (nth–column k (rest mat)))])))
```

Exercise 87.

Write a definition for

a) the function **sum–nth–column** of a natural number k and a matrix containing at least k columns that returns the sum of the kth column of the matrix.

b) the function **sum–matrix** of a matrix that returns the sum of all the numbers in the matrix. With '*widgets*' still bound to the matrix for the July 10 inventory, for example, this function should behave as follows:

(sum–matrix *widgets*) ↦ 1219 .

PROBLEM SET 8

1. The function **max** of a non-null vector returns the largest number in the vector. The following definition for the function uses an accumulator to keep track of 'the largest number so far':

```
(define max
  (λ (vec)
    (max–help vec 0)))

(define max–help
  (λ (vec acc)
    (cond
      [(null? vec) acc]
      [(less? acc (first vec)) (max–help (rest vec) (first vec))]
      [else (max–help (rest vec) acc)])))
```

Write a definition for the function **min** of a non-null vector that returns the smallest number in the vector.

[Hint: In the language introduced in Exercise 85, initialize the accumulator to one of the numbers in the vector.]

2.   a) The function **next–please** of a non-null vector is defined as follows:

(define next–please
   (λ (*vec*)
      (next–please–help *vec* (max *vec*))))

(define next–please–help
   (λ (*vec biggest*)
      (cons *biggest* (rember *biggest vec*))))

Describe the behavior of the function **next–please**.

   b) Using the function **next–please**, or otherwise, write a definition for the function **selection–sort** of a vector that sorts the contents of the vector into decreasing numerical order.

3. In Chapter 5 we show how special kinds of association list may be used to model the way the Scheme interpreter keeps track of variable bindings. The Scheme interpreter does this with the help of certain structures called **frames**, the exact nature of which depends very much on the individual interpreter. To reflect the close link that exists between a frame and our list-based model of it, we shall call the model an **L–frame**. In general terms we have the following:

An *L–binding is a pair whose first data expression is an atom.*

An *L–frame is a list that contains nothing but L–bindings and has the property that no two of the L–bindings it contains have the same first data expression.*

For example, the list '(a 1815)' is an L–binding which binds the atom 'a' to the atom '1815', and the list '((a 1815) (b 1914) (c 1941))' is an L–frame containing three L–bindings. On the other hand, the list

((a 1815) b 1914 (c 1941) (a 1))

is *not* an L–frame for two reasons: It contains something other than L–bindings (namely, the atoms 'b' and '1914') and it contains two L–bindings (namely, '(a 1815)' and '(a 1)') that have the same first data expression.

Notice that, in particular, an L–frame is an association list. If a is an atom and F is an L–frame, then we say that 'a is bound in F' if and only if one of the L–bindings in the L–frame F has the atom a as its first data expression. Further, if the atom a is bound in the L–frame F, then the L–binding of which the atom a is the first data expression is called the '**binding** for a in F'.

a) Write a definition for the predicate function **frame?** of an association list that returns the boolean '#t' if and only if the association list is an L–frame.

b) Complete the following skeleton definition for the function **bind–in–frame** of an atom a, a data expression val, and an L–frame F that returns an L–frame related to F as follows: If a is bound in F, then the function changes the binding of a in F so that a is bound to val; if there is no binding for a in F, then a new L–binding is added so that a is bound to val.

```
(define bind–in–frame
  (λ (a val F)
    (cond
      [(null? F) (cons ( _____ a val) ▽( ))]
      [(eq? a (first (first F))) (cons
                                   ( _____ a val)
                                   ( _____ F))]
      [else (cons
              ( _____ F)
              ( _____ a val ( _____ F)))])))
```

4. Scheme interpreters combine frames into more complicated structures called **environments**. As in the case of frames, the exact nature of an environment depends very much on the individual interpreter. However, in Chapter 5, we use certain kinds of lists to model environments. We call these list-based models 'L-environments', a general description of which follows:

An L–environment is a list that contains nothing but L–frames.

The null list is an L–environment, and so is the list

```
(((a 1) (b 2) (c 3) (d 4)) () ((a 4) (f 5) (r 6))).
```

The latter L–environment contains three L–frames:

```
((a 1) (b 2) (c 3) (d 4)),   (),   and   ((a 4) (f 5) (r 6))).
```

The **binding** for an atom *a* in an L–environment is the binding for *a* in the first (that is, leftmost) L–frame of the L–environment that contains such a binding. If no such binding exists, then *a* is said to be **unbound** in the L–environment. The **replacement** for the atom *a* in an L–frame or L–environment is the second data expression in the binding for *a* in that L–frame or L–environment.

Use the function **lookup** to write a definition for the function **lookup–in–env** of an atom *a* and an L–environment *E* in which *a* is bound that returns the replacement for *a* in *E*.

$$- \circ O \circ -$$

4.3 Piling Systems

It sometimes happens that botanists and zoologists are presented with an organism and asked to identify it. An experienced scientist might point unhesitatingly to the organism in question and say, "That's a young *Potamochaerus porkus*," or, "This is the larva of the *Danaus plexippus*," but even the most learned taxonomist must occasionally admit defeat—there are just too many species. Of the avenues of inquiry open to the scientist, one is to use a **taxonomic key**, a device designed to facilitate the rapid identification of an animal or plant. Using such a key, the scientist is led through a series of Yes/No questions each of which eliminates one or more possibilities until only one possibility remains and the organism is identified.

Suppose, for example, that you wish to identify the tree in your back yard. It has a smooth, laminated outer bark and a close-grained wood which suggests it is some kind of birch tree (genus *Betula*). The question now is, 'What kind of birch tree?', for there are six common species in North America alone. To find the answer, we may consult a **key** such as the one in the following figure:

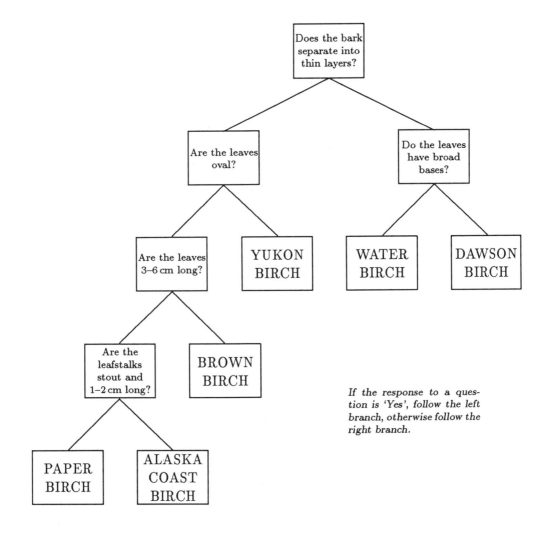

If the response to a question is 'Yes', follow the left branch, otherwise follow the right branch.

Figure 4.2: A Key for Genus *Betula*.

In this key, two branches stem from each question; the left branch corresponds to a 'Yes' answer and the right branch to a 'No' answer. Now, your back yard birch has the following characteristics:

> The bark is thin, smooth, and lustrous, peeling into papery-thin layers revealing an orange underbark. The twigs are shiny, and the leaves, which are about 6–8 cm long and 2.5–5 cm wide, hang from their stalks, are oval in shape, firm and thin, dull deep green above, and paler beneath.

The answer to the question at the top of the key, 'Does the bark separate into thin layers?', is 'Yes'. So you follow the *left* branch of the key to the next question, that is, 'Are the leaves oval?' The answer is 'Yes', so once again you follow the left branch of the key to the next question, 'Are the leaves 3–6 cm long?' This time, the answer is 'No' since some of the leaves are as long as 8 cm, so you take the *right* branch, thus identifying (or, as a botanist might say, '**keying-out**') the tree as a Brown Birch.

Exercise 88.

Use Figure 4.2 to help you key-out the trees described as follows:

a) This birch tree is 5 m tall and is found in swamps in the Yukon territory. Unlike some birch trees, its chestnut brown bark does not peel. The twigs are slender and red, the leaves have thin bases, are dark green, 2–3 cm long and 1–3 cm wide on short stalks.

b) This 10 m birch tree has slender leafstalks 2–3 cm long, with broad oval leaves. It is found from the Cook Inlet through the Kenai peninsula and Kodiak Island south to the head of the Lynn Canal. Its bark is smooth and tends to peel into thin layers. The leaves are about 5 cm long.

The key shown in Figure 4.2 is an example of a mathematical structure called a **binary tree**. Binary trees resemble the decomposition trees used in Chapter 1, but they have the special property that exactly two branches stem from each root. On the right, we show a binary tree which has an atom at each of its roots. Notice the seven 'dead twigs' on the fringes of this tree. They are not generating any further growth, that is, nothing appears at 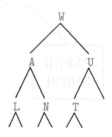 their branch ends. The empty spaces at these branch ends, where one would usually expect to find the roots of further sub-trees, are called **empty trees**. All *non-empty* binary trees, however, have exactly three components:

1. a (possibly empty) left sub-tree,

2. a data expression at the root of the tree, and

3. a (possibly empty) right sub-tree.

Binary trees have long been used by computer scientists for storing, manipulating, and retrieving information, and we devote the remainder of this chapter to looking at them in some detail. Along the way, we also introduce a new sorting strategy.

The immediate task is to design a representation for binary trees. With the above description to guide us, we naturally choose the following:

> *We represent the empty binary tree by the null list, and we represent a non-empty binary tree by a list containing exactly three data expressions, namely, the data expression at the root of the tree, the representation of the left sub-tree, and the representation of the right sub-tree, in that order.*

Taking the tree above as an example, we note that the atom 'L' lies at the root of a non-empty sub-tree both of whose sub-trees are empty, so we represent the sub-tree with the atom 'L' at its root by the list '(L () ())'. Similarly, the list '(N () ())' represents the sub-tree with the atom 'N' at its root. Then, since the atom 'A' is at the root of a tree whose left sub-tree is represented by the list '(L () ())' and whose right sub-tree is represented by the list '(N () ())', it follows that the sub-tree with the atom 'A' at its root is represented by the list '(A (L () ()) (N () ()))'. By a similar argument, the list '(U (T () ()) ())' represents the sub-tree with the atom 'U' at its root. Hence, the whole tree is represented by the list

$$(W \ (A \ (L \ () \ ()) \ (N \ () \ ())) \ (U \ (T \ () \ ()) \ ()))$$

When drawing binary trees it is customary to omit the dead wood. Thus, the tree in our example would usually be drawn like this:

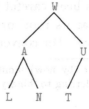

With this kind of 'trimmed tree' in mind, we say that a tree is a **leaf** if and only if it is non-empty but *both* of its sub-trees are empty, that is, it has a root, but beyond that only dead wood. Thus the tree in our example has three leaves, at whose roots appear the atoms 'L', 'N', and 'T'.

Exercise 89.

For each of the following binary trees, write the list that represents it.

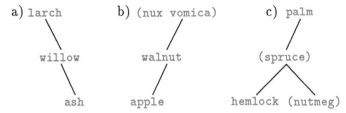

Exercise 90.

Draw the binary tree represented by the list

```
(rosewood (but () ()) (maple () (wouldnt () ())))
```

Having settled upon a way to represent binary trees, we turn our attention to the task of defining suitable constructor and data abstractor functions. We begin with a function that constructs a binary tree[8] from a root and left and right sub-trees:

$$(\text{define make–tree}$$
$$(\lambda \; (rt \; left \; right)$$
$$(\text{cons } rt \; (\text{cons } left \; (\text{cons } right \; {}^{\triangledown}()))))))$$

Next, we define three functions which select the various components of a non-empty binary tree:

(define root	(define left–tree	(define right–tree
(λ (bt)	(λ (bt)	(λ (bt)
(first bt)))	(second bt)))	(third bt)))

Thus far we have always been careful to say that a given binary tree 'has a certain data expression at its root' or that the data expression 'appears at the root of the binary tree'. For convenience, however, from this point on we

---

[8]From here on we follow our (by now) familiar practice of (almost always) omitting all mention of representation, referring to 'binary trees' rather than *representations of* binary trees'.

shall provide this kind of information by means of statements that are rather less technically correct. We shall often say, for example, that a certain data expression '*is* the root' of a given binary tree. Extending this practice a little further, we might say that the tree in Exercise 89(a) has three roots, namely, the atoms 'larch', 'willow', and 'ash'; on previous pages, we would have been careful to say '... three roots, *at which appear* the atoms ...'.

Exercise 91.

Using the above constructor and abstractor functions, write definitions for

a) the function **make–leaf** of a data expression that returns a binary tree whose root is the given data expression and both of whose sub-trees are empty.

b) the predicate function **leaf?** of a binary tree that returns the boolean '#t' if and only if the tree is a leaf.

c) the function **switch–subtrees** of a non-empty binary tree that returns the input tree with its left and right sub-trees interchanged. For example, if the input is the representation of the left-hand binary tree below then the function **switch–subtrees** should output the representation of the right-hand binary tree.

d) the function **replace–root** of a non-empty binary tree and a data expression that returns the input tree with its root replaced by the given data expression.

e) the function **replace–left–tree** of binary trees *trA* and *trB* (such that *trA* is non-empty) that returns *trA* with its left sub-tree replaced by *trB*.

f) the function **replace–right–tree** of binary trees *trA* and *trB* (such that *trA* is non-empty) that returns *trA* with its right sub-tree replaced by *trB*.

In Problem 2(b) of Problem Set 8 on page 142 you wrote a definition for the function **selection–sort** that sorts the contents of a vector into decreasing numerical order by repeatedly selecting and moving forward the largest whole number in the 'tail' of the vector. This is just one of many sorting algorithms, each with its own advantages and limitations. The selection sort, for example, has the advantage that it is simple and intuitive; indeed, it is probably the way that you go about sorting a short list of numbers. Let us check. Before reading on, sort the following numbers into decreasing numerical order, working as quickly as possible and writing the sorted list on a sheet of paper:

7   3941   17   83   9   14   10000   105   982

How did you do it? Perhaps you scanned the list for the largest number (10000), wrote it down, crossed it out from the original list (or discarded it mentally), and then repeated this process until no numbers remained to be sorted. If this was your strategy, then you were using the selection sort algorithm.

Imagine, however, that you had to sort the following numbers into decresing numerical order:

7	3941	17	83	9	14	10000	105	13
102	11021	3	73	195	740	3940	3942	3751
81	6	352	510	32105	3205	11017	1309
3307	333	4646	15	19	50	200	1591	9999

The task is now considerably more difficult, especially if you are restricted to using a selection sort, for there is no quick way to find the greatest number in a long and chaotic sequence.

Fortunately, there are many sorting algorithms that do not involve finding the greatest or least item in a sequence of items. One such algorithm is the **tree sort**, which we shall meet shortly. Rather than restricting ourselves just to sorting numbers, however, we give ourselves a change of scenery and address the problem of sorting atoms consisting only of *lower case letter* characters into alphabetical order. (For simplicity's sake, let us call atoms that consist only of lower case letter characters '**literal atoms**'.) More precisely, we shall make use of the **lexicographical** (or dictionary) order, defined in the expected way as follows:

> The literal atom **a** precedes the literal atom **b** in the lexicographical order if and only if **a** and **b** are the same atom or **a** would be listed before **b** in a dictionary.

For example, 'sprint' precedes 'sprinter' in the lexicographical order, but 'printer' precedes 'sprint'.

To help us in our task, we suppose that we have available the predicate function **order?** which inputs two literal atoms and returns the boolean '#t' if and only if the first input precedes the second in the lexicographical order.[9] Thus, for example,

- (order? $^\triangledown$apple $^\triangledown$apple) $\mapsto$ #t

- (order? $^\triangledown$sweetchestnut $^\triangledown$sweet) $\mapsto$ #f

- (order? $^\triangledown$widow $^\triangledown$window) $\mapsto$ #t

Exercise 92.

Evaluate each of these functional expressions:

a) (order? $^\triangledown$an $^\triangledown$teak)   b) (order? $^\triangledown$fir $^\triangledown$stand-news)

c) (order? $^\triangledown$sandy $^\triangledown$beech)   d) (order? $^\triangledown$poplar $^\triangledown$press)

The principle behind the tree sort is that it is possible to build a special kind of binary tree, called an **ordered binary tree**, that contains all the items to be sorted. Here is a general description of ordered binary trees:

An ordered binary tree is a binary tree with the property that each root R of the tree or of any sub-tree contained therein

- *is preceded by every root in the left sub-tree of the (sub-)tree whose root is R, and*

- *precedes every root in the right sub-tree of that (sub-)tree.*

This description is phrased in such a way that it applies in the context of any order. Of course, in our present situation, precedence is determined relative to the lexicographical order. So, for the remainder of this section, whenever you see the word 'precede' in our discussion you should understand it as abbreviating the phrase 'precede ... in the lexicographical order'. Furthermore, all the atoms we shall be sorting (and hence all the roots that feature in the ordered binary trees we display) are literal atoms. Here is an ordered binary tree:

---

[9]In fact, at the end of this chapter, you are asked to define a function **order?** that, in addition to behaving as described here, accepts *any* two atoms (whether literal or not) and determines whether or not the first precedes the second in an extended order based upon the lexicographical order.

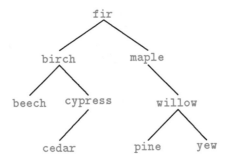

Verifying that this genuinely is an ordered binary tree involves quite a lot of checking. First, if we take the tree as a whole, we see that every root in its left sub-tree ('beech', 'birch', 'cypress', and 'cedar') precedes the root 'fir', and the root 'fir' precedes every root in the right sub-tree ('maple', 'pine', 'willow', and 'yew'). Similarly, in the sub-tree whose root is 'maple', the left sub-tree is empty, and so the condition that every root in the left sub-tree precedes the root is automatically satisfied for the simple reason that there is nothing in the left sub-tree, and therefore in particular nothing that does *not* precede the root. Furthermore, the root ('maple') of that sub-tree precedes each of the roots ('willow', 'pine', and 'yew') in the sub-tree's right sub-tree. Check every other root in the above tree until you have verified that the tree does indeed satisfy the ordered binary tree condition.

Incidentally, the empty tree (that is, the null list) is an ordered binary tree, just as it is a lat, a vector, and a matrix. It is also easy to see that every leaf is an ordered binary tree.

Exercise 93.

Which of these are (lexicographically) ordered binary trees?

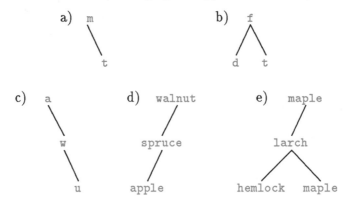

f)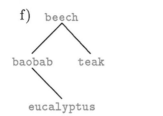

g)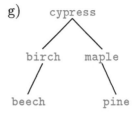

Exercise 94.

For each of the skeleton binary trees given at the top of the next page, write each of the literal atoms 'a', 'b', 'c', 'd', 'e', 'f', and 'g' in a box so that the resulting tree is ordered.

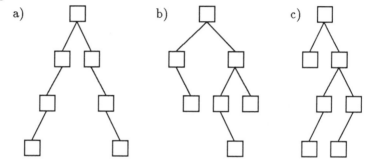

A tree sort proceeds in two stages. In the first stage, an ordered binary tree is constructed that contains all the items to be sorted, and in the second stage these items are read systematically from the tree in such a way that they emerge in order.

Obviously, we shall need to define a number of functions to perform various aspects of this task. We start with the function **tree–insert** of a literal atom and an ordered binary tree that inserts the atom into the tree in such a way that the tree remains ordered. Of course, it is possible that the tree is empty, in which case the output should be the leaf whose only root is the atom in question. Thus our definition begins as shown on the right.

```
(define tree–insert
  (λ (a obt)
    (cond
      [(null? obt)
       (make–leaf a)]
      ⋮
  )))
```

Suppose now that the tree is not empty. The question is, where should the atom go? Should we make it the root of the new tree? If we did, we would have to move the old root to some other position in the tree. If possible, of course, we would like to avoid having to do so much work! Fortunately, in the present case there are only two

possibilities: either the input atom precedes the current root of the tree or
it does not. It seems reasonable then that, in the first case, the atom should
be inserted into the left sub-tree, and in the second it should be inserted into
the right sub-tree. So we are led to the following definition:

```
(define tree–insert
  (λ (a obt)
    (cond
      [(null? obt) (make–leaf a)]
      [(order? a (root obt)) (replace–left–tree
                                obt
                                (tree–insert a (left–tree obt)))]
      [else (replace–right–tree
              obt
              (tree–insert a (right–tree obt)))])))
```

Exercise 95.

Evaluate this functional expression:

(tree–insert ▽birch ▽(beech (baobab ( ) ( )) (plum ( ) (teak ( ) ( )))))

Inserting atoms one-by-one is rather tedious, so we construct a function
that inputs a lat (containing nothing but literal atoms) and returns an ordered
binary tree whose roots are exactly the atoms in the lat. Here is a suitable
definition:

```
(define tree–insert–lat
  (λ (lat)
    (cond
      [(null? lat) ▽( )]
      [else (tree–insert (first lat) (tree–insert–lat (rest lat)))])))
```

Exercise 96.

By first compiling a trace table, or otherwise, sketch the tree that
is represented by the list to which the functional expression

(tree–insert–lat ▽(yew oak larch beech willow))

evaluates.

So much for the first stage of the tree sort; using the function **tree–insert–lat** we can build an ordered binary tree whose roots are the items to be sorted. Now we must define a function that will 'read' the sorted items from this tree in order. That is, we set about writing a definition for the function **traverse** of a binary tree that returns a list of all the roots of the tree, where this output list has the property that each root R (if any) appears in the list *after* any roots that are in the left sub-tree of the (sub-)tree whose root is R and *before* any roots that are in the right sub-tree of that (sub-)tree.

As usual, we begin the writing process by dealing with the very simplest case, that is, when the input is the empty tree:

(define traverse
  (λ (*obt*)
    (cond
      [(**null?** *obt*) $^{\triangledown}$( )]
      $\vdots$
  )))

Suppose now that the input ordered binary tree is non-empty. Then it certainly has a left sub-tree, a root, and a right sub-tree. Clearly, some type of recursion is called for, and the natural recursion probably involves the functional expressions

(traverse (left–tree *obt*))   and   **(traverse (right–tree** *obt*)).

To help us as we search for a sensible formulation of the natural recursion, we consider an example. Suppose, for a moment, that we have already succeeded in defining the function **traverse**, and suppose further that we have input into the function the list

```
(willow (beech () (larch () (oak () ())))) (yew () ())),
```

which represents the ordered binary tree you sketched in the last exercise. On the assumption that the function **traverse** behaves as we expect it to, it should turn out that, in this case,

(traverse (left–tree *obt*))   ↦   (beech larch oak)   and
(traverse (right–tree *obt*))   ↦   (yew).

Since **(root** *obt*) ↦ willow, we are faced with the task of deciding how the data expressions '(beech larch oak)', '(yew)', and 'willow' should be combined

so that the final output is correct. The solution is a natural outworking of
the basic property of ordered binary trees, namely, that everything in a tree's
left sub-tree precedes the tree's root, which in turn precedes everything in
the tree's right sub-tree. Thus, we cons the root of the tree onto the result
of traversing the right sub-tree, yielding the list '(willow yew)'. Then we
combine the contents of the lists

       (beech larch oak)   and   (willow yew)

into the single list '(beech larch oak willow yew)' using the function **append**, which you defined in Problem 8(e) of Problem Set 4 on page 93. From
our consideration of this example, it now follows easily that the definition for
the function **traverse** should be as follows:

```
(define traverse
  (λ (obt)
    (cond
      [(null? obt) ▽()]
      [else (append
              (traverse (left–tree obt))
              (cons
                (root obt)
                (traverse (right–tree obt))))])))
```

If this explanation of the derivation of the function **traverse** is a little too
glib for your liking, then you will probably benefit from taking the time to
compile a trace table showing the function in action. Unfortunately, any verbal description of a recursive process—especially one as involved as traversing
an ordered binary tree—is practically never any more convincing than the
used car salesperson who, exuding confidence, assures you that "It's perfectly
sound and reliable—you have my word on it!" Go ahead, take a test drive
anyway.

Exercise 97.

> Using the functions **tree–insert–lat** and **traverse**, write a definition
> for the function **tree–sort** of a lat containing nothing but literal
> atoms that uses the tree sort algorithm to return the lat with its
> contents sorted into lexicographical order.

We mentioned earlier that all sorting algorithms have their advantages and
disadvantages. The tree sort is no exception. Strange though it may seem,

the tree sort is particularly effective when the initial ordering of the items to
be sorted is chaotic, but it is inefficient if the items are already partially or
(worse still) completely ordered. The reason is not hard to find, for one of
the most time-consuming processes in any computer sort is the comparison
of two items to see which precedes the other. You may care to verify the fact
that the functional expression '(tree–insert–lat $^\nabla$(g c e a f b d))', in which the
lat to be sorted bears no discernible relationship to the lexicographical order,
outputs the representation of the following tree:

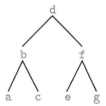

and involves exactly ten calls to the function **order?**. On
the other hand, the functional expression

(tree–insert–lat $^\nabla$(a b c d e f g))

in which the lat to be sorted is already in lexicographical
order, outputs the representation of the tree shown on the
right and involves twenty-one calls to the function **order?**,
that is, more than twice as many.

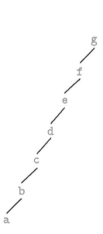

Exercise 98.

> Complete the following definition for the func-
> tion **tree–size** of a binary tree that counts how
> many roots the tree has:

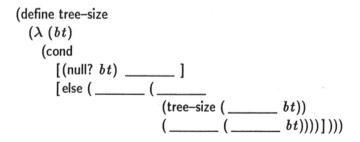

```
(define tree–size
  (λ (bt)
    (cond
      [(null? bt) _____ ]
      [else ( _____ ( _____
                       (tree–size ( _____ bt))
                       ( _____ ( _____ bt))))])))
```

Exercise 99.

> Write a definition for the function **leaf–count** of a binary tree that
> counts how many leaves the tree has.

As we have already hinted, there are other sorting algorithms based on
data structures that differ in some respects from the ordered binary tree.
Each such algorithm has its advantages and disadvantages, and once one has
become familiar with a variety of sorting procedures a suitable algorithm is
chosen for use in a given practical instance based upon the user's assessment
of which one minimizes the disadvantages and maximizes the advantages in
situations of the type in question. A more detailed look at such matters will,
however, have to wait for another occasion.

We conclude this chapter with a problem set whose problems lead to the
promised definition for the function **order?**.

PROBLEM SET 9

1. In this problem we write a definition for the function **char–to–integer** of a
   red character that outputs a whole number associated with that character.
   The function **char–to–integer** will be used in the definition for the function
   order? of two atoms that (in the case of literal atoms) determines whether
   the atoms are in lexicographical order, so it is important that the number
   associated with each (lower-case letter) character shall reflect the position
   of that character in the alphabet.

   The function **char–to–integer** may be defined in terms of the function **lookup**
   and an association list. Most likely, the association list that springs to
   mind is one in which the character 'A' is associated with the number 1, 'B'
   with 2, 'C' with 3, ... , 'Z' with 26, 'a' with 27, 'b' with 28, and so on, or
   perhaps a similar list with upper- and lower-case characters switched. We
   shall instead use a system of numerical codes known as **ASCII codes**—
   'ASCII', pronounced 'ASS-key', is an acronym for 'American Standard
   Codes for Information Interchange'—which is now regarded as standard
   by computer scientists throughout the world. The ASCII code associated
   with each red character is given in Table 4.3 on page 159.

   a) Suppose that the variable '*ascii*' is bound to an association list in
      which each red character is associated with (the W-representation of)

Character	!	#	$	*	+	–	/	0	1	2	3	4
ASCII code	33	35	36	42	43	45	47	48	49	50	51	52

Character	5	6	7	8	9	=	?	A	B	C	D	E
ASCII code	53	54	55	56	57	61	63	65	66	67	68	69

Character	F	G	H	I	J	K	L	M	N	O	P	Q
ASCII code	70	71	72	73	74	75	76	77	78	79	80	81

Character	R	S	T	U	V	W	X	Y	Z	a	b	c
ASCII code	82	83	84	85	86	87	88	89	90	97	98	99

Character	d	e	f	g	h	i	j	k	l	m	n	o
ASCII code	100	101	102	103	104	105	106	107	108	109	110	111

Character	p	q	r	s	t	u	v	w	x	y	z	
ASCII code	112	113	114	115	116	117	118	119	120	121	122	

ASCII codes lie in the range 0–127, or, in the increasingly popular extended systems, 0–255. The 'missing' codes are assigned to a variety of special punctuation marks (that we do not include in our character set, but which some Scheme interpreters may accept) and also to a number of so-called 'control' characters that do such things as make a beep on the computer's speaker (code 7), clear the screen (code 12), and so on. The extended systems also assign codes to various foreign language characters, among other things. For example, on an IBM PC, code 146 is assigned to the Scandinavian upper-case letter 'Æ'.

Table 4.3: The ASCII Codes of the Red Characters.

its ASCII code. Write a definition for the function **char–to–integer** of a red character that returns its ASCII code.

b) Evaluate each of the following functional expressions:

(i) **(char–to–integer** $^\nabla$**a)** (ii) **(char–to–integer** $^\nabla$**A)**

(iii) **(char–to–integer 4)** (iv) **(char–to–integer** $^\nabla$**?)**

2. a) Use the function **switch** (which you defined when you answered Exercise 84 on page 136) to define the function **integer–to–char** of (the W-representation of) an ASCII code that returns the corresponding red character.[10] For example,

$$\text{(integer–to–char 68)} \mapsto D; \qquad \text{(integer–to–char 99)} \mapsto c.$$

b) Write a definition for the predicate function **lowercase?** of a red character that returns the boolean '#t' if and only if the character is a lower-case letter.

c) Write a definition for the function **capitalize** of a red character that behaves as follows: If the input is a lower-case letter then the function returns its upper-case equivalent, otherwise the function returns its input.

3. In this problem, we introduce two new functions. The function **explode** of an atom returns the lat containing each of the characters in the atom, in order of appearance. Thus, for example,

- **(explode** $^\nabla$**1*3Hb5+)** $\mapsto$ (1 * 3 H b 5 +)
- **(first (explode** $^\nabla$**Fred))** $\mapsto$ F

The function **implode** of a lat containing only characters has the opposite effect; it returns the atom obtained when the characters in the lat are 'pushed up against' each other (in technical language, we say the characters are **concatenated**, which literally means 'chained together').[11] So, for example,

---

[10] In commercially available implementations of Scheme (including *EdScheme*), the character set used is more extensive than the one assumed in this book. Such implementations include the primitive functions **char->integer** and **integer->char** which do not depend upon the variable '*ascii*' being bound to a lengthy association list, which agree with our derived functions **char-to-integer** and **integer-to-char**, respectively, on all inputs mentioned in Table 4.3, and which behave similarly for all inputs corresponding to entries that are missing from that table.

[11] In *EdScheme*, **explode** and **implode** are primitive functions. In other implementations of Scheme, they are not. However, in all cases they are definable as derived functions.

- (implode $^\triangledown$(1 * 3 H b 5 +)) $\mapsto$ `1*3Hb5+`

- (implode (explode $^\triangledown$Fred)) $\mapsto$ `Fred`

a) Complete the following skeleton definition for the function **capitalize–atom** of an atom that changes any lower-case letters in the atom into their upper-case equivalents. For example,

- (capitalize–atom $^\triangledown$fred) $\mapsto$ `FRED`
- (capitalize–atom $^\triangledown$1*3Hb5c+) $\mapsto$ `1*3HB5C+`
- (capitalize–atom $^\triangledown$MArY) $\mapsto$ `MARY`

```
(define capitalize–atom
  (λ (atom)
    (implode (capitalize–atom–help (explode atom)))))
```

```
(define capitalize–atom–help
  (λ (lat)
    (cond
      [(null? lat) ▽()]
      [else (_____
               (_____ (_____ lat))
               (_____ (_____ lat)))])))
```

b) Write a definition for the function **initial–cap** of an atom containing nothing but letters that returns the atom with its first character in upper-case and all the remaining characters in lower-case.

c) Write a definition for the function **word** of two atoms that returns the concatenation of the two atoms. For example,

- (word $^\triangledown$deli $^\triangledown$very) $\mapsto$ `delivery`
- (word $^\triangledown$concert $^\triangledown$o) $\mapsto$ `concerto`

d) Write a definition for the function **count** of a data expression that returns a whole number determined as follows. If the input is an atom, the function should return the number of characters in the atom. However, if the input is a list then the function should return the number of data expressions in the list.

4. The time has come for us to write our long-awaited definition for the function **order?**. So far we have only used this function in the context of atoms composed of nothing but lower-case letters. Now that we have met

the ASCII codes of the lower-case letters, it is clear that we could order single letters alphabetically purely on the basis of their ASCII codes. But then there is no reason why we should not extend this method to *all* single-character atoms, not just those in which the characters involved are lower-case letters. This extended single-character order can then be used in the obvious way to extend the lexicographical order so that it accepts *all* atoms. This new lexicographical order has some interesting properties. For example, note that the atom '6' precedes the atom '73495' in the new lexicographical order, the atom '73495' precedes the atom '8', and the atom '$1million' precedes the atom 'penniless'. Also, note that all upper-case letters precede all lower-case letters in this new order. (We recognize that this leads to certain illogicalities. Why, for example, should the symbols '=' and '?' be placed *after* the numerals '0' through '9' rather than *before* them, like all the other non-alphanumeric symbols? It's just one of those historical accidents that an internationally agreed-upon system includes such anomalies. We could, of course, decide to iron out this wrinkle and make our order more logical. We choose instead to live with the ASCII codes as they are, 'warts and all'.) From here on, we use the term 'lexicographical order' to refer to the new, extended lexicographical order as determined by the ASCII codes given in Table 4.3.

a) Write a definition for the predicate function **order–char?** of two characters *a* and *b* that returns the boolean '#t' if and only if *a* *strictly* precedes *b* in the lexicographical order (the function should output the boolean '#f' if the characters are the same).

b) Complete the skeleton definition on the next page for the function **order?** of two atoms that returns the boolean '#t' if and only if the first atom precedes the second in the lexicographical order.

c) Test your definition in part (b) by completing trace tables showing the behavior of the function **order?** when its inputs are the atoms:

   (i) 'az' and 'Za'   (ii) 'az' and 'az'
   (iii) 'a?' and 'a?D'   (iv) 'dIeT' and 'di'.

d) Using the function **order?**, write a definition for the predicate function **strict–order?** of atoms *a* and *b* that returns the boolean '#t' if and only if the atom *a* strictly precedes the atom *b* in the new lexicographical order. [Hint: It is possible to define this function using only the functions **not** and **order?**.]

```
(define order?
  (λ (a b)
    (order?-help (explode a) (explode b))))

(define order?-help
  (λ (r s)
    (cond
      [(null? r) _____ ]
      [(null? s) _____ ]
      [(order-char? (first r) (first s)) _____ ]
      [(order-char? (first s) (first r)) _____ ]
      [else ( _____ ( _____ r) ( _____ s))])))
```

$- o \, O \, o -$

5 The Scheme Machine

5.1 The Inner Workings

When we first encountered the concept of evaluation in Chapter 1, we explained what was going on in intuitive terms. We told you that evaluation was a process whereby a black functional expression was changed into a red data expression. We gave you very little idea, however, as to exactly how this was achieved. Our purpose in this brief chapter is to provide you with a great deal more information about how the Scheme interpreter carries out the process of evaluation. After this admittedly highly theoretical interlude, we then proceed in the remaining chapters to show how the knowledge of what is going on may be exploited.

Consider the following short conversation between a schemer and the Scheme interpreter. It concerns the derived function **pair**, which you defined in Problem 1(c) of Problem Set 6 on page 117.

```
⟹ (define pair
      (lambda (a b)
        (cons a (cons b '()))))
pair
⟹ (pair #t '(Fred Jane))
(#t (Fred Jane))
⟹ (atom? (pair 1 2))
#f
⟹ _
```

165

Once a derived function such as **pair** has been defined by typing its definition into the computer, the typical schemer makes no further effort to remember all the details of that definition, and thereafter uses the function just as if it were primitive. Unfortunately, the Scheme interpreter is not so flexible. When it is called upon to evaluate a functional expression involving a derived function, the interpreter must somehow recall the details of that function's definition. Where are these details stored? In what form are they kept? These are two of the questions we answer in this chapter, for our explanation of the way in which the Scheme interpreter evaluates the functional expressions typed by schemers involves taking a look right into the heart of the interpreter.

We begin, however, by answering a much simpler question: What kinds of functional expression should we expect the interpreter to deal with? Does the interpreter use the same strategy to evaluate the functional expression '▽Fred' as it uses to evaluate the functional expressions '967' or '(pair 1 2)', say? The answer must surely be 'No', for these are different types of functional expressions. In fact, the interpreter recognizes four distinct categories of functional expression:

1. Black numerals, such as '9643824548'.

2. Blackened atoms, but not including black numerals or Scheme keywords. Such symbols are called **identifiers**. Included in this category are the symbols '#t' and '#f', and parameters and global variables such as '*a*' and '*alist*'. Although we have so far not even contemplated the possibility of evaluating a functional expression that consists solely of a function name such as 'first' or 'second', it happens that such names are also identifiers and, as such, can indeed be evaluated by the interpreter. We go into more detail about such matters later in this chapter.

3. Special forms. Included in this category are

    *   functional expressions, such as '"(a b c)'—which in this book we print as '▽(a b c)'—denoting the output from constant functions. In fact, an expression that begins with a right-hand quote mark is an abbreviation, understood and accepted by the Scheme interpreter, for a functional expression consisting of a black left parenthesis, followed by the keyword 'quote', followed by the blackened data expression that is the output from the constant function, followed by a black right parenthesis. Thus, '"(a b c)' abbreviates the functional

expression '(quote (a b c))'. (For obvious reasons, such unabbreviated functional expressions are known as **quote-expressions**.) Similarly, ''me' (or, in our usual printed form, '$^\triangledown$me') abbreviates the quote-expression '(quote me)'.

- cond-expressions such as   (cond
                                    [(null? r) #f]
                                    [else (first *alist*)]])

- lambda-expressions such as '(lambda (r) (first (rest r)))'.

- define-expressions such as

      (define *one* 1)   and   (define second
                                              (λ (r)
                                                (first (rest r))))

(Further special forms are introduced later in this and subsequent chapters.)

4. Functional expressions, such as '(second $^\triangledown$(a b c))' or '(cons a b)', that denote applications of primitive or derived functions to their inputs. Such functional expressions are called **function applications** or, simply, 'applications'.

Exercise 100.

For each of these functional expressions, state whether it is a black numeral, an identifier, a special form, or an application:

    a) $^\triangledown$(a b c d e f)   b) (xor (atom? a) (atom? b))

    c) #f   d) (cond [(null? a) b] [else #f])

    e) 638452   f) cons

We devote the remainder of this chapter to considering each of the four categories in turn, discussing how the interpreter recognizes the category to which a functional expression belongs, and explaining how it then evaluates the expression.

5.2 Numbers and Other Identification Marks

The first kind of functional expression we look at are the black numerals. Somewhere deep in the interpreter there is a package of low-level code (known as a **subroutine**) whose sole purpose is to identify those blackened atoms that name numbers. Having found such a name, the interpreter has very little else to do but to change it from black to red.[1]

Any blackened atom that is not a numeral or a Scheme keyword is assumed by the interpreter to be an identifier. Suppose, for a moment, that the identifier is a global variable; how should the interpreter evaluate it? As you know, the value of a global variable is the data expression that is its replacement. It is therefore natural to ask how the interpreter maintains records of the current replacements for global variables.

The answer is that the Scheme interpreter keeps track of variable bindings by storing them in structures called **frames**, which, in turn, are stored in structures called **environments**. The precise details of how environments are maintained and where they are stored in the computer's memory are highly implementation-dependent and are of little interest except to designers of interpreters. However, their behavior is almost identical to that of the L-frames and L-environments you met in Problems 3 and 4 of Problem Set 8. For our explanatory purposes in this chapter, it is convenient for us to suppose that *true* frames and environments actually are L-frames and L-environments. (While this pretense will not mislead you in any way, you will learn in Chapter 8 that *true* environments have an unusual feature that distinguishes them from L-environments.) We shall, however, continue to use the 'L-' prefix so that you are reminded we are simply modeling the actual situation.

There is one particular environment in which the interpreter keeps all the bindings it needs to enable it to do its work together with any bindings that have been established during the course of the work in progress. Obviously, this environment is constantly changing during the evaluation of a functional expression, so its instantaneous state at any given moment is known as the **current environment**. We shall refer to our L-environment model of this as the **current L-environment**. At the very start of each evaluation, at the instant when the schemer has typed a functional expression and has just pressed the return key, the current L-environment consists of a single frame called the **global L-frame**. (We refer to this initial current L-environment, containing the global L-frame and nothing else, as the **global L-environ-**

---

[1]This statement is true if you are using the *EdScheme* interpreter. (We invented the black/red color distinction in order to highlight the otherwise extremely mysterious distinction between evaluated expressions and unevaluated expressions.) Most other Scheme interpreters evaluate a (monochrome) numeral simply by returning that same numeral.

ment.) This L-frame takes up permanent residence as the rightmost L-frame of the current L-environment throughout the entire course of the evaluation just initiated. It serves a very special purpose, for it is here that, among other things, the bindings for global variables are stored.

By way of illustration we analyze the following brief conversation:

$\implies$ (define names '(ronald raymond herbert))
names
$\implies$ names
(ronald raymond herbert)
$\implies$ _

In response to the assignment with which the schemer starts the conversation, the interpreter adds the L-binding '(names (ronald raymond herbert))' to the global L-frame, thereby binding the identifier '*names*' to the list '(ronald raymond herbert)'. The rules followed by the interpreter as it does this are explained in a little while. Having done this, the interpreter has printed the atom 'names' to indicate that an L-binding for the corresponding identifier has been established. Next, the schemer has typed the functional expression '*names*'. The interpreter, recognizing this to be a blackened atom that is neither a black numeral nor a Scheme keyword, assumes that it is an identifier and finds its value simply by looking up its replacement in the global L-frame.

The identifiers '**#t**' and '**#f**' are dealt with in the same way as global variables, for when the interpreter is first activated it establishes a number of L-bindings in the global L-frame, among them '(#t #t)' and '(#f #f)'. Indeed, in general, the interpreter seeks to evaluate any identifier it encounters by trying to look up its replacement in the current L-environment. Of course, if the identifier in question is not bound in the current L-environment, then the interpreter signals to the schemer that an error has occurred.

5.3 Special Instructions

The Scheme interpreter recognizes a special form from the fact that it is a blackened non-null list whose first sub-expression—by which we mean the blackened first data expression of the list that results when the functional expression is painted red—is a keyword. Each special form has its own special rules for evaluation, some easy to follow and others rather more complicated.

The rules for each special form are encoded in the interpreter, and upon recognizing a particular special form by the presence of its keyword the interpreter refers to the appropriate coded set of instructions for information on how to proceed. We summarize the rules for evaluating the four kinds of special form we have met so far in Figure 5.1 below, where we refer to each special form by its keyword.

quote To evaluate a quote-expression, return the second sub-expression of the quote-expression, in red.

cond To evaluate a cond-expression, take the clauses one by one in order and evaluate their predicates until one is found whose value is the boolean '#t'. Then return the value of the corresponding consequent, and pay no attention to the remaining clauses. If no predicate expression evaluates to the boolean '#t', evaluate the alternative in the else-clause.

lambda To evaluate a lambda-expression, return a special list (called a **function descriptor**) that provides the Scheme interpreter with all the information it needs to calculate the output from the function described by the lambda-expression. Exactly what this list contains is explained in Section 5.4.

define To evaluate a define-expression, establish an L-binding in the global L-frame of the identifier that is the second sub-expression to the value of the third sub-expression. Then return the second sub-expression, in red.

Figure 5.1: Special Form Evaluation.

The time has now arrived for us to meet the two special forms we referred to in Chapter 2. During our discussion of Boolean functions in that chapter, we introduced you to the two-input functions **and2** and **inor**, whose truth tables are given at the top of the next page. We explained that, for our purposes at that time, these truth tables included all the necessary information. There are, of course, several definitions that could be written for these functions so that they behave in this way when their inputs are boolean objects. One possibility for each function is given beneath its truth table. Unfortunately,

a	b	(and2 a b)
#t	#t	#t
#t	#f	#f
#f	#t	#f
#f	#f	#f

a	b	(inor a b)
#t	#t	#t
#t	#f	#t
#f	#t	#t
#f	#f	#f

```
(define and2
  (λ (a b)
    (cond
      [a b]
      [else #f])))
```

```
(define inor
  (λ (a b)
    (cond
      [a #t]
      [else b])))
```

by defining them in this way we actually limit their usefulness! To illustrate what we mean, consider how convenient it would be if we could test whether a data expression a is an atomic element (either an atom or the null list) by evaluating the functional expression

$$\text{(inor (atom? } a\text{) (null? } a\text{))}$$

If a is the null list then this functional expression evaluates to the boolean '#t', and if a is a non-null list then it evaluates to the boolean '#f'. But if a is an atom then the functional expression above cannot be evaluated, since the function **null?** accepts only lists as its input.

Scheme gets around this problem by providing two special forms called **and-expressions** and **or-expressions**. An and-expression consists of the keyword 'and' (in black) followed by two functional expressions each of which represents the output from a predicate function, all enclosed in black parentheses, as, for example, in the functional expression

$$\text{(and (atom? } a\text{) (eq? } a\text{ }^{\triangledown}\text{Fred))}$$

An and-expression is evaluated as follows: The first functional expression following the keyword 'and' is evaluated. If it evaluates to the boolean '#f', then the and-expression evaluates to the boolean '#f'. On the other hand, if the first functional expression evaluates to the boolean '#t', then the second functional expression is evaluated. The value of the and-expression is then the boolean (either '#t' or '#f') to which this functional expression evaluates.

The most important aspect of this is that the second functional expression is only evaluated if the first functional expression evaluates to the boolean '#t'. This means, for example, that the functional expression

$$\text{(and (atom? } a \text{) (eq? } a \text{ }^{\triangledown}\text{Fred))}$$

can *always* be evaluated (even when **a** is a list). It also means that we can use an and-expression in recursive definitions where we might be reluctant to use the derived function **and2**. Consider, for example, the function **lat?** whose definition is given on page 82. Close inspection of that definition reveals that the following is an acceptable alternative:

```
(define lat?
  (λ (a)
    (cond
      [(null? a) #t]
      [else (and2 (atom? (first a))
                  (lat? (rest a)))])))
```

What happens when the list '(a (b) c)' is the input to the function **lat?** and the foregoing definition is followed? Here is the relevant trace table:

```
(lat? (a (b) c))
(and2 (atom? a) (lat? ((b) c)))
(and2 #t (lat? ((b) c)))
(and2 #t (and2 (atom? (b)) (lat? (c))))
(and2 #t (and2 #f (lat? (c))))
(and2 #t (and2 #f (and2 (atom? c) (lat? ()))))
(and2 #t (and2 #f (and2 #t #t)))
(and2 #t (and2 #f #t))
(and2 #t #f)
#f
```

Let us now see in what way the function **lat?** would perform differently if the alternative in the else-clause of the above definition were replaced by an and-expression, as shown on the right. Once again, we compile a trace table

```
(define lat?
  (λ (a)
    (cond
      [(null? a) #t]
      [else (and (atom? (first a))
                 (lat? (rest a)))])))
```

to show how the function **lat?** behaves when its input is the list '(a (b) c)' and this modified definition is followed. The trace table begins with the mixed expression '(**lat?** (a (b) c))'. Since the list '(a (b) c)' is not the null list, we must evaluate the following mixed expression:

$$\text{(and (atom? a) (lat? ((b) c)))}$$

Following the rules for evaluating an and-expression, we evaluate the functional expression '(**atom?** a)'. Since this evaluates to the boolean '#t', the and-expression evaluates to the value of the second functional expression. In other words, the trace so far is as follows:

> (**lat?** (a (b) c))
> (**and** (**atom?** a) (**lat?** ((b) c)))
> (**lat?** ((b) c))

The list '((b) c)' is clearly not the null list, so we must next evaluate the mixed expression:

$$\text{(and (atom? (b)) (lat? (c)))}$$

The first functional expression in this and-expression evaluates to the boolean '#f', so the value of the and-expression is the boolean '#f', and the completed trace table is as follows:

> (**lat?** (a (b) c))
> (**and** (**atom?** a) (**lat?** ((b) c)))
> (**lat?** ((b) c))
> (**and** (**atom?** (b)) (**lat?** (c)))
> #f

This represents a major improvement in efficiency over the definition involving the function **and2**. Although there is no gain in efficiency over the original definition on page 82, it could be argued that our modification above involving an and-expression expresses the 'rules' for evaluating the **lat?** of a list more succinctly than the original does, for it emphasizes that, for a non-null list to be a lat, its first data expression must be an atom *and* the rest of the list must be a lat.

An or-expression is similar in form to an and-expression except, of course, the keyword 'or' (in black) appears in place of the keyword 'and'. It is evaluated according to the following rules: The first functional expression following the keyword 'or' is evaluated. If it evaluates to the boolean '#t', then the or-expression evaluates to the boolean '#t'. Otherwise, the second functional expression is evaluated, and its value is the value of the or-expression. For example, the functional expression

$$(\text{or } (\text{atom? } a) \, (\text{null? } a))$$

evaluates to the boolean '#t' if *a* is an atom or the null list (or both), and it evaluates to the boolean '#f' otherwise. We remark in passing that, if *a* is an atom, then the sub-expression '(null? *a*)' is not evaluated.

Note that, in and-expressions and or-expressions, the order of appearance of the two functional expressions that follow the keyword is significant. As a general rule, it is advisable to place the most 'welcoming' of the two functional expressions in first position, that is, the expression that accepts the broader range of inputs.

Exercise 101.

Using the replacements

a : Fred	*b* : (Fred Jane)
c : ( )	*d* : #t

evaluate as many of these functional expressions as possible:

a) (and (atom? *a*) (not (atom? *b*)))

b) (or *d* (eq? *b* ▽(Jane)))

c) (and (not (atom? *b*)) (null? *d*))

d) (and #f (or *d* (eq? *a* ▽Fred)))

e) (or (not (null? *c*)) (and *d* (eq? *a* (first *b*))))

Having completed the introduction of our latest two special forms, we should extend our rules for evaluating special forms. All the important and relevant information is summarized in Figure 5.2 at the top of the next page.

Exercise 102.

Complete this skeleton definition for the function **member?** (first defined on page 82) so that it uses the special form **or**:

```
(define member?
   (λ (a s)
      (cond
         [(null? s) #f]
         [else ( _____ ( _____ ( _____ s) a)
                  ( _____ a ( _____ s)))])))
```

> **and**   To evaluate an and-expression, proceed as follows: Evaluate
> the second sub-expression.[2] If its value is the boolean '#t',
> then return the value of the third sub-expression. Otherwise
> return the boolean '#f'.
>
> **or**   To evaluate an or-expression, proceed as follows: Evaluate
> the second sub-expression. If its value is the boolean '#t',
> then return the boolean '#t'. Otherwise return the value of
> the third sub-expression.

Figure 5.2: Special Form Evaluation (continued).

5.4 Interpreting Commands

At this point in our discussion of evaluation there remains only one type of
functional expression for us to consider, namely, function applications. As
you may have guessed from the way we have organized the discussion thus
far, the Scheme interpreter identifies applications by a process of elimination.
If the functional expression typed by a schemer is neither a numeral, nor an
identifier, nor a special form, then the interpreter assumes it to be an application. Upon recognizing an application, the interpreter determines whether
the function being applied is primitive or derived. If it is primitive, then the
input(s) is/are sent to the subroutine within the interpreter itself that calculates the output from that function. On the other hand, if the function is a
derived function, then the interpreter must find out how it is defined before
it can begin to calculate the output.

Of course, all of this activity on the part of the interpreter requires a
considerable amount of information, all of which at any moment is stored
in the interpreter's current L-environment. In particular, the name of each
function is bound in the global L-frame to a **function descriptor** (or FD, for
short), which is a data expression that provides all the information about a
function that the interpreter needs to know.[3] There are two types of function

---

[2] The second sub-expression is of course the first functional expression following the keyword,
which is the first sub-expression.

[3] The function descriptors described here are those used by the *EdScheme* interpreter. Other
interpreters use FDs that *look* different, but the principle is exactly the same.

the means whereby the interpreter can distinguish between the two types of function. The FD of a primitive function is a list containing exactly two data expressions: first, the atom 'primitive' and, second, the atom that names the primitive function. For example, the FD of the primitive function **first** is the list '(primitive first)' and the FD of the primitive function **eq?** is the list '(primitive eq?)'.

When the interpreter is first activated it creates an L-binding in the global L-frame for each of the primitive functions, binding the name of each primitive function to its FD. On the other hand, a global L-binding for a derived function is only established at the time that the schemer types in the function's definition. For example, the lambda-expression in the definition

(define second
    (λ (*r*)
      (first (rest *r*))))

evaluates to the FD '(derived (r) (first (rest r)) ())'. So typing the above assignment causes the L-binding

(second (derived (r) (first (rest r)) ()))

to be established in the global L-frame.

Function descriptors of derived functions contain exactly four data expressions. The first data expression is the atom 'derived', which (obviously!) tells the interpreter that it is dealing with a derived function. The second data expression, called the **FD-parameter list**, is the lambda-parameter list, in red. The third data expression, called the **FD-body**, is the lambda-body, in red. The fourth data expression, called the **FD-environment**, is the L-environment that was current when the lambda-expression was evaluated, with the global L-frame discarded. In the next chapter we show how FDs of derived functions can be generated with non-empty FD-environments. However, when a function has been defined using a define-expression as in the example above, the FD-environment is always empty.

Exercise 103.

    a) Write the function descriptor of the primitive function **atom?**.

    b) Write the global L-binding   (define pair
        established by the define-   (λ (*a b*)
        expression on the right.   (cons *a* (cons *b* ▽()))))

To find the FD associated with a function the interpreter has only to evaluate the function name. Since a function name is an identifier, its value is simply its replacement (which is an FD) in the global L-frame.

This is perhaps an opportune moment to remark that, if the schemer has a momentary lapse and types a functional expression such as '(xqfplrt *var*)' before defining the function xqfplrt, the interpreter will quickly identify the expression as an application, but, after a fruitless search in the global L-frame, will then complain that the identifier 'xqfplrt' is not bound in the current L-environment. Such behavior on the part of the interpreter is often particularly useful in alerting the schemer to typing errors. Suppose, for example, that you have in mind to type the functional expression '(first ▽(a b c))', but in the heat of the moment you mistype 'first' as 'frist'. In a flash the Scheme intepreter will dispassionately announce that it is ignorant of how to frist anything— unless of course you have previously defined a function called 'frist', in which case some (probably) totally unexpected output will appear on the screen.

The nature of the next step in evaluating a function application depends on whether the function's FD indicates that it is primitive or derived. We consider an example of each type.

Suppose the interpreter is asked to evaluate the application

$$\text{(cons \#t } ^\triangledown\text{(4 2 and 2 4 \#t))}$$

The interpreter begins its job by evaluating each of the three sub-expressions it contains, with the following results:

$$\text{cons} \mapsto \text{(primitive cons)}$$
$$\text{\#t} \mapsto \text{\#t}$$
$$^\triangledown\text{(4 2 and 2 4 \#t)} \mapsto \text{(4 2 and 2 4 \#t)}$$

Next, the interpreter notes that the function to be applied is primitive and that, specifically, it is the function cons. Knowing that cons takes two inputs, it checks that two inputs have actually been supplied, and then sends them to the subroutine that deals with the function cons. Finally, this subroutine returns the list '(#t 4 2 and 2 4 #t)'.

Next, we look at how the interpreter behaves when it is presented with an application involving a derived function—for example, '(second ▽(a b c))'. As in our first example, the interpreter begins by evaluating each sub-expression of this functional expression.

$$\text{second} \mapsto \text{(derived (r) (first (rest r)) ())}$$
$$^\triangledown\text{(a b c)} \mapsto \text{(a b c)}$$

Then it applies the function described by the FD to its input(s) in the following manner:

Derived Function Evaluation

1. The interpreter stores a record of the current L-environment for later use.

2. It replaces the current L-environment by the L-environment that results from the following procedure:

   - Append the global L-environment to the FD-environment.

   - Onto the result cons an L-frame containing L-bindings of the parameters listed in the FD-parameter list to the function's inputs.

   (Note that the new current L-environment contains, in order, an L-frame in which each of the function's parameters is bound to a corresponding input, all the L-frames—if any—in the FD-environment, and lastly the global L-frame.)

3. It blackens the FD-body and evaluates the resulting functional expression.

4. It replaces the current L-environment by the L-environment that was stored in Step 1, thereby returning the current L-environment to its former state.

To simplify the continuation of our description, we suppose that the global L-frame in the current L-environment contains only these three bindings:

```
((second (derived (r) (first (rest r)) ()))
 (first (primitive first))
 (rest (primitive rest)))
```

(We have restricted ourselves just to the L-bindings that are used in the evaluation of the functional expression '(second $^{\triangledown}$(a b c))'. In reality, of course, the global L-frame contains L-bindings for *all* the primitive functions, derived functions, and global variables, as well as L-bindings for the identifiers '#t' and '#f'.) As the evaluation begins, the current L-environment is the global L-environment, containing only the global L-frame. Having recognized that the functional expression '(second $^\nabla$(a b c))' is an application, and having evaluated each of its sub-expressions as described above, the interpreter appends the global L-environment to the FD-environment. Since in the present case the FD-environment is null, the result is just the global L-environment. Next, the interpreter builds a new L-frame that contains L-bindings of the parameters listed in the FD-parameter list to the function's inputs. In our example, there is only one parameter listed, namely, 'r'. So this is bound to the input, '(a b c)', in the L-frame '((r (a b c)))', which is then consed onto the new L-environment to yield the two-frame L-environment

```
(((r (a b c)))
 ((second (derived (r) (first (rest r)) ()))
  (first (primitive first))
  (rest (primitive rest))))
```

The interpreter then blackens the FD-body, obtains the functional expression '(first (rest r))', and starts to evaluate it in the context of the newly modified current L-environment.

The functional expression '(first (rest r))' is recognized by the interpreter as an application, so it proceeds to evaluate this expression's two sub-expressions, 'first' and '(rest r)'. The identifier 'first' evaluates to the FD '(primitive first)', which is its replacement in the current L-environment. The interpreter now moves on to the functional expression '(rest r)'.

Since '(rest r)' is an application, the interpreter evaluates both of its sub-expressions. The identifier 'rest' evaluates to its replacement in the current L-environment, that is, the FD '(primitive rest)'. The variable 'r' is also an identifier, and is evaluated in the same way; its replacement in the current L-environment is the list '(a b c)'. The interpreter learns from the FD '(primitive rest)' that it is applying a primitive function, namely, the function **rest**. Accordingly, it sends the input, the list '(a b c)', to the appropriate subroutine, which promptly returns the list '(b c)'. Thus the interpreter has evaluated the functional expression '(rest r)' to the list '(b c)'.

Having done this, the interpreter sends the list '(b c)' to the subroutine that deals with the primitive function **first**, which responds by returning the atom 'b'. It then restores the current L-environment that was in effect just before the evaluation of the function **second** began, namely, the global L-environment containing only the global L-frame. Finally, it prints the result (that is, the atom 'b') on the screen.

In view of the involved nature of the evaluation process, we now consider a number of different examples, explaining in detail what goes on as the evaluation proceeds. Before doing so, however, we provide on page 181 a synopsis of the interpreter's evaluation strategy. This will serve both to focus our attention as we work through our sample evaluations and as a handy reference for future use. (Our description assumes that all the necessary L-bindings exist in the current L-environment. If this supposition should ever prove to be groundless, then an error would be signaled.)

We may now proceed with our promised examples. As you probably realize, one of the most tedious things in tracing the behavior of the interpreter as it evaluates a functional expression is having repeatedly to write out the contents of the global L-frame, which is a long and cumbersome list. At the start of any evaluation it contains L-bindings for all the primitive functions, the identifiers '#t' and '#f', and for any derived functions and global variables that have been defined prior to that time. To save ourselves the chore of writing out such a long list over and over again, we propose to write the upper-case Greek letter 'Φ' (phi, pronounced 'fee') in its place.[4] Notice that 'Φ' does not always abbreviate the same list; whatever list happens to be the global L-frame at the commencement of the evaluation under discussion, that is the list which 'Φ' abbreviates throughout that discussion. Notice also that, at the start of an evaluation, the current L-environment is the global L-environment, denoted by '(Φ)'.

Example 1:

Suppose that L-bindings have been created in the global L-frame for the identifiers 'pair' and 'triple' by typing the following definitions:

```
(define pair                    (define triple
  (λ (a b)                        (λ (a b c)
    (cons a (cons b ▽()))))        (cons a (pair b c))))
```

Let us evaluate the function application '(triple 1 2 3)'. The four sub-expressions of this functional expression evaluate as shown at the top of page 182.

---

[4] The symbol 'Φ' is part of the language we are using to talk about list processing, hence we regard it as being colorless. You will often have cause to write it, however, and on such occasions we suggest you use whatever color you have at hand.

The Scheme Interpreter's Evaluation Strategy

To evaluate a functional expression in the current L-environment, proceed as follows:

1. If the functional expression is a black numeral, then its value is that same numeral, but in red.

2. If the functional expression is an identifier, then its value is the replacement for that identifier in the current L-environment.

3. If the functional expression is a special form, then its value is found by following the rules of evaluation for the special form in question.

4. If the functional expression is neither a black numeral, nor an identifier, nor a special form, then it is an application. Its value is found by evaluating each of its sub-expressions in the current L-environment, and then applying the value of the first (which of necessity will be an FD) to the values of the other sub-expressions.
   To apply the FD of a primitive function, send the input(s) to the appropriate subroutine.
   To apply the FD of a derived function,

   a) store a record of the current L-environment;

   b) replace the current L-environment by the L-environment obtained by appending the global L-environment to the FD-environment, and then consing onto the result an L-frame containing L-bindings of the parameters listed in the FD-parameter list to the function's inputs;

   c) blacken the FD-body and evaluate it; and

   d) replace the current L-environment by the L-environment stored in (a).

triple $\mapsto$ (derived (a b c) (cons a (pair b c)) ())

   1 $\mapsto$ 1

   2 $\mapsto$ 2

   3 $\mapsto$ 3

After storing the current L-environment, the interpreter appends the global L-environment to the (null) FD-environment, and then conses the L-frame '((a 1) (b 2) (c 3))' onto the resulting list, obtaining the new current L-environment

$$(((a\ 1)\ (b\ 2)\ (c\ 3))\ \Phi)$$

Next, it blackens the FD-body, and begins to evaluate the resulting functional expression in the new current L-environment.

The functional expression '(cons *a* (pair *b* *c*))' is an application. The identifier '**cons**' evaluates to the FD '(primitive cons)', the identifier '*a*' evaluates to the atom '1', and the sub-expression '(pair *b* *c*)' evaluates as described in the next paragraph.

The sub-expressions of the application '(pair *b* *c*)' evaluate as follows:

pair $\mapsto$ (derived (a b) (cons a (cons b (quote ()))) ())

   b $\mapsto$ 2

   c $\mapsto$ 3

The FD-environment of the function **pair** is null, its FD-parameter list is the list '(a b)', and in this case the inputs are the atoms '2' and '3'. So, after storing the current L-environment, the new current L-environment

$$(((a\ 2)\ (b\ 3))\ \Phi)$$

is created. Notice that, in the new frame '((a 2) (b 3))', L-bindings are established between the first variable in the FD-parameter list (that is, '*a*') and the first input (that is, the atom '2'), and between the second variable in the FD-parameter list (that is, '*b*') and the second input (that is, the atom '3'). No attention is paid in this process to the fact that the atoms '2' and '3' happen to be the values (in the former current L-environment) of the variables '*b*' and '*c*', respectively. Where these values came from and the identity of the variables which gave rise to them are of no consequence; all that matters is the order of the inputs in relation to the order of appearance of the variables in the FD-parameter list.

Having thus renovated the current L-environment, the interpreter blackens the FD-body, and proceeds to evaluate the functional expression it obtains (that is, '(cons *a* (cons *b* $^\triangledown$()))') in the new L-environment. We see that the three sub-expressions of the above function application evaluate as follows:[5]

$$\text{cons} \;\mapsto\; \text{(primitive cons)}$$
$$a \;\mapsto\; 2$$
$$(\text{cons } b \; ^\triangledown()) \;\mapsto\; (3)$$

The atom '2' and the list '(3)' are then sent to the subroutine for the function **cons**, which returns the list '(2 3)', and the interpreter returns the current L-environment to its state just before the evaluation of '(pair *b* *c*)' began, that is,

$$((\text{(a 1) (b 2) (c 3)) } \Phi)$$

We have now determined that, in this L-environment, the three sub-expressions of the application '(cons *a* (pair *b* *c*))' evaluate as follows:

$$\text{cons} \;\mapsto\; \text{(primitive cons)}$$
$$a \;\mapsto\; 1$$
$$(\text{pair } b \; c) \;\mapsto\; (2\ 3)$$

So the atom '1' and the list '(2 3)' are sent to the subroutine for the function **cons**, which returns the list '(1 2 3)', the current L-environment is returned to its original state (that is, '(Φ)'), and the list '(1 2 3)' is printed on the computer's screen.

Example 2:

In this example, we investigate how the interpreter deals with applications of recursive functions. Let us suppose that the global L-frame contains the following L-binding for the function **lat?**:

---

[5] For the sake of brevity, we have omitted a detailed explanation of the evaluation of the third sub-expression. By now, you should easily be able to supply such an explanation yourself.

```
(lat? (derived
          (a)
          (cond
            [(null? a) #t]
            [else (and
                      (atom? (first a))
                      (lat? (rest a)))])
          ()))
```

We trace the interpreter's behavior as it evaluates the functional expression '(lat? $^\triangledown$(x y))'.

Since the functional expression '(lat? $^\triangledown$(x y))' is an application, the interpreter evaluates both of its sub-expressions as follows:

$$\textbf{lat?} \quad \mapsto \quad \begin{array}{l} \texttt{(derived} \\ \quad \texttt{(a)} \\ \quad \texttt{(cond} \\ \quad\quad \texttt{[(null? a) \#t]} \\ \quad\quad \texttt{[else (and} \\ \quad\quad\quad\quad \texttt{(atom? (first a))} \\ \quad\quad\quad\quad \texttt{(lat? (rest a)))])} \\ \quad \texttt{())} \end{array}$$

$$^\triangledown\textbf{(x y)} \quad \mapsto \quad \texttt{(x y)}$$

From the FD, the interpreter learns that it is dealing with a derived function, and in consequence the current L-environment is stored and replaced by the following:

$$((\texttt{(a (x y))}) \ \Phi \ )$$

The interpreter blackens the FD-body, obtains the functional expression

$$\begin{array}{l} \texttt{(cond} \\ \quad \texttt{[(null? } a \texttt{) \#t]} \\ \quad \texttt{[else (and} \\ \quad\quad\quad \texttt{(atom? (first } a \texttt{))} \\ \quad\quad\quad \texttt{(lat? (rest } a \texttt{)))])} \end{array}$$

and begins to evaluate it in the current L-environment. Having identified the expression as a cond-expression, the interpreter proceeds in accordance with the rules for evaluating this special form. Thus, it begins by evaluating the functional expression '(null? *a*)', that is, the predicate of the first clause in the cond-expression. This is an application, and its sub-expressions evaluate in the current L-environment as follows:

$$\textsf{null?} \quad \mapsto \quad \texttt{(primitive null?)}$$
$$\textbf{\textit{a}} \quad \mapsto \quad \texttt{(x y)}$$

The subroutine for the primitive function **null?** returns the boolean '#f', so, since there are no other predicates, the interpreter moves on to evaluate the alternative in the else-clause, namely, the and-expression

> (and
>   (atom? (first *a*))
>   (lat? (rest *a*)))

As you may easily verify, the functional expression '(atom? (first *a*))' evaluates to the boolean '#t'. So the interpreter must now evaluate the functional expression '(lat? (rest *a*))'.

The first sub-expression of the application '(lat? (rest *a*))' evaluates to the FD of the function **lat?** and the application '(rest *a*)' evaluates to the list '(y)', since the current L-environment is '(((a (x y))) Φ)'. As before, the interpreter learns from the FD that it is dealing with a derived function and in consequence it stores the current L-environment and replaces it by the following:

$$\texttt{(((a (y))) }\Phi\texttt{)}$$

Next, it blackens the FD-body and sets about evaluating the resulting cond-expression in the new L-environment. Once again, the application '(null? *a*)' evaluates to the boolean '#f', so the interpreter must evaluate the functional expression

> (and
>   (atom? (first *a*))
>   (lat? (rest *a*)))

Since the identifier '*a*' is now bound in the current L-environment to the list '(y)' and the functional expression '(atom? (first *a*))' evaluates to the boolean '#t', the interpreter next evaluates the application '(lat? (rest *a*))'. The replacement for the identifier 'lat?' is, of course, still its FD, and the sub-expression '(rest *a*)' evaluates to the null list. Thus the current L-environment is once again stored and replaced, this time by the following:

$$(((a\ (\ )))\ \Phi)$$

The FD-body is again blackened, and the interpreter begins to evaluate the resulting cond-expression. The identifier '*a*' is now bound to the null list, so (finally!) the functional expression '(null? *a*)' evaluates to the boolean '#t'. The corresponding consequent expression is the identifier '#t', which the interpreter evaluates to the boolean '#t'. It then restores the current L-environment to its original state of containing nothing but the global frame, and prints the boolean '#t' on the screen.

Exercise 104.

Evaluate the functional expression

a) '(first *r*)' in the L-environment

$$(((r\ (a\ b\ c))\ (s\ Fred))\ \Phi)$$

b) '(atom? *b*)' in the L-environment

$$(((a\ 1)\ (b\ (1\ 2\ 3))\ (c\ 2))\ \Phi)$$

c) '(eq? *a* *b*)' in the L-environment

$$(((b\ different)\ (c\ same)\ (a\ same))\ \Phi)$$

d) '(cons $^\triangledown$go *s*)' in the L-environment

$$((\ (\ )\ ((s\ (go\ go)))\ \Phi)$$

e) '(a b)' in the L-environment

$$(((a\ (primitive\ atom?))\ (b\ (a\ b\ c)))\ \Phi)$$

All of the function descriptors we have worked with so far in this section have had non-null FD-parameter lists. This is for the very simple reason that all of the functions we have met so far take at least one input. But it raises the question as to whether or not it is possible for an FD-parameter list to be null, and if so, what consequences this might have in the evaluation process. The answer to the first of these concerns is that there do indeed exist functions whose FDs have null FD-parameter lists. They are 'no-input' functions, and they are usually known as **thunks**. Here is an example:

```
(define alphabet
  (λ ( ) ▽(a b c d e f g h i j k l m n o p q r s t u v w x y z)))
```

As you can imagine, thunks are useful for abbreviation purposes—it is a lot easier to type '**(alphabet)**' than it is to type

$$\triangledown(\text{a b c d e f g h i j k l m n o p q r s t u v w x y z})$$

On the other hand, there are many other uses of thunks. They are, for example, of central importance to 'streams', whereby infinite sequences of numbers may be stored in a finite space. (You will become acquainted with streams in Chapter 7.) Moreover, when you finish a scheming session by typing '**(quit)**' (or, with some interpreters, '**(exit)**') you are calling on a thunk.

As our final example in this section, let us examine how a functional expression involving a thunk is evaluated.

Example 3:

Suppose that the above definition for the thunk **alphabet** has been typed into the Scheme interpreter. As a result the global L-frame contains the following replacement for the identifier '**alphabet**':

```
(derived
  ()
  (quote
    (a b c d e f g h i j k l m n o p q r s t u v w x y z))
  ())
```

(Note that, since a thunk has no parameters, the FD-parameter list in this function descriptor is null.) We further suppose that the function **second** has been defined in the usual way. Let us evaluate the functional expression '**(second (alphabet))**'.

The interpreter begins by determining that this functional expression is an application, so it proceeds to evaluate the two sub-expressions. The identifier '**second**' evaluates to the FD '`(derived (r) (first (rest r)) ())`', and the functional expression '**(alphabet)**' evaluates as follows. The interpreter evaluates the only sub-expression to the FD

```
(derived
  ()
  (quote
    (a b c d e f g h i j k l m n o p q r s t u v w x y z))
  ())
```

Then it stores the current L-environment and replaces it by one obtained as follows: The global environment is appended to the (empty) FD-environment, thereby leaving the global environment unchanged. Then an empty L-frame is consed onto the result—this L-frame is empty because the FD-parameter list is empty—producing the new current L-environment, '(( ) Φ)'. Next, the FD-body is blackened and the resulting functional expression evaluated in the new current L-environment. Since the resulting functional expression

(quote (a b c d e f g h i j k l m n o p q r s t u v w x y z))

is a quote-expression, it evaluates to the second sub-expression in red, that is, '(a b c d e f g h i j k l m n o p q r s t u v w x y z)'. The current L-environment is then restored to its original state, and we are faced with the task of evaluating (in the original current L-environment) a functional expression whose sub-expressions evaluate as follows:

$$\begin{array}{rcl}
\textbf{second} & \mapsto & \texttt{(derived (r) (first (rest r)) ())} \\
\textbf{(alphabet)} & \mapsto & \texttt{(a b c d e f g h i j k l m n o p} \\
& & \texttt{q r s t u v w x y z)}
\end{array}$$

Recognizing that it is dealing with a derived function, the interpreter stores the current L-environment, replaces it by

```
(((r (a b c d e f g h i j k l m n o p q r s t u v w x y z)))  Φ)
```

blackens the FD-body, and begins to evaluate the resulting functional expression, '(first (rest **r**))', in the new current L-environment. Since we are now dealing with primitive functions, we restrict ourselves to reporting the results. The functional expression '(rest **r**)' evaluates to the list

```
(b c d e f g h i j k l m n o p q r s t u v w x y z)
```

so the interpreter sends this list to the subroutine that deals with the primitive function **first**, which responds by returning the atom 'b'. Finally, the current L-environment is restored to its initial state of containing nothing but the global L-frame, and the result (that is, the atom 'b') is printed on the screen.

Exercise 105.

Consider the following L-environment:

```
(((a (a b c d e))
  (b begin)
  (c (primitive atom?))
  (d (derived (a b) (cons a (cons b (quote ())))) ()))
  (e (derived
         (a)
         (cons a (cons r s))
         (((r (a b c)) (s (d e f)))))))
  (g (derived
         ()
         (first a)
         (((a (s e n d)) (first (primitive rest)))))))))
 Φ)
```

Evaluate each of these functional expressions in the above L-environment:

a) **a**

b) **(c a)**

c) **(d b c)**

d) **(e a)**

e) **(e b)**

f) **(d (e b) (g))**

As a final remark in this chapter, we reiterate that virtually all the functions we have been considering have null FD-environments. In the above exercise, we have provided a couple of examples of FDs that involve non-null FD-environments, but have given no hint as to how such FDs may be generated. All will be revealed in the next chapter!

− o O o −

6 Automation

In Chapter 5 we have seen how the interpreter processes function applications by evaluating *all* the sub-expressions of the application and then applying the value of the first sub-expression (which must evaluate to a function descriptor) to the values of the remaining sub-expressions. In this chapter we explore ways in which the interpreter's strategy may be exploited.

6.1 Machines That Use Machines

The predicate function **lat?**, defined on page 172 by

```
(define lat?
  (λ (r)
    (cond
      [(null? r) #t]
      [else (and
              (atom? (first r))
              (lat? (rest r)))])))
```

is just one of a number of 'list-checking' functions we first met in Chapter 2. Other functions of this type include **lili?** (see Problem 1 of Problem Set 3) which checks whether every data expression in a list is itself a list, and the function **latel?** (see Problem 2 of Problem Set 3) which checks whether every data expression in a list is an atomic element. These functions may be defined as follows:

191

```
(define lili?                           (define latel?
  (λ (r)                                   (λ (r)
    (cond                                    (cond
      [(null? r) #t]                           [(null? r) #t]
      [else (and                               [else (and
              (list? (first r))                        (atomic? (first r))
              (lili? (rest r)))])))                    (latel? (rest r)))])))
```

These three functions have many features in common, so many in fact that they differ only in the predicate function that is used to inspect the first data expression in the input. In the case of the function **lat?**, the predicate function used is the primitive function **atom?**, while the functions **lili?** and **latel?** use the derived predicate functions **list?** and **atomic?**, respectively (see Exercise 45(c) and Problem 2(a) of Problem Set 3).

It is not hard to imagine circumstances in which we might write a program that calls upon all three of the above functions. Before we could use it, however, we would be faced with the tedious task of typing the three almost-identical definitions into the computer. Think how much easier it would be if we could say to the computer, 'This is what a definition for a general list-checking function looks like. Whenever the need arises, I'll tell you exactly which predicate function to use.' We now investigate this approach, which, as you will see, is surprisingly powerful.

Our aim is to give the computer a general definition for list-checking functions—something like this:

```
(define list–checker?
  (λ (r)
    (cond
      [(null? r) #t]
      [else (and
              (⋆ (first r))
              (list–checker? (rest r)))])))
```

When using the function **list–checker?** we would like the '⋆' in the definition to be replaced by the name of the appropriate predicate function. For example, if we require the function **list–checker?** to identify a lat, then we want '⋆' to be replaced by the identifier '**atom?**'. Unfortunately, we have no mechanism for replacing symbols like '⋆' by function names. However, we *do* have a mechanism for replacing parameters by data expressions, and this suggests a possible way out of our difficulty. We could replace '⋆' by a variable and then take steps to ensure that the variable in question is bound to the desired function descriptor. For example, the function defined by

```
(define list–checker?
  (λ (r)
    (cond
      [(null? r) #t]
      [else (and
             (f (first r))
             (list–checker? (rest r)))])))
```

will behave like the function **lat?** provided that the replacement for 'f' is given by 'f : (primitive atom?)'. On the other hand, if[1]

$$f : \text{(derived (r) (or (atom? r) (null? r)) ())}$$

then the function **list–checker?** will behave just like the function **latel?**. To make it possible for us to bind the variable 'f' to any data expression of our choice we include it in the lambda-parameter list of the function **list–checker?** as follows:

```
(define list–checker?
  (λ (f r)
    (cond
      [(null? r) #t]
      [else (and
             (f (first r))
             (list–checker? f (rest r)))])))
```

Note that we have not only added the variable 'f' to the list of parameters, but, because the function now expects two inputs (of which the first must be an FD and the second must be a list), we have also had to insert the variable 'f' into the natural recursion in the last line of the definition.

To verify that this function behaves as required, at the top of the next page we evaluate the functional expression '(list–checker? atom? ∇(a b c))'. Since (lat? ∇(a b c)) ↦ #t, the output obtained is exactly as expected. Note that, in this trace table, we have used the function name **atom?** throughout rather than replacing it by the data expression to which it is bound, that is, its FD, '(primitive atom?)'. This is almost universal practice, and it

---

[1] Notice that in this case the data expression to which 'f' is bound is an FD of the derived function **atomic?**. (See the discussion on pages 171–174.)

```
(list-checker? atom? ▽(a b c))
(list-checker? atom? (a b c))
(and
   (atom? a)
   (list-checker? atom? (b c)))
(list-checker? atom? (b c))
(and
   (atom? b)
   (list-checker? atom? (c)))
(list-checker? atom? (c))
(and
   (atom? c)
   (list-checker? atom? ( )))
(list-checker? atom? ( ))
#t
```

perhaps explains why it is usual to make statements such as 'The inputs to the function **list-checker?** must be a function and a list.' We propose to adopt these common notational and linguistic practices and suggest that you do the same.[2] You should bear in mind, however, that, technically speaking, the first input to the function **list-checker?** is a function *descriptor* rather than an actual function.

Having a general function like **list-checker?** available, we could in retrospect define the more specific functions **lat?**, **lili?**, and **latel?** in terms of it:

```
(define lat?                        (define lili?
   (λ (r)                              (λ (r)
      (list-checker? atom? r)))           (list-checker? list? r)))
```

```
(define latel?
   (λ (r)
      (list-checker? atomic? r)))
```

Such redefinitions will of course influence the manner in which functional expressions involving these functions are evaluated, but the results of such evaluations will be unaffected. The following trace table, for example, shows

---

[2]The title of this section owes its origins to this kind of 'loose' use of language.

how '(latel? $^\triangledown$(a (b) c))' would be evaluated if latel? were defined in terms of
list–checker? as above:

```
(latel? ▽(a (b) c))
(latel? (a (b) c)))
(list–checker? atomic? (a (b) c))
(and
   (atomic? a)
   (list–checker? atomic? ((b) c)))
(list–checker? atomic? ((b) c))
(and
   (atomic? (b))
   (list–checker? atomic? (c)))
          #f
```

Exercise 106.

a) Using the functions list–checker? and number?, write a definition for the predicate function vector? of a list that returns the
boolean '#t' if and only if the list is a vector (see page 137).

b) Let the predicate function null–list? of a data expression be
defined as follows:

$$\text{(define null–list?}$$
$$(\lambda\,(a)$$
$$(\text{equal? } a \,^\triangledown(\,))))$$

Write a definition, using the functions list–checker? and null–
list?, for the predicate function W2? of a list that returns the
boolean '#t' if and only if the list is a W2-representation of
a whole number (see page 99).

c) Why could we not use the primitive function null? in place of
null–list? in part (b)?

Exercise 107.

(All the definitions you write in this exercise should involve the
function list–checker?. Any other functions you might need are
either primitive or were introduced in Problem Set 5.)

a) Using the predicate function even?, write a definition for
the predicate function all–even? of a vector that returns the

boolean '#t' if and only if every number in the vector is an even number.

b) Write a definition for the predicate function **all–zero?** of a vector that returns the boolean '#t' if and only if every number in the vector is zero.

c) Write a definition for the predicate function **all–divide–24?** of a vector that returns the boolean '#t' if and only if every number in the vector is a divisor of 24.

Let us reflect upon what we have achieved so far in this chapter. We began with the simple function **lat?** and replaced the occurrence of a function name by a parameter. (This process is known as **function abstraction, procedural abstraction**, or simply **abstraction**.) By so doing, as the foregoing examples and exercises show, we have unexpectedly generated solutions to a whole class of problems, some of which may previously have seemed unrelated. With this in mind, let us begin again with another simple function and apply the same technique.

On page 82 we defined the predicate function **member?** so that, when given an atom '*a*' and a lat '*r*', it returns the boolean '#t' if and only if one of the atoms in the lat '*r*' is the atom '*a*'. Here is a definition for this function that uses an or-expression (see Exercise 102 on page 174):

```
(define member?
  (λ (a r)
    (cond
      [(null? r) #f]
      [else (or (eq? (first r) a)
                (member? a (rest r)))])))
```

With hindsight, we may decide that the function **member?** is unnecessarily restrictive. If the predicate function **equal?** had been used instead of **eq?**, for example, then we could have used it to test for membership even when the first parameter is not bound to an atom. That is, if the function **member?** had been defined as follows:

```
(define member?
  (λ (a r)
    (cond
      [(null? r) #f]
      [else (or (equal? (first r) a)
                (member? a (rest r)))])))
```

then, when given any data expression a and any list r, it would return the boolean '#t' if and only if one of the data expressions in the list r is the data expression a.

There is, however, a distinct *dis*advantage in defining the function **member?** in terms of **equal?** instead of **eq?**, namely that **equal?** is a complex recursive function and in consequence is relatively inefficient. Therefore, the performance of the function **member?** (defined in this way) would not be optimal if we were certain that the first input was an atom and the second input was a lat. We could, of course, define *two* functions, an efficient version for use when checking for occurrences of atoms in lats, and a less efficient one that deals with the more general case. A far better solution, though, is to *abstract* the occurrence of the predicate function that tests for equality. We can then delay specifying which test to use until we know the nature of the inputs. Here is a definition for the function **member?** from which the occurrence of the test for equality has been abstracted:

```
(define member?
  (λ (f a r)
    (cond
      [(null? r) #f]
      [else (or (f (first r) a)
                (member? f a (rest r)))])))
```

(Note once again that the variable 'f' has been inserted into both the list of parameters and the natural recursion.) Let us verify that this function behaves as we expect. Suppose we wish to check whether the atom 'rose' occurs in the lat '(thorn rose thorn)'. Having observed that the inputs are an atom and a lat, we evaluate the functional expression

```
(member? eq? ▽rose ▽(thorn rose thorn))
```

as follows:

```
(member? eq? ▽rose ▽(thorn rose thorn))
(member? eq? rose (thorn rose thorn))
(or (eq? thorn rose)
    (member? eq? rose (rose thorn)))
(member? eq? rose (rose thorn))
(or (eq? rose rose)
    (member? eq? rose (thorn)))
#t
```

Exercise 108.

    Compile a trace table showing the evaluation of the functional expression '(member? equal? $^\triangledown$(a) $^\triangledown$(a (a) ((a))))'. (You may wish to review your solution to Problem 7 of Problem Set 3 on page 86, where you wrote a definition for the function **equal?**.)

    Of course, now that we have produced the above generalized **member?** function, there is no reason why we should restrict ourselves to the FDs of **eq?** and **equal?** when it comes to the replacements of the first parameter.

Exercise 109.

    Evaluate each of these functional expressions:

    a) (member? = 3 $^\triangledown$(1 2 3 4 5))

    b) (member? eqlat? $^\triangledown$(a b) $^\triangledown$((c) (b a) (d e f)))

    c) (member? less? 0 $^\triangledown$(1 2 3 4 5))

    d) (member? less? 2 $^\triangledown$(1 2 3 4 5))

    e) (member? less? 6 $^\triangledown$(1 2 3 4 5))

Exercise 110.

    Let the predicate functions **K** and **L** be defined as follows:

```
(define K                      (define L
   (λ (a r)                       (λ (a r)
      (member? less? a r)))           (not (K a r)))))
```

Describe the behavior of each of these functions in words.

Exercise 111.

    Let the predicate function **does–not–divide?** of the whole numbers m and n be defined as follows:

```
(define does-not-divide?
   (λ (m n)
      (not (divides? m n)))))
```

    Use the functions **member?** and **does–not–divide?** to write a definition for the predicate function **all–divisors?** of a whole number n and a vector ***vec*** that returns the boolean '#t' if and only if every member of ***vec*** is a divisor of n.

PROBLEM SET 10

Problems 1–3 use the function accumulate, *which is defined as follows:*

```
(define accumulate
  (λ (op init r)
    (cond
      [(null? r) init]
      [else (op (first r)
                (accumulate op init (rest r)))])))
```

Note that the first input to accumulate *must be the FD of a 2-input function.*

1. Let the function S be defined as follows:

```
(define S
  (λ (v)
    (accumulate + 0 v)))
```

   a) Evaluate each of these functional expressions:

   (i) (S ▽(1 2 3 4 5))   (ii) (S ▽(2 4 6 8))

   b) Describe in words the behavior of the function S when its input is a
   vector. What is the usual name for the function S?

2. a) Evaluate each of these functional expressions:

   (i) (accumulate * 1 ▽(1 2 3 4 5))   (ii) (accumulate * 1 ▽(2 4 6 8))

   b) Use the function accumulate to define the function product of a vector
   that returns the product of the numbers in the vector.

3. a) Evaluate each of these functional expressions:

   (i) (accumulate cons ▽( ) ▽(a b c))

   (ii) (accumulate cons ▽(d) ▽(a b c))

   (iii) (accumulate cons ▽(a b c) ▽(d e f))

   b) Use the function accumulate to define the functions

   (i) append of lists *r* and *s* that appends *s* to *r* (see Problem 8(e) of
   Problem Set 4 on page 93).

   (ii) cons–to–end of a data expression *a* and a list *r* that inserts *a* as
   the last data expression in *r* (see Problem 8(a) of Problem Set 4
   on page 92).

Problems 4–7 use the function **modify**, *which is defined as follows:*

```
(define modify
  (λ (f old new r)
    (cond
      [(null? r) ▽( )]
      [(equal? (first r) old) (f old new (rest r))]
      [else (cons (first r) (modify f old new (rest r)))])))
```

4. Let the function **Q** be defined as follows:

```
(define Q                        (define R
  (λ (old new r)                   (λ (old new s)
    (modify R old new r)))           (cons old (cons new s))))
```

a) Evaluate each of these functional expressions:

  (i) **R**   (ii) **(Q ▽a ▽z ▽(a b a c))**

  (iii) **(Q ▽b ▽z ▽(a b a c))**   (iv) **(Q ▽c ▽z ▽(a b a c))**

b) What is the usual name for the function **Q**?
   [Hint: It is one we have met earlier in this book.]

5. Use the function **modify** to define the functions:

a) **insertl** of data expressions *old* and *new* and a list *r* that returns the list *r* with the data expression *new* inserted to the left of the first occurrence of the data expression *old* (see Problem 3 of Problem Set 4 on page 91 for an 'atomic' version of this function).

b) **subst** of data expressions *old* and *new* and a list *r* that replaces the first occurrence in *r* of the data expression *old* by the data expression *new* (see Problem 5 of Problem Set 4 on page 91 for an 'atomic' version of this function).

c) **rember** of a data expression *a* and a list *r* that removes the first occurrence of the data expression *a* from the list *r* (see page 87 for an 'atomic' version of this function).

6. Let the function **W** be defined as follows:

```
(define W                        (define X
  (λ (old r)                       (λ (old new s)
    (modify X old #f r)))            (W old s)))
```

a) Evaluate each of these functional expressions:

(i) X   (ii) (W $^\triangledown$a $^\triangledown$(c a b a c))

(iii) (W $^\triangledown$b $^\triangledown$(c a b a c))   (iv) (W $^\triangledown$c $^\triangledown$(c a b a c))

b) How does the function W differ in behavior from the function **rember**? Suggest a more descriptive name for the function W.

7. Using the technique developed in the previous problem, we may define the function **insertl–all** of data expressions *old* and *new* and a list *r* that returns the list *r* with the data expression *new* inserted to the left of *every* occurrence of the data expression *old*, as follows:

> (define insertl–all
>   (λ (*old new r*)
>   (modify Z *old new r*)))

> (define Z
>   (λ (*old new s*)
>   (cons *new* (cons *old* (insertl–all *old new s*)))))

Using the function **modify**, write similar definitions for the functions:

a) **insertr–all** of data expressions *old* and *new* and a list *r* that returns the list *r* with the data expression *new* inserted to the *right* of every occurrence of the data expression *old*.

b) **subst–all** of data expressions *old* and *new* and a list *r* that returns the list *r* with every occurrence of the data expression *old* replaced by the data expression *new* (see Problem 6 of Problem Set 4 on page 92 for an 'atomic' version of this function).

$- \circ\, \mathrm{O} \circ -$

6.2 Machines That Build Machines

The time has come for us to make good on the promise we made at the end of the previous chapter to explain how to define functions that return function descriptors with non-null FD-environments. In order to motivate our presentation of the way in which Scheme deals with the matter, we provide a short introduction in which we explain what would be required if we were to do all the work by hand. Then, when we introduce the automated method that is a built-in feature of Scheme, you will have a greater appreciation for what is involved.

The simplest method of returning an FD is, of course, to output it explicitly, as for example in the following definition for the one-input function **first–maker** of an data expression which returns the FD for the primitive function **first**:

$$\text{(define first–maker}$$
$$(\lambda\ (a)\ ^\triangledown\text{(primitive first)))}$$

We note that (**first–maker** $^\triangledown$**Fred**) $\mapsto$ (primitive first). This definition may be simplified further, however, if we recall that the identifier '**first**' is bound in the global L-environment to its FD, so we may replace the quote-expression by the identifier '**first**'. Furthermore, the function has no need of its input, so we could define it as a thunk, as follows:

$$\text{(define first–maker}$$
$$(\lambda\ (\ )\ \text{first))}$$

When the function **first–maker** is defined in this way, then it follows that (**first–maker**) $\mapsto$ (primitive first). In view of the fact that the functional expression '(**first–maker**)' evaluates to a function descriptor, we may use it as the first sub-expression of a function application. For example, the functional expression '((**first–maker**) $^\triangledown$(a b c d e))' evaluates as follows:[3]

$$\text{((first–maker)}\ ^\triangledown\text{(a b c d e))}$$
$$\text{(first (a b c d e))}$$
$$\text{a}$$

Of course, it would have been much easier if we had just used the function **first** instead of the function **first–maker**. In fact, it appears that all we have

---

[3]Note, once again, that in this trace table we write the function name '**first**' in place of its function descriptor.

managed to do is create extra work for ourselves! We therefore aim a little
higher and attempt to write a definition, using the method of Problem 1 of
Problem Set 1, for a function that actually *constructs* an FD. We define the
function **make–cons–fcn** which inputs a data expression a and returns the FD
of a function that inputs a list s and returns the cons of a onto s. That is,
it operates as follows:

(make–cons–fcn ▽Fred) ↦ (derived (s) (cons (quote Fred) s) ())

(make–cons–fcn ▽(a b)) ↦ (derived (s) (cons (quote (a b)) s) ())

Here is one possible definition for the function **make–cons–fcn**:

```
(define make–cons–fcn
  (λ (a)
    (cons
      ▽derived
      (cons
        ▽(s)
        (cons
          (cons
            ▽cons
            (cons
              (cons
                ▽quote
                (cons
                  a
                  ▽()))
              ▽(s)))
          ▽(()))))))
```

Assuming that FDs are data expressions of the type we described in Chapter 5, the FD returned by the function **make–cons–fcn** may be applied to an
input. Thus, the functional expression '((make–cons–fcn ▽Fred) ▽(a b c))', for
example, may be evaluated as follows:

((make–cons–fcn ▽Fred) ▽(a b c))

((make–cons–fcn ▽Fred) (a b c))

((derived (s) (cons (quote Fred) s) ()) (a b c))

(cons ▽Fred (a b c))

(cons Fred (a b c))

(Fred a b c)

(Note that, since the FD returned by the function **make–cons–fcn** is not necessarily bound to an identifier in the current L-environment—it is an 'anonymous' FD—we must refer explicitly to the FD in the trace table.)

Exercise 112.

Using the above definition for the function **make–cons–fcn**, evaluate the following functional expressions in the global L-environment:

a) (make–cons–fcn $^\nabla$(a b c d e))

b) ((make–cons–fcn $^\nabla$(a b c d e)) $^\nabla$(Fred Jane Mary))

The definition for the function **make–cons–fcn** is, to put it mildly, rather complicated! Imagine the effort that would be required to output the FD of a more involved function. As a first step toward simplifying its definition (and those of other functions that return FDs) we note that the functional expressions '(cons $^\nabla$Fred *s*)' and '(cons *a* *s*)' evaluate to the same data expression provided that the latter is evaluated in an L-environment in which the variable '*a*' is bound to the atom 'Fred'. We can use this fact to help us write an alternative definition for the function **make–cons–fcn**.

Recall from Section 5.4 that the frames in the FD-environment (the fourth data expression of an FD) form part of the new current L-environment in which the (blackened) FD-body is evaluated. Therefore, instead of placing the input to the function **make–cons–fcn** in a quote-expression embedded in the FD, we could construct the FD-body in such a way that it includes a variable which, in turn, is bound in the FD-environment. Suppose, for example, that the input to the function **make–cons–fcn** is the atom 'Fred'. Then, as an alternative to constructing the FD

```
(derived (s) (cons (quote Fred) s) ())
```

we may construct the FD '(derived (s) (cons a s) (((a Fred))))'. (In this expression, we could, of course, use any identifier in place of '*a*', with the exception of '*s*' and 'cons'.)

Exercise 113.

The foregoing discussion leads to the alternative definition for the function **make–cons–fcn** given at the top of the next page. (See Problem 1(c) of Problem Set 6 on page 117 for the function **pair**.) Using this definition, evaluate the functional expression

((make–cons–fcn $^\nabla$Jim) $^\nabla$( ))

in the global L-environment.

```
(define make–cons–fcn
  (λ (a)
    (cons
      ▽derived
      (cons
        ▽(s)
        (cons
          ▽(cons x s)
          (cons
            (cons
              (cons
                (pair ▽x a)
                ▽( ))
              ▽( ))
            ▽( )))))))
```

Functions such as **make–cons–fcn**, as defined in the exercise above, are undeniably complex and difficult to work with. Fortunately, there is a much less cumbersome way of achieving our goal, based on the fact that lambda-expressions evaluate to function descriptors.

You may recall from our work in Chapter 5 that each lambda-expression evaluates to an FD as follows: The first data expression in the FD is the atom 'derived'; this is followed by the lambda-parameter list and the lambda-body, both in red. The fourth and last data expression, the FD-environment, is the L-environment that was current at the moment the lambda-expression was evaluated, with the global L-frame discarded. It is usually convenient to give names to derived functions, but there is no reason why we cannot apply functions anonymously. For example, when evaluated in the global L-environment, the lambda-expression '(λ (a) (∗ 2 a))' evaluates to the FD

```
(derived (a) (* 2 a) ())
```

It may therefore be applied to an input as follows:

```
((λ (a) (∗ 2 a)) 14)
((derived (a) (* 2 a) ()) 14)
(∗ 2 14)
28
```

Exercise 114.

Evaluate each of these functional expressions in the global L-environment:

a) $((\lambda\ (a\ b)\ (\text{cons}\ a\ b))\ {}^{\triangledown}(\text{a b c})\ {}^{\triangledown}(\text{d e f}))$

b) $((\lambda\ (x)$

    (cond

      [(null? x) #t]

      [else (null? (rest x))]]))

  ${}^{\triangledown}$(a b c))

c) $((\lambda\ (a\ b)$

    (cond

      [(atom? a) b]

      [(atom? b) a]

      [else (cons a b)]]))

  ${}^{\triangledown}$(Jan Pete)

  ${}^{\triangledown}$Mary)

d) $((\lambda\ (vec)$

    (cond

      [(null? vec) 0]

      [(null? (rest vec)) 1]

      [else 2]))

  ${}^{\triangledown}$(2))

e) $((\lambda\ (a\ b\ c)$

    (cond

      [(null? a) ${}^{\triangledown}$()]

      [(lat? a) b]

      [else c]))

  ${}^{\triangledown}$(Fred Jane (Paul Mary (Ron)) Mike Ed) ${}^{\triangledown}$Fred ${}^{\triangledown}$Jane)

f) $((\lambda\ (m\ n)\ (=\ (+\ m\ 5)\ n))\ 49\ 44)$

g) $((\lambda\ (x\ y)\ (-\ (*\ x\ x)\ (*\ y\ y)))\ 5\ 3)$

h) $((\lambda\ (a\ b\ c)\ ((\lambda\ (x)\ (*\ x\ x))\ b))\ 5\ 10\ 15)$

All the lambda-expressions we have evaluated to this point have been evaluated in the global L-environment and, in consequence, the resulting FDs have empty FD-environments. The time has come to explore the evaluation of lambda-expressions in L-environments that contain other L-frames in addition to the global L-frame. Consider, for example, the value of '$(\lambda\ (b)\ (+\ a\ b))$' in the L-environment '$(((\text{a 3})\ (\text{c 5}))\ \Phi)$'. Discarding the global L-frame from this L-environment leaves the L-environment '$(((\text{a 5})\ (\text{c 3})))$', so '$(\lambda\ (b)\ (+\ a\ b))$' evaluates to

    (derived (b) (+ a b) (((a 5) (c 3))))

You may recall that when an FD is applied to its inputs, the interpreter appends the FD-environment to the global L-environment (thus reinstating the global L-frame), and onto the result a new L-frame is consed that contains binding(s) of the input(s) to the parameter(s). So, for example, in the environment '$(((a\ 5)\ (c\ 3))\ \Phi)$', the functional expression '$((\lambda\ (b)\ (+\ a\ b))\ 7)$' evaluates as follows:

> $((\lambda\ (b)\ (+\ a\ b))\ 7)$
> ((derived (b) (+ a b) (((a 5) (c 3)))) 7)
> $(+\ 5\ 7)$
> 12

When evaluated in the L-environment '$(((a\ 25))\ \Phi)$', however, the same functional expression evaluates to the atom '37'. (Check this.)

Exercise 115.

   a) In the L-environment '$(((r\ one)\ (s\ two))\ \Phi)$', evaluate the functional expressions

   (i) $(\lambda\ (a)\ (eq?\ a\ r))$

   (ii) $((\lambda\ (a)\ (eq?\ a\ r))\ {}^\triangledown one)$

   (iii) $((\lambda\ (a)\ (eq?\ a\ r))\ {}^\triangledown two)$

   b) In the L-environment '$(((a\ 3)\ (b\ 5))\ ((c\ 0))\ \Phi)$', evaluate the functional expressions

   (i) $((\lambda\ (x)\ (+\ x\ a))\ 12)$

   (ii) $((\lambda\ (x\ y)\ (+\ x\ (*\ y\ c)))\ 9\ 2)$

When the function **make–cons–fcn** is defined as in Exercise 113 on page 204, the functional expression '(**make–cons–fcn** ${}^\triangledown$**Jim**)' evaluates to the FD

> (derived (s) (cons x s) (((x Jim))))

But this is precisely the FD that is returned when the lambda-expression '$(\lambda\ (s)\ (cons\ x\ s))$' is evaluated in the L-environment '$(((x\ Jim))\ \Phi)$', and this, in turn, is the L-environment that is created to serve in the evaluation of the lambda-body of the function **make–cons–fcn** when the input to that function is the atom 'Jim'. We may therefore redefine the function **make–cons–fcn** as follows:

> (define make–cons–fcn
> $(\lambda\ (x)$
> $(\lambda\ (s)$
> $(cons\ x\ s))))$

Computer scientists tend to speak of functions that output *functions*, that is, **function-valued functions**. Technically speaking, such functions actually output *the FDs of* functions, but the usual 'loose' form of language is very convenient, and we adopt it too. Furthermore, we propose whenever possible to write mixed lambda-expressions in place of the FDs of derived functions. Consider, for example, the FD

$$\texttt{(derived (s) (cons x s) (((x Fred))))}$$

When this is applied to an input, the interpreter evaluates the functional expression '(cons *x* *s*)' in an L-environment in which '*x*' is bound to the atom 'Fred', 'cons' is bound to its FD, and '*s*' is bound to the input. It therefore seems reasonable to replace the FD by the mixed expression

$$(\lambda\ (s)\ ((\text{primitive cons}) \text{Fred}\ s))$$

In fact, we can take this one stage further by writing the identifier 'cons' in place of its FD, thereby obtaining the mixed expression

$$(\lambda\ (s)\ (\text{cons Fred}\ s))$$

From this mixed expression it is easy to see that we are dealing with a one-input function of a list that conses the atom 'Fred' onto the input; this information is not so immediately clear from the FD itself.

Using the above simplified definition for the function **make–cons–fcn**, the functional expression

$$(\textsf{make–cons–fcn}\ {}^{\triangledown}\text{(a b c d e)})$$

evaluates to the function $(\lambda\ (s)\ (\textsf{cons}\ \text{(a b c d e)}\ s))$ in the global L-environment, and so the functional expression

$$((\textsf{make–cons–fcn}\ {}^{\triangledown}\text{(a b c d e)})\ {}^{\triangledown}\text{(Fred Jane)})$$

evaluates in the global L-environment as follows:

```
((make–cons–fcn (a b c d e)) (Fred Jane))
((λ (s) (cons (a b c d e) s)) (Fred Jane))
(cons (a b c d e) (Fred Jane))
((a b c d e) Fred Jane)
```

Exercise 116.

Evaluate each of the following functional expressions in the global L-environment, writing mixed lambda-expressions in place of FDs:

a) (make–cons–fcn $^\triangledown$( ))   b) ((make–cons–fcn $^\triangledown$( )) $^\triangledown$(Fred))

As a further example of a function that returns a function, consider the function **A**, whose definition is as follows:

$$\text{(define A}$$
$$(\lambda \ (r)$$
$$(\lambda \ ( )$$
$$(r \ ^\triangledown(\text{a b c})))))$$

We begin by ascertaining what the suitable inputs are to this function. We note that it accepts exactly one input represented by the variable 'r'. The function **A** then returns a function which applies r to the list '(a b c)'. Thus the replacement for 'r' must be a one-input function that—at the very least—accepts the list '(a b c)' as an input. Since the function **first** is a one-input function for which the list '(a b c)' is an acceptable input, let us experiment by using it as the input to the function **A**. The functional expression '(A first)' evaluates in the global L-environment to the function $(\lambda \ ( ) \ (\text{first} \ ^\triangledown(\text{a b c})))$, which is a nameless thunk that always returns the atom 'a', as the following trace table illustrates:

$$((\text{A first}))$$
$$((\lambda \ ( ) \ (\text{first} \ ^\triangledown(\text{a b c}))))$$
$$(\text{first} \ ^\triangledown(\text{a b c}))$$
$$(\text{first} \ (\text{a b c}) \ )$$
$$\text{a}$$

Exercise 117.

Let **A** be the function defined above. Evaluate each of the following functional expressions in the global L-environment:

a) **(A rest)**   b) **((A rest))**

c) **(A atom?)**   d) **((A atom?))**

e) **(A second)**   f) **((A second))**

6.3 On the Assembly Line

Let us turn our attention once again to the function **make–cons–fcn** whose definition was given on page 207 as follows:

(define make–cons–fcn
   (λ (x)
      (λ (s)
         (cons x s))))

In what sense does the behavior of this function resemble that of the function **cons**? One difference is immediately apparent: the function **cons** is a two-input function, whereas the function **make–cons–fcn** takes one input only. On the other hand, either function may be used, for example, to cons the atom 'a' onto the list '(b c)' to produce the list '(a b c)'. In the case of the function **cons** this is achieved by passing the atom 'a' and the list '(b c)' as inputs to the function:

(cons a (b c)) $\mapsto$ (a b c)

The same is true in the case of the function **make–cons–fcn**, except that in this instance the inputs must be passed 'one at a time':

((make–cons–fcn a) (b c)) $\mapsto$ (a b c)

The function **make–cons–fcn** is an example of a **curried function**,[4] that is, a function that corresponds to a function of two or more inputs but which takes the inputs 'one at a time'. We explore this new idea by developing the curried version of another function of two inputs. Specifically, we shall write a curried version of the function **pair** of data expressions *a* and *b* that returns a list containing the data expressions *a* and *b*, in that order, and nothing more. Here is a definition for the function **pair**:

(define pair
   (λ (a b)
      (cons a (cons b $\triangledown$()))))

---

[4]So named to honor the American mathematical logician Haskell Brooks Curry (1900–1982). In fact, functions of this kind were first used by the mathematician Moses Schönfinkel (died 1942), but Curry was the one who recognized the significance of Schönfinkel's work and systematized it.

Our task is to define a one-input function that will input the data expression
a and return a one-input function which, when given the data expression **b** as
its input, returns the list containing just the data expressions **a** and **b**, in that
order. We shall call this function '**pair–curry**'. Here is a possible definition:

$$\text{(define pair–curry}$$
$$(\lambda\ (a)$$
$$(\lambda\ (b)$$
$$\text{(cons}\ a\ \text{(cons}\ b\ ^{\triangledown}(\,)))))) $$

Let us check that this function behaves as expected by evaluating the mixed
expression '**((pair–curry** Fred**)** Mary**)**'.

$$\text{((pair–curry Fred) Mary)}$$
$$((\lambda\ (b)\ \text{(cons Fred (cons}\ b\ ^{\triangledown}(\,))))\ \text{Mary})$$
$$\text{(cons Fred (cons Mary (\,)))}$$
$$\text{(cons Fred (Mary))}$$
$$\text{(Fred Mary)}$$

We observe that this is in agreement with our expectations, since

$$\text{(pair}\ ^{\triangledown}\textbf{Fred}\ ^{\triangledown}\textbf{Mary)}\ \mapsto\ \text{(Fred Mary)}$$

Exercise 118. Write a curried version of the primitive function **eq?**.

Exercise 119.
>   Let the function **B** be defined as follows:
>
> $$\text{(define B}$$
> $$(\lambda\ (x\ y)$$
> $$\text{(cons (first}\ x)\ \text{(second}\ y)))) $$
>
>   Write a curried version of the function **B**.

Exercise 120.
>   Let the curried function **D–curry** of a data expression be defined
>   as follows:
>
> $$\text{(define D–curry}$$
> $$(\lambda\ (a)$$
> $$\text{(cond}$$
> $$[\text{(atom?}\ a)\ \text{first}]$$
> $$[\text{else}\ (\lambda\ (b)\ \text{(cons}\ b\ ^{\triangledown}(\,)))]))) $$

a) Evaluate each of these functional expressions:

   (i) **((D–curry** ▽**Fred)** ▽**(a b c))**

   (ii) **((D–curry** ▽**(Fred Mary))** ▽**(a b c))**

b) Let the function **D** be a *non*-curried version of the function
   D–curry. Then, for example, since

$$((\mathbf{D\text{–}curry}\ (a\ b\ c)\,)\,\mathrm{Fred}\,) \mapsto (\mathrm{Fred})$$

it follows that we want $(\mathbf{D}\ (a\ b\ c)\ \mathrm{Fred}\,) \mapsto (\mathrm{Fred})$. Write
a definition for the function **D**.

Exercise 121.

Let the curried function **E–curry** of a list be defined as follows:

```
(define E–curry
  (λ (r)
    (cond
      [(null? r) (λ (s) (cons s r))]
      [else (λ (s) (cons (first r) s))])))
```

a) Evaluate each of these functional expressions:

   (i) **((E–curry** ▽**( ))** ▽**(Fred Jane Mary))**

   (ii) **((E–curry** ▽**(a b c))** ▽**(Fred Jane Mary))**

b) Write a non-curried version **E** of the function **E–curry**.

So far we have only curried functions of two inputs. It is also possible
to curry functions of three or more inputs. To illustrate, we write a curried
version of the function **triple** of data expressions *a*, *b*, and *c*, defined as follows:

```
(define triple
  (λ (a b c)
    (cons a (cons b (cons c ▽( ))))))
```

Modeling our work on the relationship between the definitions for **pair** and
pair–curry on page 211, we propose the following:

```
(define triple–curry
  (λ (a)
    (λ (b)
      (λ (c)
        (cons a (cons b (cons c ▽( ))))))))
```

To verify that this function really works as expected, we note that

$$\text{(triple } burning\ red\ hot) \mapsto (burning\ red\ hot)$$

and

(((triple–curry burning) red) hot)
(((λ (b) (λ (c) (cons burning (cons b (cons c $^{\triangledown}$())))))) red) hot)
((λ (c) (cons burning (cons red (cons c $^{\triangledown}$())))) hot)
(cons burning (cons red (cons hot ( ))))
(burning red hot)

Exercise 122.

Let the function **F** be defined as shown on the right. Write a curried version of this function.

(define F
 (λ (x y z)
  (* x (+ y z)))))

Exercise 123.

Let the function **H–curry** be defined as shown on the right. Evaluate each of these functional expressions:

a) **(H–curry 1)**

b) **((H–curry 1) 2)**

c) **(((H–curry 1) 2) 3)**

(define H–curry
 (λ (p)
  (λ (q)
   (λ (r)
    (+ (* p q) (* p r)))))))

PROBLEM SET 11

1. Evaluate each of these functional expressions:

a) ((λ (x) (add1 (fib x))) 6)

b) ((λ (a) ((λ (x) (add1 x)) a)) 8675)

c) ((λ (a b c d) (* d (+ c a))) 1 2 3 4)

d) ((λ (r s) (= (* r 3) (* s 2))) 2 3)

2. Evaluate each of these functional expressions, writing mixed lambda-expressions in place of FDs:

  a) $((\lambda\,(x)\,(\lambda\,(a)\,(\text{cons } a\,(\text{cons } x\ ^{\triangledown}(9\ 8\ 7))))))\ 5)$

  b) $(((\lambda\,(x)\,(\lambda\,(a)\,(\text{cons } a\,(\text{cons } x\ ^{\triangledown}(9\ 8\ 7))))))\ 5)\ 364)$

  c) $((\lambda\,(a\ b)\,(\lambda\,(c\ d)\,(+\ a\,(+\ d\,(*\ b\ c))))))\ 10\ 7)$

  d) $(((\lambda\,(a\ b)\,(\lambda\,(c\ d)\,(+\ a\,(+\ d\,(*\ b\ c))))))\ 10\ 7)\ 12\ 50)$

3. Evaluate this functional expression:

```
(((λ (a)
    (cond
      [(null? a) (λ (x) (cons x ▽()))]
      [(null? (rest a)) (λ (x) (cons (first x) ▽()))]
      [(null? (rest (rest a))) (λ (x) (pair (first x) (last x)))]
      [else (λ (x) (λ (x) (cons (pair (first x) (last x)) ▽())))]))
  ▽(99 100))
  ▽(a 2 z))
```

4. Let the function **map** be defined as follows:

```
(define map
  (λ (f r)
    (cond
      [(null? r) ▽()]
      [else (cons (f (first r))
                  (map f (rest r)))])))
```

  a) Evaluate each of these functional expressions:

   (i) $(\text{map square }\ ^{\triangledown}(1\ 2\ 3\ 4\ 5))$

   (ii) $(\text{map add1 }\ ^{\triangledown}(1\ 2\ 3\ 4\ 5))$

   (iii) $(\text{map factorial }\ ^{\triangledown}(1\ 2\ 3\ 4\ 5))$

   (iv) $(\text{map }(\lambda\,(x)\,(\text{sub1 }(\text{fib } x)))\ ^{\triangledown}(1\ 2\ 3\ 4\ 5))$

   (v) $(\text{map }(\lambda\,(x)\,(-\,(*\ x\ x)\ x))\ ^{\triangledown}(1\ 2\ 3\ 4\ 5))$

   (vi) $(\text{map }(\lambda\,(x)\,(\text{gcd } x\ 6))\ ^{\triangledown}(1\ 2\ 3\ 4\ 5))$

   (vii) $(\text{map }(\lambda\,(x)\,((\lambda\,(y)\,y)\ x))\ ^{\triangledown}(1\ 2\ 3\ 4\ 5))$

  b) Describe the behavior of the function **map** in words.

5. Let the function **J** be defined as follows:

$$(\text{define } \mathbf{J}$$
$$(\lambda\,(a)$$
$$(\text{cond}$$
$$[(\text{atom? } a)\,(\lambda\,(r)\,(\text{cons } a\ r))]$$
$$[\text{else }(\lambda\,(r)\,(\text{cons } r\ a))])))$$

Evaluate each of these functional expressions:

a) **(J** $^\triangledown$**Fred)**   b) **((J** $^\triangledown$**Fred)** $^\triangledown$**(a b c))**

b) **(J** $^\triangledown$**(Jane))**   d) **((J** $^\triangledown$**(Jane))** $^\triangledown$**(a b c))**

6. Write a definition for a function **K** that behaves as follows:[5] It inputs a data expression r and returns a function that takes one input, which may be any data expression, and returns the data expression r. For example,

- **((K** $^\triangledown$**oriole)** $^\triangledown$**cardinal)** $\mapsto$ `oriole`
- **((K** $^\triangledown$**oriole)** $^\triangledown$**((sparrow) hawk))** $\mapsto$ `oriole`
- **((K** $^\triangledown$**(wren (starling)))** **#f)** $\mapsto$ `(wren (starling))`

7. Write a definition for a function **constant-maker** of a data expression r which returns a thunk whose output is the data expression r.

8. Let the function **P** be defined as follows:

$$(\text{define } \mathbf{P}$$
$$(\lambda\,(x)$$
$$(\lambda\,(y)$$
$$(\mathbf{P}\ x))))$$

Each of these functional expressions evaluates to an FD. Using mixed lambda-expressions, write the FD to which each evaluates.

a) **(P** $^\triangledown$**pom)**   b) **((P** $^\triangledown$**pom)** $^\triangledown$**pom)**

c) **(((P** $^\triangledown$**pom)** $^\triangledown$**pom)** $^\triangledown$**pom)**

9. We may define a curried version of the function **map** (see Problem 4 above) as follows:

---

[5]This function is the kestrel in the bird forest that features in Professor Smullyan's entertaining book, mentioned in the Foreword. It plays a central role in the λ-calculus.

```
(define transform
  (λ (f)
    (λ (r)
      (cond
        [(null? r) ▽()]
        [else (cons (f (first r))
                    ((transform f) (rest r)))]))))
```

(Note how the natural recursion has been changed to its curried form.)

a) Use this function to redefine the function **map**.

b) Recall that in Exercise 65 on page 90 you defined the function **getfirsts** of a list containing nothing but non-null lists that returns a list made up of the first data expressions of the internal lists of the input, in order. We observe that this function may be redefined as follows:

```
(define getfirsts
  (λ (r)
    ((transform first) r)))
```

Notice, however, that in words this definition tells us that the function **getfirsts** behaves just like the function **(transform first)**. (Check that **(transform first)** is indeed a one-input function.) Furthermore, the suitable inputs to both functions are exactly the same. It follows that '**getfirsts**' and '**(transform first)**' are simply different names for the same function. In recognition of this fact, we may shorten our redefinition even further by removing all mention of variables, as follows:

```
(define getfirsts
  (transform first))
```

Write a definition involving no variables for the function **cutfirsts** that inputs a list containing nothing but non-null lists and returns the list with the first data expression removed from each of the internal lists.

10. Let the function **filter** be defined as shown at the top of the next page.

a) Evaluate each of these functional expressions:

(i) **(filter atom? ▽(a (b) (c d) e))**

(ii) **(filter (λ (a) (equal? a ▽(b))) ▽(a (b) (c d) e))**

(iii) **(filter (λ (c) (even? (fib c))) ▽(1 2 3 4 5 6 7 8 9))**

```
(define filter
  (λ (f s)
    (cond
      [(null? s) ▽()]
      [(f (first s)) (cons (first s) (filter f (rest s)))]
      [else (filter f (rest s))])))
```

b) Describe the behavior of the function **filter** in words.

11. Write a definition for the function **filter–curry**, a curried version of the function **filter**. Then use this function to

   a) redefine the function **make–lat** of a list that removes all internal lists from the input, thereby producing a lat. (See Problem 8(c) of Problem Set 4 on page 93.)

   b) the function **make–vec** of a list that removes all non-numerals from the input, thereby making a vector.

12. Let the function **compose** be defined as follows:

```
(define compose
  (λ (f g)
    (λ (x)
      (g (f x)))))
```

   a) Evaluate each of these functional expressions:
   - (i) **(compose rest first)**
   - (ii) **((compose rest first) ▽(a b c))**
   - (iii) **((compose null? not) ▽())**
   - (iv) **((compose square add1) 5)**
   - (v) **((compose reverse first) ▽(a b c d e))**
   - (vi) **((compose (transform first) sum) ▽((1 2) (3 4) (5 6)))**
   - (vii) **((compose (transform (λ (x) (+ x 10))) sum) ▽(1 2 3 4 5))**
   - (viii) **((compose (filter–curry even?) (transform add1)) ▽(1 2 3 4 5 6))**

   b) Use the function **compose** to write new definitions for the following functions, doing without variables wherever possible:
   - (i) **second**
   - (ii) **last**
   - (iii) **list?**

13. Let the function **assoc–f** be defined as follows:

```
(define assoc-f
  (λ (r alist succ fail)
    (cond
      [(null? alist) (fail r)]
      [(equal? r (first alist)) (succ r)]
      [else (assoc-f r (rest alist) succ fail)])))
```

a) Evaluate each of these functional expressions:

(i) (assoc-f   (ii) (assoc-f

    ▽c   ▽e

    ▽((a 1) (b 2) (c 3) (d 4))   ▽((a 1) (b 2) (c 3) (d 4))

    (λ (p) (+ (second p) 5))   (λ (p) p)

    (λ (r) #f))   (λ (r) (pair r 5)))

b) The two-input function **assoc** takes any data expression r as its first input and any association list *alist* as its second input. If any pair in *alist* has r as its first data expression, then the function returns the first such pair, otherwise it returns the boolean '#f'. Write a definition for the function **assoc** in terms of the function **assoc-f**.

c) Write a new definition for the function **lookup** (see page 135) in terms of the function **assoc-f**.

14. Let the function **qsort** be defined as follows:

```
(define qsort
  (λ (ord r)
    (cond
      [(null? r) ▽()]
      [else (append (qsort ord
                           (filter (λ (x) (ord x (first r))) (rest r)))
                    (cons (first r)
                          (qsort ord
                                 (filter (λ (x) (not (ord x (first r))))
                                         (rest r)))))])))
```

Evaluate the functional expression '(qsort less? ▽(5 1 4 2 3 6 1))'.

$$- \text{o O o} -$$

7 Perpetual Motion Machines

In this chapter we study a type of data structure that may be used to organize computations on collections of data and that helps us clarify the underlying structure of our programs. It is important for the schemer to strive toward writing programs that not only work correctly and efficiently, but whose behavior is readily apparent, for in this way he or she will have much greater freedom to test, modify, and improve those programs.

The data structure to which we refer is the **stream**. In computing in general, a stream is just a sequence of data objects, which might be the cards dealt in a card game, the daily price of gold in dollars on the Tokyo bullion market, images on a laserdisk, names on a roster, and so on. In particular, the word 'stream' appears in such common phrases as 'input stream' and 'output stream'. In Scheme, however, the word 'stream' has a very specialized meaning. A Scheme stream is not actually a sequence of data objects; it is related to such a sequence, though, in that we 'know' what the current object is and we 'know' how to find out what the next object in the sequence is. In a sense, then, it is more a *method* of generating the sequence than it is the sequence itself. (These rather nebulous general remarks will become more meaningful as soon as we introduce streams and examine some examples.)

Before we make our official introduction, however, we turn our attention to some general techniques of program design that are not only useful for us to bear in mind when programming in Scheme, but also essential when, later on, we shall be interested in manipulating streams.

219

7.1 Interlocking, Multi-purpose Machines

Consider the following definition for the function **product–even–fibs** of natural numbers m and n that returns the product of the even numbers among the mth through nth Fibonacci numbers:

```
(define product–even–fibs
  (λ (m n)
    (cond
      [(less? n m) 1]
      [(even? (fib m)) (* (fib m) (product–even–fibs (add1 m) n))]
      [else (product–even–fibs (add1 m) n)])))
```

(See Problem 16(a) of Problem Set 5 for the definition of the function **fib**.) Having typed this definition into the computer, it is then an easy matter to discover the product of the even numbers among the first ten Fibonacci numbers: we simply have to evaluate the functional expression

(product–even–fibs 1 10)

But there is an alternative—and, in our view, preferable—approach to the problem.

The task we are attempting to perform may be broken down into three distinct parts. First, we calculate some Fibonacci numbers; second, we identify which of them are even; and last, we multiply these even Fibonacci numbers together. Each of these sub-tasks may be dealt with independently. It is, for example, easy to define a function **fibnums** of a vector which returns the vector of the Fibonacci numbers corresponding to the numbers in the input vector, and a function **pick–evens** of a vector which returns the vector of the even numbers in the input vector. These functions would behave like this:

(fibnums ▽(1 2 3 4 5 6 7 8 9 10)) ↦ (1 1 2 3 5 8 13 21 34 55)
(pick–evens ▽(1 1 2 3 5 8 13 21 34 55)) ↦ (2 8 34)

Recalling that in Problem 2(b) of Problem Set 10 you defined a function **product** of a vector that returns the product of the numbers in the vector, it follows that an alternative way to determine the product of the even numbers among the first ten Fibonacci numbers is to evaluate the functional expression

(product (pick–evens (fibnums ▽(1 2 3 4 5 6 7 8 9 10))))

For the sake of emphasis, we reiterate that, in the definition for the function **product–even–fibs** on the previous page, all the various sub-tasks are intertwined as the recursive process unravels, whereas in the analysis which gave rise to our alternative functional expression we have separated out the subtasks and dealt with them individually. This sub-division process is one aspect of good programming practice.

Another, equally important, aspect of good practice is to be concerned about broadening the applicability of the functions we define. What we have in mind here will become apparent as our illustration continues. We begin by asking you to write a definition for the function **interval** of the whole numbers m and n that returns a vector containing, in order, all of the whole numbers m through n. We shall denote such a vector by '$[m; n]$', which we read as 'the interval from m through n'. Thus,

$$\textbf{(interval 1 10)} \mapsto \texttt{(1 2 3 4 5 6 7 8 9 10)} = [1; 10].$$

Exercise 124.

a) Complete the following skeleton definition for the function
   interval:

   ```
   (define interval
     (λ (m n)
       (cond
         [(_____ n m) ▽()]
         [else (_____ m (_____ (_____ m) n))]))))
   ```

b) Evaluate each of the following functional expressions. (In
   part (v), we remind you of Problem 6 in Problem Set 5.)
   (i) **(interval 200 15)**   (ii) **(interval 700 700)**
   (iii) **(interval 0 10)**   (iv) **(first (interval (10 1000)))**
   (v) **(nth 15 (rest (interval 574 85642)))**

We now turn our attention to writing a definition for the function **fibnums** of a vector which returns the vector of the Fibonacci numbers corresponding to the numbers in the input vector. A natural way to proceed is as follows:

```
(define fibnums
  (λ (vec)
    (cond
      [(null? vec) ▽()]
      [else (cons (fib (first vec))
                  (fibnums (rest vec)))])))
```

This would be fine if all we ever wanted to do was to find Fibonacci numbers, but the above definition is evidently a specific instance of a more generally applicable function. We can, for example, abstract the function **fib**, whereupon we discover that the function of which this is a specific instance is the function **map**, which was defined in Problem 4 of Problem Set 11:

```
(define map
  (λ (f vec)
    (cond
      [(null? vec) ▽()]
      [else (cons (f (first vec))
                  (map f (rest vec)))])))
```

Exercise 125.

> Evaluate each of the following functional expressions. (See Problem Set 5 for the definitions of the functions **factorial** and **remainder**.)
>
> a) (map fib (interval 3 7))
>
> b) (map factorial (interval 2 6))
>
> c) (map (λ (x) (remainder x 4)) (interval 0 10))
>
> d) (nth 7 (map (λ (x) (* x (+ x 5))) (interval 12 7685)))

Exercise 126.

> Let the function **A** of a natural number n and a vector *vec* be defined as follows (refer to Problem 13(a) of Problem Set 5):
>
> ```
> (define A
>   (λ (n vec)
>     (map (λ (x) (gcd x n)) vec)))
> ```
>
> Evaluate the functional expression '(A 12 (interval 1 12))'.

Exercise 127.

> Using the function **map**, write a new definition for the function **fibnums**.

Moving on to the function **pick–evens**, a natural way to proceed is as follows:

```
(define pick–evens
  (λ (vec)
    (cond
      [(null? vec) ▽()]
      [(even? (first vec)) (cons (first vec) (pick–evens (rest vec)))]
      [else (pick–evens (rest vec))])))
```

Inspired by the above reminder of our work on function abstraction, we realize that we can abstract the function—in this case **even?**—that is used to test each data expression in the input vector. As a result we obtain the generalized filtering function **filter**, which we defined in Problem 10 of Problem Set 11:

```
(define filter
  (λ (f vec)
    (cond
      [(null? vec) ▽()]
      [(f (first vec)) (cons (first vec) (filter f (rest vec)))]
      [else (filter f (rest vec))])))
```

Exercise 128.

Using the function **filter**, write a new definition for the function **pick–evens**.

Exercise 129.

Evaluate each of these functional expressions:

a) (map fib (filter even? (interval 1 10)))

b) (filter even? (map fib (interval 1 10)))

c) (filter (λ (x) (divides? x 24)) (interval 1 24))

d) (nth 8 (filter (λ (x) (= 1 (gcd 24 x))) (interval 1 24)))

Exercise 130.

There is a function that is important in the Theory of Numbers and that may be defined in terms of the function **filter** as follows:

```
(define sieve
  (λ (vec)
    (cond
      [(null? vec) ▽()]
      [else (cons
              (first vec)
              (sieve
                (filter
                  (λ (x) (not (divides? (first vec) x)))
                  (rest vec))))])))
```

a) Evaluate the functional expression '(sieve (interval 2 30))'.

b) Describe in words what appears to be the behavior of the function **sieve**.

In answering Exercise 130(b) you probably referred to prime numbers.[1] Thus far in this book we have not introduced a predicate function that recognizes prime numbers. We rectify this omission in the next exercise, thereby providing ourselves with a source of many interesting problems for later in the chapter.

Exercise 131.

a) Let the function **prime–div–list** of a natural number n greater than 1 be defined as follows:

```
(define prime–div–list
  (λ (n)
    (prime–div–aux n ▽() 2)))
```

```
(define prime–div–aux
  (λ (n list div)
    (cond
      [(= n div) (cons div list)]
      [(divides? div n)
       (prime–div–aux (quotient n div) (cons div list) div)]
      [else (prime–div–aux n list (add1 div))])))
```

(i) Make a trace table for the evaluation of the functional expression '(prime–div–list 60)'.

---

[1] A whole number is said to be prime if and only if it has exactly *two* divisors. Thus, 5 is prime since its divisors are 1 and 5. Note however that 0 and 1 are *not* prime since 0 has an infinite number of divisors and 1 has only one.

(ii) Evaluate the functional expressions '(prime–div–list 48)' and '(prime–div–list 11)'.

(iii) Why do you think this function is called 'prime–div–list'?

b) Using the function **prime–div–list**, write a definition for the predicate function **prime?** of a whole number n, which returns the boolean '#t' if and only if n is a prime number. (The whole numbers 0 and 1 will need separate treatment in your definition.)

c) In practice, we prefer the following definition for the predicate function **prime?** to the one you gave in part (b):

```
(define prime?
  (λ (n)
    (cond
      [(less? n 2) #f]
      [(even? n) (= n 2)]
      [else (prime?–help n 3)])))
```

```
(define prime?–help
  (λ (n div)
    (cond
      [(less? n (square div)) #t]
      [(divides? div n) #f]
      [else (prime?–help n (+ 2 div))])))
```

Describe in words the strategy employed by this definition, explain why it works, and say why you think it might be preferable to the definition given in part (b).

Exercise 132.

a) Evaluate the functional expression

(filter prime? (interval 2 30))

and compare your answer with the one you obtained in Exercise 130(a).

b) Let the function **L** of a natural number n be defined as follows:

```
(define L
  (λ (n)
    (filter
      prime?
      (filter
        (λ (x) (divides? x n))
        (interval 1 n)))))
```

(i) Evaluate the functional expression '(L 50)'.

(ii) Describe the behavior of the function L in words.

(iii) Compare and contrast the effects of the functions L and prime–div–list.

You will recall that at the beginning of Problem Set 10 you were introduced to the general function **accumulate**, defined as follows:

```
(define accumulate
  (λ (op init r)
    (cond
      [(null? r) init ]
      [else (op (first r)
                (accumulate op init (rest r)))])))
```

Exercise 133.

Evaluate each of these functional expressions. (In part (d), refer to Problem 14 of Problem Set 5.)

a) (accumulate * 1 (interval 1 5))

b) (accumulate * 2 (filter prime? (interval 1 10)))

c) (accumulate + 0 (filter
                     prime?
                     (filter
                       (λ (x) (divides? x 24))
                       (interval 1 24))))

d) (accumulate lcm 1 (filter prime? (interval 1 10)))

e) (accumulate cons ▽( ) (interval 1 10))

Exercise 134.

Using the functions **accumulate**, **map**, **filter**, and **interval**,

a) write a functional expression that evaluates to the product of all the distinct prime divisors of 30.

b) write a definition for a function of a natural number n greater than 1 which returns the product of all the distinct prime divisors of n.

Exercise 135.

Write a definition for a function of whole numbers m and n which returns the sum of all the numbers in the interval $[m; n]$ that are one less than a prime number.

Exercise 136.

a) Evaluate the functional expression

$$(\text{map } (\lambda \ (x) \ (\text{remainder } 10 \ x)) \ (\text{interval } 1 \ 10))$$

b) Write a definition for a function of a natural number n which returns the vector containing just the *even* remainders that are obtained when each of the numbers in the interval $[1; n]$ is divided into n.

c) Write a definition for a function of a natural number n which returns the sum of the squares of the *even* remainders that are obtained when each of the numbers in the interval $[1; n]$ is divided into n.

7.2 Put Off Till Tomorrow What You Can Do Without Delay

Compare the following two functions. Each one accepts as its input a natural number n greater than 1 and returns the smallest prime divisor of n. The first function is given by a standard, tail-recursive definition:

```
(define first–prime–divisor–A
  (λ (n)
    (first–prime–divisor–aux n 2)))
```

```
(define first–prime–divisor–aux
  (λ (n try)
    (cond
      [(= n try) n]
      [(and (divides? try n) (prime? try)) try]
      [else (first–prime–divisor–aux n (add1 try))])))
```

The second function makes use of the technique we developed in the last section of separating out the sub-tasks:

```
(define first–prime–divisor–B
  (λ (n)
    (first
      (filter
        prime?
        (filter
          (λ (x) (divides? x n))
          (interval 2 n))))))
```

Perhaps the easiest way to compare the behavior of these two functions is to compile trace tables. The following table shows the behavior of the first function as it attempts to find the smallest prime divisor of 4235:

```
(first–prime–divisor–A 4235)
(first–prime–divisor–aux 4235 2)
(and (divides? 2 4235) (prime? 2))
(first–prime–divisor–aux 4235 3)
(and (divides? 3 4235) (prime? 3))
(first–prime–divisor–aux 4235 4)
(and (divides? 4 4235) (prime? 4))
(first–prime–divisor–aux 4235 5)
(and (divides? 5 4235) (prime? 5))
5
```

How does the second function deal with the same task? The relevant trace table is given at the top of the next page. At one point it involves a rather long list, so we have used an ellipsis to save space and make it more readable. We trust that the intended meaning is clear.

How do the two approaches compare? The first function is clearly much more efficient than the second. The function **first–prime–divisor–A** tests whether

```
(first–prime–divisor–B 4235)
(first
  (filter
    prime?
    (filter
      (λ (x) (divides? x 4235))
      (interval 2 4235))))
(first
  (filter
    prime?
    (filter
      (λ (x) (divides? x 4235))
      (2 3 4 5 6 7 8 9 10 11 12 13 14 ... 4233 4234 4235))))
(first (filter prime? (5 7 11 35 55 77 121 385 605 847 4235)))
(first (5 7 11))
5
```

or not the numbers 2, 3, 4, and 5 are divisors of 4235 and then tests the first divisor it finds (that is, 5) to see if it is prime—a total of five tests. On the other hand, the function **first–prime–divisor–B** checks four thousand two hundred and thirty four whole numbers to see if they are divisors of 4235, and then checks each of the eleven divisors to see if it is prime—a total of four thousand two hundred and forty five tests! However, to its credit, the second function is easier to write and—what is very important—the way in which it achieves its goal is eminently clear from its definition, a claim which is open to dispute in the case of the first function.

It would be nice if we could have the best of both worlds, that is, a means of representing and manipulating sequences of whole numbers which both lends itself to the technique of separating out the sub-tasks and at the same time avoids unnecessary calculation. This could be achieved if we could somehow *delay* certain evaluations. Suppose, for example, that we could say to the function **interval**, 'I would like the sequence of consecutive whole numbers from 2 through 4235, ... but not all at once, please. Give me one number now, and if I need another, I'll get back to you!' This idea of **delayed evaluation** is at the heart of the concept of a stream.[2] Just as a

---

[2]Delayed evaluation was first described by Peter Landin in 1965, and was used by Daniel Friedman and David Wise in 1976 to implement streams in Lisp.

vector represents a sequence of numbers, so a stream represents a sequence of data objects, but instead of providing all the objects at the same time, a stream provides just one object to the calling function along with information about how to obtain the next object in the sequence. In a sense, a vector provides all the information at once, whereas a stream provides it on a 'need to know' basis.

We define a **stream**[3] as follows:

A list is a stream if and only if either

>   (i) *it is the null list, or*

>   (ii) *it is a non-null list containing at least two data expressions such that the* **first** *of this list is a red numeral and the* **rest** *of the list is the FD of a thunk which, when invoked,*[4] *evaluates to a stream.*

For obvious reasons, the null list is known as the **empty stream**. A non-empty stream, on the other hand, is a non-null list with the property that its first data expression is a number[5] and when we invoke the **rest** of the list the result is a new stream. If this new stream is non-empty, then its first data expression is a number and when we invoke the **rest** of it we get yet another stream. And so on. There are only two possibilities: either we eventually obtain the empty stream in this process or we do not. In the first case we say that the original stream *generates* a finite sequence of numbers, or alternatively that the original stream is finite. In the second case the original stream is said to *generate* an infinite sequence of numbers, or in other words the stream is infinite. It is common to extend this vocabulary to the empty case and say that the empty stream *generates* the empty sequence of numbers. Using this language, we may describe a non-empty stream like this: It is a non-null list with the property that its first data expression is the first number in the sequence it generates and the **rest** of the list is the FD of a thunk which, when invoked, returns the stream that generates the rest of the sequence.

As a very simple example, consider the stream

---

[3] What we describe here are streams of numbers. Scheme interpreters also admit streams of other kinds of data objects. However, our work with streams of numbers is representative of all the important stream-handling techniques.

[4] We usually speak of functions being *applied* to their inputs. However, a thunk has no inputs, so we prefer to say that such a function is *invoked*.

[5] We are adopting the usual lax terminology of saying 'number' when we really ought to say 'representation of a number' or 'numeral'.

```
(1 derived () (cons 2 (lambda () (quote ())))  ())
```

The first data expression of this list is the atom '1', so the first number in the sequence generated by the stream is 1. The **rest** of the list is the FD

```
(derived () (cons 2 (lambda () (quote ())))  ())
```

When this thunk is invoked it evaluates as follows:

((derived () (cons 2 (lambda () (quote ()))) ()))
(cons 2 (λ () $^{\triangledown}$()))
(cons 2 (derived () (quote ()) ()))
(2 derived () (quote ()) ())

which is another non-empty stream. Its first data expression is the atom '2', so this is the second number in the sequence generated by the original stream. The **rest** of our new non-empty stream is the FD

```
(derived () (quote ()) ())
```

which, when invoked, returns the empty stream. So the stream

```
(1 derived () (cons 2 (lambda () (quote ())))  ())
```

generates a finite sequence that corresponds to the vector '(1 2)'. That is, we are dealing with the stream version of the interval [1; 2].

We shall need some data abstractor functions for streams; the following four will suffice:[6]

- The predicate function **stream–empty?** of a stream. This function returns the boolean '#t' if and only if the stream is the empty stream, and we define it as follows:

(define stream–empty? null?)

- The function **stream–cons** of a whole number n and (the FD of) a thunk f that evaluates to a stream when invoked. This function returns the stream with the property that its first data expression is n and the **rest** of the stream is the thunk f. We define it as follows:

---

[6]There are many ways to implement streams, all of them variations on the same Scheme theme. While it is true that all Scheme interpreters provide primitive functions for manipulating streams, you should be warned that those functions may not necessarily coincide with the ones described here. *EdScheme* does use the implementation we describe; indeed, it provides the functions **head** and **tail** as primitives and in addition it includes various advanced functions and special forms that are geared specifically toward facilitating stream-handling.

(define stream–cons cons)

- The function **head** of a non-empty stream. This function returns the stream's first data expression, and we define it as follows:

(define head first)

- The function **tail** of a non-empty stream. This function returns the result of invoking the thunk whose FD is the **rest** of the stream. We define it as follows:

(define tail
  (λ (*s*)
    ((rest *s*))))

(It is important for our later work to note that, whenever its input is a non-empty stream, the function **tail** always returns a stream.)

Exercise 137.

Evaluate these functional expressions:

a) (stream–empty? ▽(1 derived ( ) (cons 2 (λ ( ) (quote ( )))) ( )))

b) (head ▽(1 derived ( ) (cons 2 (λ ( ) (quote ( )))) ( )))

c) (tail ▽(1 derived ( ) (cons 2 (λ ( ) (quote ( )))) ( )))

d) (stream–cons 2 (λ ( ) (stream–cons 5 (λ ( ) (quote ( ))))))

e) (head
      (tail
        (stream–cons
          8
          (λ ( )
            (stream–cons
              13
              (λ ( ) (stream–cons 21 (λ ( ) (quote ( )))))))))))

Thinking back to the example with which we began this section, we would like to define a function **stream–interval** that behaves in much the same way as the function **interval** except that, instead of returning the vector of the numbers that make up the interval, it returns a stream which generates the sequence of those numbers. Let the inputs to the function **stream–interval**

be the whole numbers m and n. Of course, if $n < m$, then the function
stream–interval should return the empty stream. So our definition starts like
this:

$$(\text{define stream–interval}$$
$$(\lambda \ (m \ n)$$
$$(\text{cond}$$
$$[(\text{less? } n \ m) \ ^\triangledown()]$$
$$[\text{else} \dots])))$$

Suppose now that $m \leq n$. The function **stream–interval** must return a non-null
list with the property that its first data expression is m and the **rest** of the
list is a thunk. So our definition continues like this:

$$(\text{define stream–interval}$$
$$(\lambda \ (m \ n)$$
$$(\text{cond}$$
$$[(\text{less? } n \ m) \ ^\triangledown()]$$
$$[\text{else (stream–cons } m \ (\lambda \ () \dots))])))$$

Now, the thunk has to be such that, when it is invoked, it returns all the rest
of the stream, namely, the stream that generates the sequence of numbers in
the interval $[m+1; n]$. But this is given by '(stream–interval (add1 m) n)'. So
the complete definition for the function **stream–interval** is as follows:

$$(\text{define stream–interval}$$
$$(\lambda \ (m \ n)$$
$$(\text{cond}$$
$$[(\text{less? } n \ m) \ ^\triangledown()]$$
$$[\text{else (stream–cons } m \ (\lambda \ () \ (\text{stream–interval (add1 } m) \ n)))])))$$

To illustrate the behavior of this function, we trace the evaluation of
the functional expression '(**stream–interval** 1 2)'. Since 2 is not less than 1,
the definition for the function '**stream–interval**' tells us to evaluate the mixed
expression

$$(\text{stream–cons } 1 \ (\lambda \ () \ (\text{stream–interval (add1 } 1) \ 2)))$$

Recalling that the lambda-expression '(λ () (stream–interval (add1 1) 2)' is an
abbreviation for the FD

```
(derived () (stream-interval (add1 m) n) (((m 1) (n 2))))
```

we may trace the complete evaluation as follows:

(stream–interval 1 2**)**
(stream–cons 1 **(λ ()** **(stream–interval (add1** 1**)** 2**)))**
(stream–cons 1 ⟨derived
                ()
                (stream-interval (add1 m) n)
                (((m 1) (n 2))))**)**
(1 derived () (stream-interval (add1 m) n) (((m 1) (n 2))))

It now only remains for us to check that this stream generates the sequence of numbers in the interval [1; 2]. If the stream **(stream–interval 1 2)** is the replacement for the variable '**s**', then we clearly have that **(head s)** ↦ 1. That is, the first number generated by the stream returned by the function stream–interval is 1. The functional expression '**(tail s)**' evaluates as follows:

(tail *s***)**
((rest (1 derived
        ()
        (stream-interval (add1 m) n)
        (((m 1) (n 2)))))**)**
((derived () (stream-interval (add1 m) n) (((m 1) (n 2)))))
(stream–interval (add1 1**)** 2**)**
(stream–interval 2 2**)**
(2 derived () (stream-interval (add1 m) n) (((m 2) (n 2))))

If we denote this stream by the variable '**r**', then the functional expression '**(head r)**' evaluates to the atom '2'. Thus the second number generated by the stream returned by the function stream–interval is 2. Finally, the functional expression '**(tail r)**' evaluates to the empty stream:

(tail *r***)**
((rest (2 derived
        ()
        (stream-interval (add1 m) n)
        (((m 2) (n 2)))))**)**
((derived () (stream-interval (add1 m) n) (((m 2) (n 2)))))
(stream–interval (add1 2**)** 2**)**
(stream–interval 3 2**)**
()

Thus the stream (stream–interval 1 2) generates the finite sequence consisting only of the two numbers 1 and 2 in that order. But this is exactly the sequence of numbers in the interval [1; 2], so our function is behaving as expected.

Exercise 138.
 Evaluate these functional expressions:

a) (stream–interval 1 3)   b) (stream–interval 2 10)

c) (head (stream–interval 1 3))   d) (tail (stream–interval 2 10))

You will have noticed that having to write out the FD when naming a stream is a major inconvenience—in fact, not much is convenient when it comes to 'showing our work' as we deal with streams—so we propose to replace the FD by the corresponding mixed lambda-expression whenever possible. So, for example, we use the mixed expression[7]

$$(5 \ \lambda \ (\ ) \ (\text{stream–interval (add1 } 5) \ 10000))$$

to represent the stream with the property that its first data expression is the atom '5' and the **rest** of the stream is the thunk

```
(derived () (stream-interval (add1 m) n) (((m 5) (n 10000))))
```

To emphasize the power and efficiency of streams, we now evaluate the functional expression '(head (tail (stream–interval 1 1000000)))'. Since the functional expression '(stream–interval 1 1000000)' evaluates to the stream

$$(1 \ \lambda \ (\ ) \ (\text{stream–interval (add1 } 1) \ 1000000))$$

the functional expression '(tail (stream–interval 1 1000000))' evaluates as follows:

(tail (stream–interval 1 1000000))
((rest (1 λ ( ) (stream–interval (add1 1) 1000000))))
((λ ( ) (stream–interval (add1 1) 1000000)))
(stream–interval (add1 1) 1000000)
(stream–interval 2 1000000)
(2 λ ( ) (stream–interval (add1 2) 1000000))

Since the first data expression of this stream is the atom '2', it follows that

---

[7]This represents an extension of the notion of 'mixed expression' which we introduced on page 208 in our explanation of the evaluation of lambda-expressions.

$$\text{(head (tail (stream--interval 1 1000000)))} \mapsto 2.$$

We interpret this piece of information as saying that the second number in the interval $[1; 1000000]$ is the number 2. We could also have come up with this fact using the vector methods discussed in the last section by evaluating the functional expression

$$\text{(first (rest (interval 1 1000000)))}$$

However, this would have involved constructing a vector containing a million whole numbers, which, if it did not dramatically exceed the memory capacity of your computer, would have taken a considerable amount of time!

Exercise 139.

Evaluate these functional expressions:

a) **(stream--interval 12345 10000000)**

b) **(head (stream--interval 12345 1000000))**

c) **(tail (stream--interval 12345 1000000))**

d) **(head**
      (tail
        (tail
          (tail
            (stream--interval 12345 1000000)))))

Exercise 140.

a) Write a definition for the function **stream--nth** which inputs a natural number k and a stream s that generates a sequence containing at least k whole numbers and which returns the kth number in the sequence generated by the stream s.

b) Compile a trace table showing the evaluation of the functional expression '**(stream--nth 3 (stream--interval 5 1000))**'.

We now turn our attention to writing definitions for stream-processing functions that correspond to the functions **accumulate**, **filter**, and **map**. Here is our definition for the function **stream--filter** of a predicate function and a stream:

```
(define stream–filter
  (λ (f s)
    (cond
      [(stream–empty? s) ▽()]
      [(f (head s))
       (stream–cons (head s)
                    (λ () (stream–filter f (tail s))))]
      [else (stream–filter f (tail s))])))
```

To illustrate how the function **stream–filter** behaves, we work carefully through the evaluation of the functional expression

$$\text{(stream–filter even? (stream–interval 1 1000))}$$

First, we note that the functional expression '**(stream–interval 1 1000)**' evaluates to the stream

$$\text{(1 λ () (stream–interval (add1 1) 1000))}$$

We denote this stream by 's', and we pass the function **even?** and the stream s to the function **stream–filter**. We observe that s is not the empty stream. The first data expression of s is the atom '1', and so

$$\text{(even? (head } s)) \mapsto \text{\#f}$$

We therefore move to the last clause in the definition of the function **stream–filter**, which evaluates as follows:

```
(stream–filter even? (tail s))
(stream–filter even? (tail (1 λ () (stream–interval (add1 1) 1000))))
(stream–filter even? (2 λ () (stream–interval (add1 2) 1000)))
```

For convenience, we denote the stream

$$\text{(2 λ () (stream–interval (add1 2) 1000))}$$

by the variable 'r'. Once again, r is not the empty stream. So, since its first data expression is the atom '2', we have that

$$\text{(even? (head } r)) \mapsto \text{\#t}$$

According to the definition for **stream–filter**, this means that we must now evaluate the functional expression

(stream–cons (head *r*)
                    (λ ( ) (stream–filter even? (tail *r*))))

thereby obtaining the stream

(2 λ ( ) (stream–filter
                 even?
                 (tail (2 λ ( ) (stream–interval (add1 2) 1000)))))

This then is the stream returned by the function **stream–filter** when its inputs are the function **even?** and the stream (**stream–interval 1 1000**).

The first data expression of this stream is the atom '2'—which, we remark, is indeed the first even number in the interval [1; 1000]. Suppose now that we require the next number in the sequence generated by this stream. Then we must invoke the **rest** of the stream, that is, the thunk

(λ ( ) (stream–filter
             even?
             (tail (2 λ ( ) (stream–interval (add1 2) 1000)))))

We invoke this thunk as follows:

((λ ( ) (stream–filter
               even?
               (tail (2 λ ( ) (stream–interval (add1 2) 1000)))))
(stream–filter even? (tail (2 λ ( ) (stream–interval (add1 2) 1000))))
(stream–filter even? ((λ ( ) (stream–interval (add1 2) 1000))))
(stream–filter even? (stream–interval (add1 2) 1000))
(stream–filter even? (stream–interval 3 1000))
       ⋮

By an argument similar to the one given above, we see that this process yields the stream

(4 λ ( ) (stream–filter
                 even?
                 (tail (4 λ ( ) (stream–interval (add1 4) 1000)))))

Hence,

(head (tail (stream–filter even? (stream–interval 1 1000)))) ↦ 4

which is indeed the second even number in the interval [1; 1000].

Exercise 141.

Evaluate the functional expression

(tail (tail (stream–filter even? (stream–interval 1 1000))))

It is a relatively simple task to modify the definition of the function **accu-mulate** so that it inputs a stream instead of a vector. Here is our version:

```
(define stream–accumulate
  (λ (op init str)
    (cond
      [(stream–empty? str) init]
      [else (op (head str)
                (stream–accumulate op init (tail str)))])))
```

As the next exercise shows, the function **stream–accumulate** enables us to 'translate' from streams to vectors.

Exercise 142.

Evaluate these functional expressions:

a) **(stream–accumulate cons ▽( ) (stream–interval 1 10))**

b) **(stream–accumulate**
   cons
   ▽( )
   (stream–filter even? (stream–interval 1 10)))

Exercise 143.

Complete the following definition for the function **stream–map** of a function and a stream that applies the function to each number generated by the stream:

```
(define stream–map
  (λ (f s)
    (cond
      [(_____ s) ▽()]
      [else (_____
              (f (_____ s))
              (_____ () (_____ f (_____ s)))))])))
```

Exercise 144.

Write the stream to which each of these functional expressions evaluates:

  a) (stream–interval 50000 1000000)

  b) (stream–filter prime? (stream–interval 1 1000000))

  c) (stream–filter zero? (stream–interval 1 1000000))

  d) (stream–map add1 (stream–interval 1 1000000))

  e) (stream–map (λ (x) (* x (* x x)))) (stream–interval 1 1000000))

  f) (stream–nth 154 (stream–interval 50000 1000000))

  g) (head
        (tail
          (tail
            (stream–filter prime? (stream–interval 1 1000000)))))))

  h) (stream–nth 256 (stream–map
                        (λ (x) (* x (* x x)))
                        (stream–interval 1 1000000)))

7.3 ... And So On Forever

In the last section we mentioned the theoretical possibility that a stream might generate an infinite sequence of numbers, but so far we have provided no evidence that such a possibility can indeed be realized. The fact that it can is one of the major strengths of Scheme. Consider, for example, the function **wholes** of a whole number n whose definition is as follows:

```
(define wholes
  (λ (n)
    (stream–cons n (λ () (wholes (add1 n)))))))
```

We easily see that the functional expression '**(wholes 0)**' evaluates to the stream

$$(0 \; \lambda \; () \; (wholes \; (add1 \; 0)))$$

The first number generated by the stream is therefore 0. The second is the number 1, as the following evaluation shows:

```
(head (tail (0 λ ( ) (wholes (add1 0)))))
(head ((λ ( ) (wholes (add1 0)))))
(head ((λ ( ) (wholes 1))))
(head (wholes 1))
(head (1 λ ( ) (wholes (add1 1))))
1
```

In general, it may be shown that, for all whole numbers n, the nth number in the sequence generated by the stream **(wholes 0)** is $(n-1)$. Thus, the stream **(wholes 0)** generates the sequence containing all the whole numbers in order. For convenience, we may give the name 'W' to this stream by writing the following assignment:

$$\text{(define } W \text{ (wholes 0))}$$

We call W the 'stream of the whole numbers'. Obviously, it is an infinite stream.

Exercise 145.

a) Write an assignment that binds the identifier 'N' to the stream of the natural numbers.

b) Evaluate the functional expression '(stream–nth 295 N)'.

PROBLEM SET 12

1. We may define the infinite stream of the even whole numbers as follows:

$$\text{(define } evens \text{ (stream–filter even? } W))$$

Alternatively, we may define it in terms of the function add2–stream–maker of a whole number n, which in turn is defined as follows:

```
(define add2–stream–maker
  (λ (n)
    (stream–cons
      n
      (λ ( ) (add2–stream–maker (+ 2 n))))))
```

The stream *evens* may then be defined as follows:

(define *evens* (add2–stream–maker 0))

Use the function **add2–stream–maker** to define the infinite stream *odds* of the odd natural numbers.

2.   a) Complete the following definition for the function **M–stream–maker** of a whole number m that returns the infinite stream of the whole number multiples of m:

(define M–stream–maker
  (λ (m)
    (M–stream–maker–aux m 0)))

(define M–stream–maker–aux
  (λ (m n)
    (_____

    _____
      (_____ () (M–stream–maker–aux m (_____ m n))))))

   b) Evaluate the functional expression

(stream–nth 8 (M–stream–maker 5))

3. Let the function **fib–stream–maker** be defined as follows:

(define fib–stream–maker
  (λ (a b)
    (stream–cons
      b
      (λ () (fib–stream–maker b (+ a b))))))

   a) Write the stream that results when each of the following functional expressions is evaluated

   (i) (fib–stream–maker 0 1)   (ii) (tail (tail (fib–stream–maker 0 1)))
   (iii) (tail (tail (tail (fib–stream–maker 0 1))))

   b) Let the infinite stream *fibs* be defined as follows:

(define *fibs* (fib–stream–maker 0 1))

Evaluate each of the following functional expressions:

  (i) (head *fibs*)   (ii) (stream–nth 3 *fibs*)

  (iii) (stream–nth 10 *fibs*)

4. Let the stream *ones* be defined as follows:

$$\text{(define } ones \text{ (stream–cons 1 } (\lambda \text{ ( ) } ones)))$$

Evaluate the functional expression '(stream–nth 102 *ones*)'.

5. Let the function **stream–add** of two streams be defined as follows:

```
(define stream–add
  (λ (r s)
    (cond
      [(stream–empty? r) s]
      [(stream–empty? s) r]
      [else (stream–cons
              (+ (head r) (head s))
              (λ ( ) (stream–add (tail r) (tail s))))])))
```

  a) Evaluate the functional expression '(stream–add *evens ones*)'.

  b) Let the stream *naturals* be defined as follows:

```
(define naturals
  (stream–cons
    1
    (λ ( ) (stream–add ones naturals))))
```

Evaluate these functional expressions:

  (i) *naturals*   (ii) (tail (tail *naturals*))

  (ii) (head (tail (tail (tail *naturals*))))

6. Write a definition for the function **stream–start** which inputs a whole number n and a stream that generates a sequence of at least n whole numbers and which returns the vector containing the first n numbers in the sequence generated by the stream.

7. In Exercise 130 on page 223 we defined the function **sieve**. This function has the property that, for each natural number n greater than 1, if **sieve** is applied to the interval $[2; n]$ of whole numbers, then it returns the vector containing all the prime numbers in that interval. The function is based on an algorithm known as the *Sieve of Eratosthenes*.[8]

a) Write an assignment that binds the variable *two-up* to the stream that generates the natural numbers starting at 2.

b) Write a definition for the function **stream–sieve** which, when given as its only input the stream *two-up* returns the infinite stream of the prime numbers.

c) Use the functions **stream–start** and **stream–sieve** to write a functional expression that evaluates to the vector containing the first 100 prime numbers.

$$- o\ O\ o -$$

---

[8] Eratosthenes (c. 276–194 BC) was a Greek mathematician and astronomer who worked at the University of Alexandria in Egypt. He was the first person to calculate the circumference of the earth.

8 A Game-playing Machine

Our purpose in this chapter is to show you how to build a complex piece of machinery, made up of an interlocking system of smaller, less complicated components. The final construction will be a machine that is capable of playing a game, either between two schemers, or against you, or even against itself! Because the visible action of the game takes place on the computer monitor, in a very real sense you will be designing and implementing the computer software system for a video game. Before venturing out upon such a grandiose scheme, however, there are a number of technical matters we must alert you to and some new pieces of information with which we must provide you.

8.1 By-products and Environmental Control

It may already have occurred to you that the role played by define-expressions is quite unlike that played by other types of functional expressions. The most significant feature of a define-expression is what is known as its **side-effect**, that is, the binding that it creates in the global frame. The overriding importance of this aspect of a define-expression may be discerned from the fact that the designers of the language Scheme do not specify what the value of a define-expression should be; that is a decision which is left entirely in the hands of those who produce actual implementations of Scheme. Often, as in this book and the *EdScheme* interpreter, the value of a define-expression is the identifier (in red) for which a binding has been created. However, you will notice that no use is ever made of the value of a define-expression (as the

245

input to a function, for example). In the next section we introduce three new special forms, one of which is similarly only important for its side-effect.

Shifting gears rather abruptly, we now return briefly to the question of environments. You will have noticed that we have been going to a good deal of trouble—particularly in Chapter 5—to speak of L-bindings, L-frames, and L-environments, and to remind you continually that we are doing no more than modeling actual bindings, frames, and environments by means of certain kinds of data expressions. We have always shied away from coming clean and telling you how the Scheme interpreter manages environments. We have only said that the exact details vary from implementation to implementation. While we do not propose to go any further into those unspecified 'exact details', it is nevertheless now appropriate that we explain to you the specifics of the strategy employed by Scheme interpreters.

You will recall that, during the course of an evaluation, the current environment may become very large in the sense that it contains many frames each of which may contain many bindings. To save space and time, the interpreter uses an interesting system to keep track of the current environment. Instead of continually making a new environment each time a frame is added or discarded, the interpreter keeps a table of **pointers** each of which specifies where a frame may be found in the computer's memory. In the next section, we consider an example of this use of pointers. We can, however, immediately illustrate the procedure by tracing the evaluation of the functional expression '(F $^\nabla$(like a fox))', where F is bound in the global environment to the FD

```
(derived (r) (cons s r) (((m lazy)) ((p hazy) (s crazy))))
```

Before beginning the evaluation, the interpreter's table of pointers contains a single entry, a pointer that indicates the location in the computer's memory of the global frame. The interpreter notices that the functional expression '(F $^\nabla$(like a fox))' is neither a black numeral nor an identifier nor a special form. It must therefore be a function application. The identifier F evaluates to its FD, and the special form '$^\nabla$(like a fox)' evaluates to the list '(like a fox)'. According to our description in Chapter 5, the computer now appends the global environment to the FD-environment, which in this case is the list '(((m lazy)) ((p hazy) (s crazy)))'. In fact, since this extension to the global environment contains two frames, the interpreter adds two more pointers to its table of pointers, the first being a pointer to the location of the frame '((p hazy) (s crazy))' and the second to the frame '((m lazy))'. (It stores the pointers in this order because when the time comes to look up the value of an identifier, it must read the table in reverse order, starting with the most recently-added frame.) Note that each of these new frames belongs to an FD-environment that is part of an FD which is bound to the identifier **F** in the global frame, so the corresponding pointers point to locations *within the global frame*. (This observation takes on more significance in the next section.)

The interpreter then creates a brand new frame containing a binding of the variable '*r*' to the list '(like a fox)', stores this frame in a free section of its memory, and adds a new pointer to its table indicating the location of the new frame.[1] The body of the function **F**—that is, the functional expression '(cons *s* *r*)'—is then evaluated in the environment determined by the current table of pointers. The identifiers '**cons**', '*s*' and '*r*' evaluate to the data expressions '(primitive cons)', 'crazy' and '(like a fox)', respectively, and thus the value of the original functional expression is found to be the list '(crazy like a fox)'. At this point the interpreter discards the three pointers that have been added during the course of its evaluation of the function application, leaving only the pointer to the global frame, and finally it prints the list '(crazy like a fox)' on the screen.

8.2 Some New Components

In Chapter 6 we explained that, by evaluating a lambda-expression in a current environment that contains more than just the global frame, we obtain a function descriptor whose FD-environment is non-null. We have already shown how to introduce new bindings into the global frame by means of define-expressions, and we now describe some other ways of 'augmenting' the current environment.

Suppose we wish to write a function that inputs whole numbers a and b and returns the whole number $(ab)^3 + (ab)^2 + (ab)$. The simple approach of translating this expression into Scheme symbol by symbol results in the definition shown on the right. While this is perfectly acceptable in the sense that we are sure

```
(define f
  (λ (a b)
    (+ (power (* a b) 3)
      (+ (square (* a b))
        (* a b)))))
```

---

[1] Notice that the order in which these frame pointers have been added to the interpreter's list of pointers corresponds exactly to the order implied by our 'storing/appending/consing' description under item 4 in The Scheme Interpreter's Evaluation Strategy on page 181.

the required value will always be returned, it does suffer from an apparent deficiency, namely, that the product '*ab*' is calculated three times. One method of avoiding this repetition is to use a lambda-expression to abstract the occurrence of the functional expression '(* *a b*)' as follows:

```
(define f
  (λ (a b)
    ((λ (x) (+ (power x 3) (+ (square x) x)))
     (* a b))))
```

The effect is that instead of calculating '$(ab)^3 + (ab)^2 + (ab)$' directly, we let $x = ab$ and then calculate '$x^3 + x^2 + x$'. As a result, the product '*ab*' is only calculated once.

Exercise 146.

  a) Use an internal lambda-expression to rewrite the following procedure for the function **g** of the whole numbers x and y so that the sum '$x + y$' is calculated just once:

```
(define g
  (λ (x y)
    (+ (* 2 (+ x y))
       (square (+ x y)))))
```

  b) Consider the function **h** of the whole numbers x and y, which is defined as follows:

```
(define h
  (λ (x y)
    (+ (+ (+ 1 x) (+ 2 y))
       (+ (square (+ 1 x))
          (+ (square (+ 2 y)) (+ 1 x))))))
```

  (i) Write an expression in terms of 'x' and 'y' that describes the output from the function **h**.

  (ii) Rewrite the function **h** so that the sums '$1+x$' and '$2+y$' are each calculated just once.

The technique just illustrated is so useful that Scheme provides a special form which simplifies the task of producing procedures with internal lambda-expressions. The new special form is called a **let-expression**. Here is an example:

$$(\text{let } ((a \ 1) \ (b \ {}^{\triangledown}\text{Fred}))$$
$$(\text{pair } a \ b))$$

Each let-expression has three sub-expressions. The first is the keyword 'let', and this is followed by a blackened, possibly null, list of pairs called the **let-frame**. Each pair in the let-frame consists of an identifier followed by a functional expression. In the example above, the let-frame is the blackened list '$((a \ 1) \ (b \ {}^{\triangledown}\text{Fred}))$'. The third sub-expression of a let-expression is a functional expression, known as the **let-body**. In our example, the let-body is the functional expression '$(\text{pair } a \ b)$'.

The Scheme interpreter evaluates let-expressions as follows:

> **let**   To evaluate a let-expression, form a lambda-expression whose lambda-parameter list is the blackened list which contains, in order, the first components from all the blackened pairs in the let-frame, and whose lambda-body is the let-body. Then apply the lambda-expression to the functional expressions that form the second components of the blackened pairs in the let-frame (taken in order of appearance).

Thus, to evaluate the functional expression in our example above, the interpreter forms a lambda-expression whose lambda-parameter list is '$(a \ b)$' and whose lambda-body is the functional expression '$(\text{pair } a \ b)$'. That is, it creates the lambda-expression

$$(\lambda \ (a \ b) \ (\text{pair } a \ b))$$

which it then applies to the functional expressions '**1**' and '${}^{\triangledown}\text{Fred}$', in that order:

$$((\lambda \ (a \ b) \ (\text{pair } a \ b)) \ 1 \ {}^{\triangledown}\text{Fred}) \mapsto (\texttt{1 Fred})$$

Hence, the let-expression in our example evaluates to the pair '$(\texttt{1 Fred})$'.

As a second example, consider the functional expression

$$(+ \ (\text{let } ((a \ 1)) \ (\text{add1 } a)) \ 4)$$

According to the foregoing description, this is transformed by the interpreter into the functional expression

$$(+ \ ((\lambda \ (a) \ (\text{add1 } a)) \ 1) \ 4)$$

which evaluates to the atom '6'.

If the let-frame is empty, then the interpreter transforms the let-expression into the invocation of a thunk; for example, the let-expression

$$\text{(let ( ) (* 2 4))}$$

is transformed into the application '$((\lambda \ () \ (* \ 2 \ 4)))$' which evaluates to the atom '8'.

Exercise 147.

For each of these functional expressions,

(i) write the functional expression into which the given functional expression is transformed by the Scheme interpreter, and hence

(ii) evaluate the functional expression.

a) (let ((a (+ 1 3)) (b 5))
    (* a b))

b) (let ((a 3) (b 2))
    (power a b))

c) (let ((a 1) (b 2))
    (λ ( ) (pair b a)))

d) (let ((d (λ (x) (gcd 12 x))))
    (d 20))

e) (+
    (let ((a 4) (b 5) (c (* 12 10)))
     (+ c (* a b)))
    (let ((i (fib 2)) (j (factorial 3)))
     j))

From a different point of view, we remark that let-expressions have the effect of temporarily adding a new frame (namely, the let-frame with the second component of each pair evaluated) to the current environment, evaluating the let-body in the resulting new environment, and then discarding the temporarily-added frame. This way of thinking about the behavior of let-expressions often makes it easier to see at a glance how they evaluate.

Exercise 148.

Evaluate these functional expressions:

a) (cons (let ((a $^\triangledown$confusing))
     a)
    (let ((a $^\triangledown$(variables)))
     a))

b) (let ((x 4))
    (let ((x (+ x 2)))
     (+ x (* x 2))))

Notice that our description of how let-expressions are evaluated implies that the function **f** with which we began this section may be defined as follows:

> (define f
>   (λ (*a b*)
>   (let ((*x* (* *a b*)))
>   (+ (power *x* 3) (+ (square *x*) *x*)))))

Compare this with the definition given on page 248 which involves an embedded lambda-expression.

Exercise 149.
   Use let-expressions to rewrite the definitions of the functions **g** and **h** defined in Exercise 146.

To illustrate the fact that let-expressions allow us to define functions whose FDs have non-null FD environments, let us evaluate the let-expression

> (let ((*a* 1))
>   (λ (*x*) (+ *x a*)))

in the global environment. First, the let-expression is transformed into the functional expression '((λ (*a*) (λ (*x*) (+ *x a*))) 1)'. Since this is a function application, we evaluate both of its sub-expressions. The lambda-expression '(λ (*a*) (λ (*x*) (+ *x a*)))' evaluates in the current environment (which contains only the global frame at this point) to the FD

```
(derived (a) (lambda (x) (+ x a)) ())
```

and, of course, 1 ↦ 1. Next, a record of the current environment is stored for later use. Then the global environment is appended to the FD-environment, and onto the result—which, since the FD-environment is null, is just the global environment—we cons a new frame in which the variable *a* is bound to the input, namely, the atom '1'. The result, that is, '(((a 1)) Φ)', is the new current environment.

Finally, the blackened FD-body, that is, the functional expression

$$(\lambda \ (x) \ (+ \ x \ a))$$

is evaluated in this new environment, and the result is the FD

```
(derived (x) (+ x a) (((a 1))))
```

We remark that this is the FD of a function that inputs a whole number x and returns $x + 1$. But, more importantly for the purposes of this illustration, it is an FD whose FD-environment is non-null. Notice that, in effect, the non-null FD-environment stores information that is 'local' to the function; unlike the information in the global environment, the contents of a non-null FD-environment are not available 'outside' the function.

Exercise 150.

Evaluate each of the following functional expressions:

a) (let ((x 5) (y 2))   b) (let ((x (add1 5)))
      (λ (d) (+ d (* x y)))))   (λ (a) (sub1 a)))

c) (let ((x 2))
      (let ((y 3))
        (λ (a) (* x (+ a y))))))

The following definition[2] gives the name 'j' to a function whose descriptor, thanks to the involvement of a let-expression, has a non-null FD-environment containing the L-frame '`((a Costello) (b Hardy))`':

(define j
  (let ((a $^\nabla$Costello) (b $^\nabla$Hardy))
    (λ (m)
      (cond
        [(eq? m $^\nabla$Abbott) a]
        [(eq? m $^\nabla$Laurel) b]))))

The let-expression in this definition evaluates to a one-input function that responds in a sensible and predictable fashion to the input of either of the atoms '`Abbott`' and '`Laurel`'. Given either of the two anticipated inputs the function evaluates as follows:

(j $^\nabla$Abbott) $\mapsto$ Costello
(j $^\nabla$Laurel) $\mapsto$ Hardy

---

[2]Observe that this definition includes a cond-expression that has no else-clause. Such expressions are permitted in Scheme, but the designers of the language do not specify what the result should be if none of the predicates evaluates to the boolean '`#t`'. Hence, different Scheme interpreters may react in different ways to such a situation. *EdScheme* produces an error message informing the schemer in so many words that no predicate clause evaluates to '`#t`'.

Functions whose FDs contain non-null FD-environments and which respond only to certain 'messages' (such as the atoms 'Abbott' and 'Laurel' in the exercise above) are sometimes called **objects**, since they can be made to behave like independent entities.[3] By way of illustration, let us make an object that (in an extremely restricted way) acts like a person. Our simple 'person-object' will know just two things: its name and its age. Moreover, it will respond to just two messages; when it receives the atom 'get-name' as an input it will return its name, and when given the atom 'get-age' it will return its age. For example, **PersonA** is a newborn baby named 'Des':

```
(define PersonA
  (let ((my-name ▽Des) (my-age 0))
    (λ (message)
      (cond
        [(eq? message ▽get-name) my-name]
        [(eq? message ▽get-age) my-age]))))
```

To find the name and age of **PersonA**, we send it the messages 'get-name' and 'get-age', respectively:

$$(\text{PersonA } {}^\triangledown\text{get-name}) \mapsto \text{Des} \qquad (\text{PersonA } {}^\triangledown\text{get-age}) \mapsto 0$$

Here is a second person-object:

```
(define PersonB
  (let ((my-name ▽Mona) (my-age 0))
    (λ (message)
      (cond
        [(eq? message ▽get-name) my-name]
        [(eq? message ▽get-age) my-age]))))
```

We could of course find **PersonB**'s name by evaluating the functional expression '**(PersonB** ▽get-name)', but a better strategy is to define a function that inputs a person-object and returns its name. Here is such a function:

---

[3] Programming with the help of objects, that is, 'object-oriented programming', is becoming increasingly important in present-day computer science. It provides a means to 'cobble together' a custom-made software package from previously-written 'plug-in software modules', thus avoiding having to write all the code from scratch. In addition, it gives programmers a framework for modeling aspects of the real world and organizing their thoughts as they develop solutions to real-world problems.

```
(define get–name
  (λ (person)
     (person ▽get–name)))
```

With the help of this function, we can find the name of **PersonB** by evaluating the functional expression '(get–name PersonB)':

```
(get–name PersonB)
(PersonB ▽get–name)
(PersonB get-name)
Mona
```

The function **get–name** is an example of a **syntax-switching function**, since its only purpose is to rearrange the syntax of a function application—here the application '(get–name *person*)' is switched to '(*person* ▽get–name)'. Syntax-switching functions often ease communication with objects.

Exercise 151.

Write a definition for the syntax-switching function **get–age** of a person that returns the person's age. Then evaluate the functional expression '(get–age PersonB)'.

In view of the great similarity between the definitions of **PersonA** and **PersonB**, we observe that we can automate the process of creating person-objects. The function **make–person** defined below, for example, inputs a name and returns a new person-object whose name is the given name and whose age is 0.[4]

```
(define make–person
  (λ (person–name)
     (let ((my–name person–name) (my–age 0))
        (λ (message)
           (cond
              [(eq? message ▽get–name) my–name]
              [(eq? message ▽get–age) my–age])))))
```

To show how this function works, let us evaluate the functional expression

(make–person ▽Frankenstein)

---

[4] We could have arranged for the function to input the person's age as well, but instead we have opted for initializing the variable '*my–age*' to zero. After all, apart from Athena, most people are 0 years old when they come into the world!

Since this expression is an application, we evaluate each of its two sub-
expressions. The first sub-expression evaluates to the FD of the derived function **make–person** and the second sub-expression to the atom 'Frankenstein'.
Next, we append the global environment to the FD-environment and onto
the result—which, since the FD-environment is null, is the same as the global
environment—we cons a frame containing a binding of the identifier *'person–
name'* to the input, the atom 'Frankenstein'. As a result, the current environment is now '(((person-name Frankenstein)) Φ)'. We then blacken
the FD-body of the function **make–person** to obtain the functional expression

$$\text{(let } ((my\text{–}name\ person\text{–}name)\ (my\text{–}age\ 0))$$
$$(\lambda\ (message)$$
$$(\text{cond}$$
$$[(\text{eq? } message\ ^\triangledown\text{get–name})\ my\text{–}name\ ]$$
$$[(\text{eq? } message\ ^\triangledown\text{get–age})\ my\text{–}age\ ])))$$

and evaluate this in the new environment. The let-expression has the effect of
adding the frame '((my-name Frankenstein) (my-age 0))' to the current
environment, which therefore becomes

```
(((my-name Frankenstein) (my-age 0))
 ((person-name Frankenstein)) Φ)
```

Finally, we evaluate the lambda-expression in this environment, thereby producing the following FD:

```
(derived
 (message)
 (cond [(eq? message (quote get-name)) my-name]
       [(eq? message (quote get-age)) my-age])
 (((my-name Frankenstein) (my-age 0))
  ((person-name Frankenstein))))
```

So this is the value of the functional expression '(make–person ᐁFrankenstein)'.
Identifiers that are bound in FD-environments are known as **local state
variables**. Thus the variables *'my–age'*, *'my–name'*, and *'person–name'*,
for example, are local state variables for the function

(make–person ᐁFrankenstein)

As you will have noticed, 'Frankenstein' is bound *twice* in the FD-environment of the above function descriptor, and we would agree with you that

this is a little excessive. To avoid such gratuitous bondage, we simplify the definition for **make–person** as follows:

```
(define make–person
  (λ (my–name)
    (let ((my–age 0))
      (λ (message)
        (cond
          [(eq? message ▽get–name) my–name]
          [(eq? message ▽get–age) my–age])))))
```

Exercise 152.

Let us add a third person-object to our growing population by evaluating the functional expression

```
(define PersonC (make–person ▽(Mona Lisa)))
```

Evaluate

a) **(get–name PersonC)**   b) **(get–age PersonC)**

Exercise 153.

a) Write a definition for the function **make–personality** of two inputs, a name and a nationality, that returns an object with three local state variables, namely, '*my–name*', '*my–nation*' and '*my–age*', the last of these being bound initially to the atom '0'. The object produced should respond in the same way as a person-object to the messages 'get-name' and 'get-age', and should return its nationality when sent the message 'get-nation'.

b) Write a definition for the syntax-switching function **get–nation** of this new type of object that returns its nationality.

Unfortunately, our person-objects never age because they have no way to change the binding for the variable '*my–age*' once it has been set by the function **make–person**. The time has come, therefore, for us to introduce a new special form, called 'a set-expression', that allows such a change to be made. A **set-expression** looks just like an assignment, the only difference being that the keyword '**define**' is replaced by the keyword '**set!**'.[5] The keyword is

---

[5]It is the convention among schemers to pronounce the black symbol '!' as 'bang'. Thus 'set!' is read 'set-bang'.

followed by two sub-expressions, the first being an identifier and the second being any functional expression, and the whole expression is enclosed in a pair of black parentheses. Like define-expressions, set-expressions are only evaluated for their side-effects, never for their value. They *do* have a value, but the designers of the Scheme language do not specify what it should be. This vagueness about the value of a set-expression can lead to problems when they are used within definitions. There is, however, an easy way to overcome this difficulty, as we explain in a little while. For the moment, though, we concentrate only on the side-effects of set-expressions.

The side-effect of a set-expression is to change the binding for the identifier in the current environment so that it is bound to the value of the functional expression. For example, suppose the current environment is

$$\text{(((a plus) (b proud)) ((a minus) (c me)) } \Phi\text{)}$$

Evaluating the set-expression '(set! *a* ▽winner)' changes the binding for *a* so that the current environment becomes

$$\text{(((a winner) (b proud)) ((a minus) (c me)) } \Phi\text{)}$$

(Note that only the first binding for '*a*' is changed.) If we now evaluate the set-expression '(set! *c* ▽urchin)' the current environment becomes

$$\text{(((a winner) (b proud)) ((a minus) (c urchin)) } \Phi\text{)}$$

There are three very important points to note regarding the side-effect of a set-expression:

1. Set-expressions may only be used to change bindings that already exist. Unlike define-expressions, they may not be used to create new bindings; indeed, the Scheme interpreter will complain if the identifier in a set-expression is not already bound in the current environment.

2. Unlike the define-expressions we have met so far in this book, set-expressions can be used to change bindings in frames other than the global frame.

3. Set-expressions can be used to make *permanent* changes to bindings in FD-environments. Recall that during the evaluation of an application, the current environment is temporarily extended to include the FD-environment of the function being applied; this is achieved by adding

new pointers—one for each frame of the FD-environment—to the interpreter's table of pointers. Evaluating a set-expression changes a binding
in one of the frames in the current environment. If this frame happens
to be part of the FD-environment of an FD that is currently bound to
an identifier in the global environment, then the new binding remains
in force even after the evaluation is complete and the added pointers
have been discarded.

As an illustration of this last point, consider the function **m**, defined as
follows:

$$\text{(define m}$$
$$\text{(let }((a\ 1))$$
$$(\lambda\ (d)\ \text{(set! }a\ d))))$$

Evaluating this definition causes the identifier '**m**' to be bound to the FD

```
(derived (d) (set! a d) (((a 1))))
```

in the global frame. Suppose we now evaluate the functional expression
'**(m 2)**', keeping a close eye on how the interpreter behaves as it manipu-
lates its environments. At the outset, the interpreter has just one pointer in
its table of pointers indicating the physical location in the computer's memory of the global frame. Let us denote this pointer by 'P_1' and depict the
global frame as follows (the global frame contains a large number of bindings,
so we only display the binding for the identifier in which we are interested,
that is, '**m**'):

```
( ... (m (derived (d) (set! a d) (((a 1))))) ... )
  ↑P₁
```

Since the functional expression '**(m 2)**' is clearly a function application, the
Scheme interpreter adds to its table a pointer to the location of each frame in
the FD-environment (in this case there is only one such frame). We denote
this pointer by 'P_2'; it points to the memory location of the frame '**((a 1))**'
in the binding for '**m**' in the global frame:

```
( ... (m (derived (d) (set! a d) (((a 1))))) ... )
  ↑P₁                                  ↑P₂
```

Next, the interpreter creates a new frame containing bindings of the parameters listed in the FD-parameter list (in this case there is only one, namely, 'd')

to the inputs to the function **m** (in this case there is only one input, namely, the atom '2') and adds a new pointer (P_3, say) to its table, indicating the beginning of this new frame:

```
( ... (m (derived (d) (set! a d) (((a 1)))))  ... )        ((d 2))
↑P₁                                        ↑P₂              ↑P₃
```

Then the interpreter evaluates the functional expression '(**set!** *a d*)' in the environment consisting of the frames indicated by P_3, P_2, and P_1, in that order. The set-expression has the side-effect of changing the binding for '*a*' in this environment so that '*a*' ends up bound to the atom '2':

```
( ... (m (derived (d) (set! a d) (((a 2)))))  ... )        ((d 2))
↑P₁                                        ↑P₂              ↑P₃
```

The interpreter then completes the evaluation by discarding pointers P_2 and P_3 and returning the value of the set-expression—whatever that might be. At this stage, the only pointer remaining signals the beginning of the global frame:

```
(... (m (derived (d) (set! a d) (((a 2))))) ...)
↑P₁
```

Notice that the evaluation of the set-expression has had the side-effect of permanently changing the binding for the variable '*a*' in the FD-environment. In fact, the old value of '*a*'—that is, the atom '1'—has been *overwritten*; it is lost forever. The FD-environment in which the variable '*a*' is bound lies within an FD which is itself assigned in the global frame to the identifier '**m**', so the binding for '**m**' in the global frame has been changed! In fact, the identifier '**m**' is now bound in the global frame to the FD

```
(derived (d) (set! a d) (((a 2))))
```

With the help of set-expressions, objects may be provided with a means of changing the values of their local state variables. Suppose, for example, that we modify our definition for the function **make–person** by adding a third clause to the cond-expression:

```
(define make–person
  (λ (my–name)
    (let ((my–age 0))
      (λ (message)
        (cond
          [(eq? message ▽get–name) my–name]
          [(eq? message ▽get–age) my–age]
          [(eq? message ▽birthday) (set! my–age (add1 my–age))])))))))
```

Suppose also that we define **PersonD** to be an object of this new type:

(define PersonD (make–person ▽Leonardo))

By then immediately evaluating the identifier '**PersonD**', we obtain the FD

```
(derived
 (message)
 (cond [(eq? message (quote get-name)) my-name]
       [(eq? message (quote get-age)) my-age]
       [(eq? message (quote birthday))
        (set! my-age (add1 my-age))])
 (((my-age 0)) ((my-name Leonardo))))
```

Next, we define the syntax-switching function **birthday** as follows:

```
(define birthday
  (λ (person)
    (person ▽birthday)))
```

Then the functional expression '**(birthday PersonD)**' evaluates as follows:

```
(birthday PersonD)
(PersonD ▽birthday)
(PersonD birthday)
(set! my–age (add1 0))
(set! my–age 1)
```

As it evaluates the expression '**(set! *my–age* 1)**', the Scheme interpreter changes the binding of '*my–age*' in the FD-environment of **PersonD**'s FD. The old value of '*my–age*' (that is, the atom '0') is overwritten by the new value, '1'. Indeed, it is just as though the function **PersonD** had originally been defined with '*my–age*' bound to the atom '1', for if we now evaluate the identifier '**PersonD**' we obtain the FD

```
(derived
 (message)
 (cond [(eq? message (quote get-name)) my-name]
       [(eq? message (quote get-age)) my-age]
       [(eq? message (quote birthday))
        (set! my-age (add1 my-age))]])
 (((my-age 1)) ((my-name Leonardo))))
```

Furthermore, the functional expression '(get–age PersonD)' now evaluates to the atom '1' rather than '0', as previously. Unlike its predecessors, **PersonD** does not have eternal youth!

Exercise 154.

Let the function **A** be defined as follows:

> (define A
>   (let ((*count* 0))
>   (λ ()
>   (set! *count* (add1 *count*)))))

a) Write the FD to which '**A**' is bound in the global frame directly after the above definition is evaluated.

b) Suppose that the functional expression '(**A**)' is evaluated. Write the FD to which '**A**' is now bound.

c) Give a general description of the changes that occur in the FD of the function **A** each time the function is invoked.

We now return to the problems we mentioned earlier that arise from the fact that the value of a set-expression is not specified by the language's designers. From our point of view, this is an unsatisfactory situation since we like to be able to predict the output from each function that we define. To extricate ourselves from this difficulty we introduce a new special form called 'a **begin-expression**'. Each begin-expression consists of a black left parenthesis, then the keyword '**begin**' followed by one or more functional expressions, and finally a black right parenthesis. The Scheme interpreter evaluates a begin-expression by evaluating each of its functional expressions one by one in order of appearance, and returning the value of the last functional expression. Consider, for example, the begin-expression

> (begin (cons ▽waste ▽(of effort)) (first ▽(BOO)))

As the interpreter evaluates this functional expression, it first evaluates

$$\text{(cons }^\triangledown\text{waste }^\triangledown\text{(of effort))}$$

and obtains the list '(waste of effort)'. This list is then discarded and the interpreter goes on to evaluate '(first $^\triangledown$(BOO))'. Since this is the final functional expression in the begin-expression, the interpreter returns the atom 'BOO'. Such behavior may seem remarkably wasteful—even stupid!—until one realizes that it is perfectly possible for the functional expressions whose values are discarded to have side-effects. So by listing the functional expressions in a begin-expression in a sensible order we can arrange matters so that the lasting side-effects we desire are achieved *and* a predictable output is returned. For example, if the variable '*my–age*' is bound to a number in the current environment, then the functional expression

$$\text{(begin (set! } my\text{–}age \text{ (add1 } my\text{–}age\text{)) } my\text{–}age\text{)}$$

evaluates as follows. First, the Scheme interpreter evaluates the functional expression '(set! *my–age* (add1 *my–age*))' with the side-effect that the binding for '*my–age*' is changed. In fact, the replacement for '*my–age*' will be increased by 1. The value of this set-expression—whatever it may be—is then discarded, and the interpreter evaluates the functional expression '*my–age*' with the result that the begin-expression returns the new value of the variable '*my–age*'.

For the record, let us summarize the manner in which the Scheme interpreter evaluates set-expressions and begin-expressions:

> **set!**   To evaluate a set-expression, change the binding for the identifier (the first sub-expression following the keyword '**set!**') in the current environment so that it is bound to the value of the functional expression (the second sub-expression following the keyword).
>
> **begin**   To evaluate a begin-expression, evaluate the sub-expressions that follow the keyword '**begin**' one by one in the order in which they are listed, and return the value of the last sub-expression.

By modifying the final clause of our definition of the function **make–person** so that it involves a suitably chosen begin-expression, we can arrange things so that the function **birthday** of a person-object returns the new age of the person-object. Here is the modified definition:

```
(define make–person
  (λ (my–name)
    (let ((my–age 0))
      (λ (message)
        (cond
          [(eq? message ▽get–name) my–name]
          [(eq? message ▽get–age) my–age]
          [(eq? message ▽birthday)
           (begin
             (set! my–age (add1 my–age)) my–age)])))))
```

Let us define 'PersonE' to be a person-object of this new type:

(define PersonE (make–person ▽Amy))

The following conversation shows PersonE in action:

```
⟹ (get–name PersonE)
Amy
⟹ (get–age PersonE)
0
⟹ (birthday PersonE)
1
⟹ (birthday PersonE)
2
⟹ (get–age PersonE)
2
⟹ _
```

Exercise 155.

Write a definition for the function **make–vain–person** of an data expression (the person's name) which returns a person-object having the local state variables '*my–name*' and '*my–age*', that responds to the messages 'get-name' and 'get-age' in the usual way, and that responds to the message 'birthday' as follows: If the value of '*my–age*' is currently less than 21 then the number bound to '*my–age*' is incremented by 1, otherwise it is left unchanged; in either case the new value of '*my–age*' is returned.

Suppose now that **PersonE** decides to change its name from 'Amy' to 'Zoe'. Is it possible to modify our definition for **make–person** so that the value of the local state variable '*my–name*' can be changed to a new name? The answer is 'Yes', but the solution is not straightforward. Ideally, we would like to send to the new type of person-object some suitable message, such as 'set-name', together with a new name. Unfortunately, the function returned by **make–person** is a one-input function; it cannot accept two inputs, a message *and* a new name. This suggests that perhaps we should change the definition of **make–person** so that, if the input is a list, then it dissects the list to retrieve all the information it needs. We could then input the name-changing information in the form—in the case of our example—of the pair '(set-name Zoe)'.

There is, however, an easier way to solve this problem. We arrange things so that, when the person-object receives the message 'set-name', it returns a function that inputs the new name and changes the binding of the local state variable '*my–name*' so that its value is the new name. Here is a suitable modification of our definition for the function **make–person**:

```
(define make–person
  (λ (my–name)
    (let ((my–age 0))
      (λ (message)
        (cond
          [(eq? message ▽get–name) my–name]
          [(eq? message ▽get–age) my–age]
          [(eq? message ▽birthday)
           (begin (set! my–age (add1 my–age)) my–age)]
          [(eq? message ▽set–name)
           (λ (new–name)
             (begin (set! my–name new–name) my–name))])))))
```

We then define the syntax-switching function **set–name** as follows:

```
(define set–name
  (λ (person name)
    ((person ▽set–name) name)))
```

(Notice that, because of the way we have caused person-objects to react to the message 'set-name', in this definition '(*person* ▽set–name)' evaluates to a one-input function which is then applied to the current value of the variable '*name*'.)

Exercise 156.

Let the person-object **PersonF** be defined as follows, using the new definition for the function **make–person**:

(define PersonF (make–person ▽(Samuel Clemens)))

a) Evaluate the functional expression

(set–name PersonF ▽(Mark Twain))

b) After the application in part (a) has been evaluated, what is the value of the functional expression '(get–name PersonF)'?

PROBLEM SET 13

1. a) In computing, a **stack** is an object in which data expressions are stored and retrieved in such a way that the first data expression to be stored is always the last data expression to be retrieved. Thus, in general, data expressions are retrieved from a stack in the reverse of the order in which they were stored. It is an example of a so-called 'First-In-Last-Out' (or FILO) object. The following function makes stacks:

```
(define make–stack
  (λ ()
    (let ((st ▽()))
      (λ (message)
        (cond
          [(eq? message ▽push)
           (λ (a)
             (begin (set! st (cons a st)) ▽done))]
          [(eq? message ▽pop)
           (let ((item–removed (first st)))
             (begin (set! st (rest st)) item–removed))])))))
```

The appropriate syntax-switching functions for stacks are the functions **push** and **pop**, defined as follows:

```
(define push                    (define pop
  (λ (stack s)                    (λ (stack)
    ((stack ▽push) s)))             (stack ▽pop)))
```

Complete the following conversation by providing the missing data expressions:

```
⟹ (define S (make-stack))
S
⟹ (push S 'bedrock)
_____

⟹ (push S 'clay)
_____

⟹ (pop S)
_____

⟹ (push S 'limestone)
_____

⟹ (pop S)
_____

⟹ (pop S)
_____

⟹ _
```

b) A **queue** is similar to a stack in that it is an object used to store data expressions. In the case of a queue, however, the first data expression to be stored is always the first to be retrieved and, in general, the data expressions are retrieved in the order in which they are stored. Queues are examples of 'First-In-First-Out' (or FIFO) objects. The function **make-queue** makes a queue, and the syntax-switching functions **add-to-queue** and **fetch-from-queue** are used when storing and retrieving data expressions in the queue. The conversation in Figure 8.1 on page 267 demonstrates how a queue operates. Write definitions for the functions **make-queue**, **add-to-queue** and **fetch-from-queue**.

2. a) The definition in Figure 8.2 on page 267 makes objects that are intended to behave like bank accounts. The associated syntax-switching functions are **withdraw** and **deposit**, defined as follows:

$$
\begin{aligned}
&\textbf{(define withdraw} \\
&\quad (\lambda\ (account\ amount) \\
&\qquad ((account\ {}^{\triangledown}\textbf{withdrawal})\ amount)))
\end{aligned}
$$

```
⟹ (define Q (make–queue))
Q
⟹ (add–to–queue Q '(early bird))
done
⟹ (add–to–queue Q '(on time))
done
⟹ (fetch–from–queue Q)
(early bird)
⟹ (add–to–queue Q '(late arrival))
done
⟹ (fetch–from–queue Q)
(on time)
⟹ (fetch–from–queue Q)
(late arrival)
⟹ _
```

Figure 8.1: *See Problem 1(b).*

```
(define make–account
  (λ ()
    (let ((balance 0))
      (λ (message)
        (cond
          [(eq? message ▽deposit)
           (λ (amount)
             (begin
               (set! balance (+ balance amount))
               balance))]
          [(eq? message ▽withdrawal)
           (λ (amount)
             (cond
               [(less? balance amount) ▽insufficient–funds ]
               [else (begin
                       (set! balance (– balance amount))
                       balance)]))])))))
```

Figure 8.2: *See Problem 2(a).*

```
(define deposit
  (λ (account amount)
    ((account ᐁdeposit) amount)))
```

Complete the following conversation:

```
⟹ (define A (make–account))
A
⟹ (deposit A 100)
_____

⟹ (withdraw A 75)
_____

⟹ (withdraw A 50)
_____

⟹ (deposit A 250)
_____

⟹ _
```

b) Rewrite the definitions for the functions **make–account**, **withdraw** and **deposit** so that accounts may only be accessed through the use of a password. For example, if the password for account **A** is 'sa14tv', then the functional expression '(**withdraw A 75** ᐁsa14tv)' subtracts 75 from the current balance (provided of course that the balance is sufficiently large) and returns the new balance (or the dreaded message 'insufficient-funds'), whereas the functional expression '(**withdraw A 75** ᐁabcdef)' evaluates to the atom 'access-denied' and leaves the balance unchanged. An account's password should be defined when the account is created; that is, the function **make–account** should be a one-input function that inputs a password and returns an account.

$$- \circ O \circ -$$

8.3 The Rules Of The Game

Our purpose in the remainder of this chapter is to design and produce a major Scheme program which will enable the computer to play a simple game of strategy. The program will be flexible enough that we can arrange for the computer to play the game against a schemer, for it to be the arbiter in a game played between two schemers, or even for it to play the game against itself. The most interesting feature of the program, however, is that it will be written in such a way that the more games the computer plays, the better it becomes at winning. By thus producing a program that is capable of learning from its mistakes, we will have ventured into the exciting, up-to-the-minute field of artificial intelligence.

In this section we begin simply by describing the game itself. In subsequent sections we develop some useful utility functions and then, finally, we put together the overall game-playing program.

The game is inspired by the Milton-Bradley game **Connect Four**™ and it is played on a 4-by-4 grid whose columns are labeled as follows:

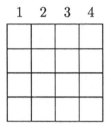

There are two players, Player 1 and Player 2, who use the characters 'o' and 'x', respectively. Each player attempts to be the first to achieve three of his or her characters side by side in a single row (either horizontal, vertical, or diagonal) by making moves in accordance with the following rules.

A player moves by choosing a column in which at least one box is still empty and marking his or her character in the lowest empty box of that column.[6] Player 1 goes first. Suppose, for example, that Player 1 begins by playing in column 2, thus creating the game position shown on the left below:

---

[6]This insistence upon the lowest available box distinguishes the game from tic-tac-toe, and corresponds to the effect of gravity on the game pieces in the commercially available game.

If Player 2 now also selects column 2, then the game position is transformed into the one shown on the right above.

As is implied in the above description, no player may place a character in a box that already contains a character. This means that, once all the boxes in a column contain characters, that column may no longer be selected; it is said to be 'full'. Play alternates between Player 1 and Player 2 until one of two situations arises:

1. A player places his or her character in such a way that three of the same characters form an unbroken line, either horizontal, vertical, or diagonal. The player who makes such a move wins the game. Each of these game positions, for example, is a winning position for Player 1 (whose character is 'o'):

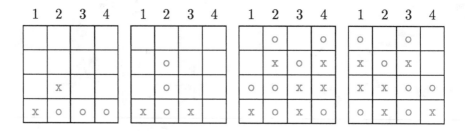

2. All the columns are full (there are no empty boxes) and neither player has a winning position. The game is a tie.

Before attempting the next exercise, use pencil and paper to play the game a few times with a friend, trying as you do so to figure out some of the strategy involved.

Exercise 157.

It is Player 2's turn to play. In each of these game positions, if the right move is made, Player 2 will win. In each case, where should Player 2 mark an 'x'?

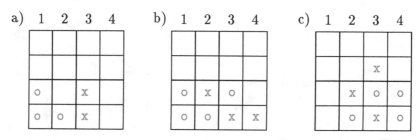

d)

1	2	3	4
		o	
x		x	
o	x	o	o

e)

1	2	3	4
	x	x	
	o	o	
	o	x	o
x	x	o	o

f)

1	2	3	4
o			
x			x
o	x		o
o	o		x

8.4 Game Positions

In order for the computer to become involved in playing the game we have just described, we must introduce a way to represent game positions using data expressions. There are several possibilities, but we choose the following. We represent each column in a game position by a list containing four atoms that indicate the contents of the column's four boxes in order from bottom to top and using the character '-' to indicate an empty box. Thus the list '(x x o -)' represents a column in which each of the bottom two boxes contains an 'x', the third box up contains an 'o', and the top box is empty. A representation of a game position consists of a list of the four data expressions that represent the contents of the game grid's four columns in order from left to right. Thus the game position shown on the right is represented by the list

1	2	3	4
o			
x			x
o	x		o
o	o		x

$$((o\ o\ x\ o)\ (o\ x\ -\ -)\ (-\ -\ -\ -)\ (x\ o\ x\ -))$$

Exercise 158.

   a) Write the list that represents this game position:

1	2	3	4
	x	x	
	o	o	
	o	x	o
x	x	o	o

b) Sketch the game position represented by the list

$$((o \ o \ x \ -) \ (o \ x \ x \ -) \ (x \ o \ o \ -) \ (o \ x \ x \ -))$$

From here on, we intend to 'lighten up' our language and speak as though functions manipulate game positions, whereas in reality, of course, they input and output *representations* of game positions. In addition, we shall refer to 'o' and 'x' collectively as 'game characters'.

Exercise 159.

a) Using the function **duplicate**, or otherwise, write a definition for the thunk **make–grid** that returns the representation of the initial game position in which no characters have yet been placed.

b) Write a definition for the predicate function **column–full?** of a game position *game–pos* and a whole number *n* from 1 through 4 that returns the boolean '#t' if and only if column *n* contains no empty boxes.

c) Write a definition for the function **tie?** of a game position *game–pos* that returns the boolean '#t' if and only if all the columns in the game position are full.

d) Write a definition for the function **play** of a game position *game–pos*, a whole number *n* from 1 through 4 (such that column *n* of the game position is not already full), and a game character *char* that returns the new game position that results when game character *char* is placed in column *n* of the game position *game–pos*.

Our chosen representation of game positions makes it possible for the computer to manipulate such representations in ways that correspond to making a move, checking for a winning line, and so on. Indeed, in a little while we write functions that perform some of these tasks. Unfortunately, our representations of game positions do not look very much like the 4-by-4 grid on which the game is played. We therefore now take time to write a definition for the function **display–game** of a game position that displays that position on the computer monitor in grid-like form.

The function **display–game** will only ever be evaluated for its side-effect, which is to print a 'picture' of a given game position on the monitor. In fact, it will achieve this effect by calling on the primitive Scheme function **display**.

The value of this function, which takes one input, is unspecified but its side-effect is to display the input data expression on the monitor. As a matter of style and to ensure that a functional expression involving the function **display** returns a predictable value, we always embed the function within a begin-expression.

The following conversation illustrates how the function **display** behaves:

```
⟹ (define f
      (lambda (a)
        (begin (display (cons a '())) 'done)))
f
⟹ (f 'well)
(well)done
⟹ (begin (display '(sol)) (display (null? '(M T))) (cons 'ah '()))
(sol)#f(ah)
⟹ _
```

Notice that the computer does *not* go to the beginning of a new line on the monitor after printing the data expression that is input to the function **display**. To achieve this result we require yet another primitive function, namely, the thunk **newline**. When it is evaluated, the functional expression '(newline)' causes the cursor on the monitor to move to the beginning of a fresh line. Here is a conversation showing how the functions **display** and **newline** interact:

```
⟹ (define f
      (lambda (a)
        (begin (display (cons a '())) (newline) 'done)))
f
⟹ (f 'well)
(well)
done
⟹ (begin
      (display '(sol)) (newline)
      (display (null? '(M T))) (newline)
      (cons 'ah '()))
(sol)
#f
(ah)
⟹ _
```

Exercise 160.

Write a definition for the function **display–list** of a list that prints each data expression in the list on a new line and returns the atom 'done'. The function should behave as illustrated by the following conversation:

```
⟹ (display–list '(nice Lee))
nice
Lee
done
⟹ (display–list '((think about it) ()))
(think about it)
()
done
⟹ (display–list '())
done
⟹ _
```

Exercise 161.

Recall from Problem 9 of Problem Set 11 that the functions **get-firsts** (which accepts any list of non-null lists and returns the list of the first data expressions of the input's internal lists, in order) and **cutfirsts** (which accepts any list of non-null lists and returns the input list with the first data expression removed from each of the internal lists) may be defined in terms of the curried function **transform** as follows:

$$\text{(define getfirsts (transform first))}$$

$$\text{(define cutfirsts (transform rest))}$$

a) Use the functions **getfirsts** and **cutfirsts** to write a definition for the function **transpose** which inputs a list containing nothing but non-null lists such that all the internal lists have the same number of data expressions and returns a list of lists formed as follows: The first internal list of the output is the list of the first data expressions (in order of appearance) of the lists in the input; the second internal list of the output is the list of the second data expressions (in order of appearance) of the lists in the input; and so on. For example,

(transpose $^\triangledown$((1 2 3) (1 3 2) (2 1 3) (2 3 1) (3 1 2) (3 2 1)))
$\longmapsto$ ((1 1 2 2 3 3) (2 3 1 3 1 2) (3 2 3 1 2 1))

b) Use the functions **transpose** and **reverse** (see Problem Set 4, Problem 8(d)) to write a definition for the function **transform–game** of a game position that outputs a list built up as follows:

- Its first data expression is the list '(1 2 3 4)'.

- Its second data expression is a list containing four atoms that indicate the contents of the four boxes in the top row of the game position in order from left to right, using the character '–' to indicate an empty box.

- Similarly, the third, fourth, and fifth data expressions are lists indicating the contents, respectively, of the next-to-top, next-to-bottom, and bottom rows of the game position.

Consider, for example, this game position:

	1	2	3	4
	o			
	x			x
	o	x		o
	o	o		x

which is represented by the list

((o o x o) (o x – –) (– – – –) (x o x –))

When this list is input to the function **transform–game**, the output should be the list

((1 2 3 4) (o – – –) (x – – x) (o x – o) (o o – x))

c) Write a definition for the function **display–game** of a game position that displays that position in a grid-like form, and returns the atom 'done'.

For the remainder of this section, we devote our attention to designing a definition for the predicate function **winner?** of a game position *game–pos* and a game character *char* that returns the boolean '#t' if and only if the game position is a winning position for the player whose character is *char*, and to a small number of useful functions that call upon the function **winner?**.

Recall that winning lines come in four varieties: horizontal, vertical, rising diagonally to the right, and sinking diagonally to the right. (For these last two possibilities, see Figure 8.3 below.) It is therefore natural to define the

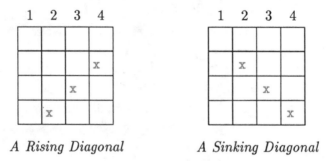

A Rising Diagonal   A Sinking Diagonal

Figure 8.3: Winning Diagonals.

function **winner?** in such a way that each of these possibilities is considered in turn:

```
(define winner?
  (λ (game-pos char)
    (cond
      [(win-column? game-pos char) #t]
      [(win-row? game-pos char) #t]
      [else (or (win-riser? game-pos char)
                (win-sinker? game-pos char))]])))
```

Of course, this definition presupposes that the functions **win-column?**, **win-row?**, **win-riser?**, and **win-sinker?** have already been defined. By answering the next few exercises you will see to it that this supposition is well-founded.

Exercise 162.

> a) Complete the following skeleton definition for the predicate function **win-in-this-column?** of a representation of a column *col*—whose contents, you will recall, are listed in order from bottom to top—a game character *char*, and a counter n, initially zero, that returns the boolean '#t' if and only if the column contains a winning line for the player using game character *char*:

```
(define win-in-this-column?
  (λ (col char n)
    (cond
      [(= n 3) _____ ]
      [(null? col) _____ ]
      [(eq? ( _____ col) char)
       (win-in-this-column?
         ( _____ col) char ( _____ n))]
      [else (win-in-this-column? ( _____ col) char 0)])))
```

b) Write a definition for the predicate function **win-column?** of a
   game position *game-pos* and a game character *char* that
   returns the boolean '#t' if and only if the game position
   contains a winning vertical line for the player whose game
   character is *char*.

c) Use the function **win-column?** to write a definition for the
   function **win-row?** of a game position *game-pos* and a game
   character *char* that returns the boolean '#t' if and only if
   the game position contains a winning horizontal line for the
   player whose game character is *char*.
   [Hint: Use the function **transpose** defined in Exercise 161(a).]

It may have come as a pleasant surprise to you that the problem of discovering whether a game position contains a winning horizontal line can be
reduced to that of looking for a winning vertical line. As it happens, we can
similarly reduce the search for diagonal lines to a task we already know how
to perform. What is more, there is a very simple transformation of the game
position that makes such a reduction possible. We deal first with the identification of *rising* diagonal lines of game characters. Each of the game positions
shown in Figure 8.4 at the top of the next page contains a winning rising
diagonal for the player whose character is 'x'. In both cases, the winning
diagonal line will be turned into a winning row by the following transformation: Move column 1 of each game position *up* by one square, leave column 2
unchanged, move column 3 *down* by one square, and move column 4 *down*
by two squares. The transformed grids are shown in Figure 8.5. Note that in
each case the 'x's are now in a horizontal line. We must therefore find anal-
ogous transformations of the representations of these game positions which
will produce data expressions that can be tested for the presence of winning
lines using the function **win-row?**.

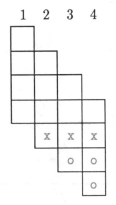

Figure 8.4: Rising diagonals (before grid transformation).

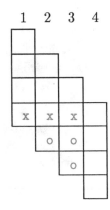

Figure 8.5: Rising diagonals (after grid transformation).

Exercise 163.

a) Let the function **adjust–column** of a representation of a column
col and a whole number *n* from 0 through 3 be defined as
follows:

```
(define adjust–column
  (λ (col n)
    (cond
      [(zero? n) (cons ▽– (butlast col))]
      [(one? n) col]
      [else (adjust–column (cons–to–end ▽– (rest col))
                           (sub1 n))])))
```

Evaluate

(i) (adjust–column $^\triangledown$(o o x –) 0)

(ii) (adjust–column $^\triangledown$(o o x –) 1)

(iii) (adjust–column $^\triangledown$(o o x –) 2)

(iv) (adjust–column $^\triangledown$(o o x –) 3)

b) Complete the following skeleton definition for the function **adjust–game** of a game position *game–pos* that transforms the game position according to the algorithm described in the text preceding this exercise:[7]

```
(define adjust–game
  (λ (game–pos)
    (adjust–game–aux game–pos _____ )))
```

```
(define adjust–game–aux
  (λ (game–pos n)
    (cond
      [(null? game–pos) _____ ]
      [else ( _____ (adjust–column (first game–pos) n)
                      (adjust–game–aux (rest game–pos)
                                       ( _____ n)))])))
```

c) Write a definition for the predicate function **win–riser?** of a game position *game–pos* and a game character *char* that returns the boolean '#t' if and only if the game position contains a winning rising diagonal for the player whose game character is *char*.

To plug the last remaining gap in our definition of the function **winner?** we must write a definition for a function that identifies winning sinking diagonal lines. But this is simplicity itself! There is an extremely easy way to transform a game position that contains a winning sinking diagonal into one containing a winning *rising* diagonal, namely, to look at the game position in a mirror. Such a 'reflected image' may be achieved using the function **reverse**, which you defined in Problem 8(d) of Problem Set 4.

---

[7]In fact, it also performs operations corresponding to discarding the topmost box and the lowest three boxes of the transformed grid and inserting empty boxes in the upper right and lower left corners of what remains, thereby turning the result of the transformation into a 4-by-4 grid. Such actions are acceptable since the contents of the discarded boxes cannot possibly form part of a winning horizontal line in the transformed grid. (Why not?)

Exercise 164.

Use the function **win–riser?** to write a definition for the predicate function **win–sinker?** of a game position *game–pos* and a game character *char* that returns the boolean '#t' if and only if the game position contains a winning sinking diagonal for the player whose game character is *char*.

PROBLEM SET 14

1. Evaluate each of the following functional expressions:

   a) (winner? $^\triangledown$((o x – –) (x x – –) (o x o –) (o – – –)) $^\triangledown$x)

   b) (winner? $^\triangledown$((x – – –) (o x x o) (x o x o) (o o – –)) $^\triangledown$o)

   c) (winner? $^\triangledown$((x o o o) (o x – –) (– – – –) (x o x –)) $^\triangledown$o)

   d) (winner? $^\triangledown$((x o o x) (o o x o) (x x o x) (o o x x)) $^\triangledown$x)

2. Let the predicate function **winning–move?** of a game position *game–pos*, a game character *char*, and a whole number n from 1 through 4 such that column n is not already full be defined as follows:

   > (define winning–move?
   >   (λ (*game–pos char n*)
   >   (winner? (play *game–pos n char*) *char*)

   a) Evaluate each of the following functional expressions:

      (i) (winning–move? $^\triangledown$((o o – –) (o – – –) (x x – –) (– – – –)) $^\triangledown$x 3)

      (ii) (winning–move? $^\triangledown$((– – – –) (o x – –) (o x – –) (– – – –)) $^\triangledown$o 1)

      (iii) (winning–move? $^\triangledown$((– – – –) (– – – –) (x o – –) (o o x –)) $^\triangledown$x 2)

      (iv) (winning–move? $^\triangledown$((– – – –) (x o x –) (o x o –) (– – – –)) $^\triangledown$o 1)

   b) Describe in words the behavior of the function **winning–move?**.

3. Write a definition for the predicate function **exists–winning–move?** of a game position *game–pos* and a game character *char* that returns the boolean '#t' if and only if there exists a winning move for the player whose game character is *char*. (Be sure to take account of the fact that columns which are already full may not be selected.)

4. Write a definition for the predicate function **losing–move?** of a game position *game–pos*, game characters *ch1* and *ch2*, and a whole number n
from 1 through 4 such that column n is not already full that returns the
boolean '#t' if and only if, by choosing to move in col-
umn n, the player whose character is *ch1* opens the
way for his or her opponent to win in a single move.
For example, in the game position on the right the
player whose character is '○' must play in column 1 to
avoid losing. This amounts to saying that columns 2
and 4 are losing moves for this player. So if the function **losing–move?** is defined correctly,

1	2	3	4
		o	
		x	
	x	o	
	o	x	

$$(\text{losing–move? } {}^{\triangledown}((-\,-\,-\,-)\ (\text{o x}\,-\,-)\ (\text{x o x o})\ (-\,-\,-\,-))\ {}^{\triangledown}\text{o } {}^{\triangledown}\text{x } 1) \mapsto \text{\#f}$$

$$(\text{losing–move? } {}^{\triangledown}((-\,-\,-\,-)\ (\text{o x}\,-\,-)\ (\text{x o x o})\ (-\,-\,-\,-))\ {}^{\triangledown}\text{o } {}^{\triangledown}\text{x } 2) \mapsto \text{\#t}$$

$$(\text{losing–move? } {}^{\triangledown}((-\,-\,-\,-)\ (\text{o x}\,-\,-)\ (\text{x o x o})\ (-\,-\,-\,-))\ {}^{\triangledown}\text{o } {}^{\triangledown}\text{x } 4) \mapsto \text{\#t}$$

5. a) Here is a skeleton definition for the function **game–report** of a game
position *game–pos* and game characters *ch1* and *ch2*:

```
(define game-report
  (λ (game-pos ch1 ch2)
    (game-report-aux game-pos ch1 ch2 4 ▽(ok ok ok ok))))
```

```
(define game-report-aux
  (λ (game-pos ch1 ch2 n report)
    (cond
      [(zero? n) report]
      [(column-full? game-pos n)
       (game-report-aux game-pos ch1 ch2 (sub1 n)
                        (replace-nth n ▽full report))]
      [(winning-move? game-pos ch1 n)
       (game-report-aux game-pos ch1 ch2 (sub1 n)
                        (_____ n _____ report))]
      [(_____ _____ _____ _____ _____ )
       (_____ _____ _____ _____ (_____ _____ )
                        (replace-nth n _____ report))]
      [else (_____ game-pos ch1 ch2 (sub1 n) report)])))
```

This function returns a list (called 'a **game report**') containing four atoms that correspond in order from left to right to the four columns in the game position, as follows:

- If a column is full, the corresponding atom is 'full'.
- If the column is such that the player whose game character is *ch1* will win by playing in that column, the corresponding atom is 'win'.
- If the column is such that the player whose game character is *ch1* will, by playing in that column, make it possible for the other player (whose character is *ch2*) to win on the following move, the corresponding atom is 'lose'.
- If none of the first three conditions applies, the corresponding atom is 'ok'.

Consider, for example, the game position shown on the left below:

```
 1   2   3   4        1   2   3   4
+---+---+---+---+    +---+---+---+---+
|   | x | x |   |    |   |   |   |   |
+---+---+---+---+    +---+---+---+---+
|   | o | o |   |    |   |   |   |   |
+---+---+---+---+    +---+---+---+---+
|   | o | x | o |    |   |   | o |   |
+---+---+---+---+    +---+---+---+---+
| x | x | o | o |    | o | o | x | x |
+---+---+---+---+    +---+---+---+---+
```

Columns 2 and 3 are full. For the player whose character is 'x' to play in column 1 would be to invite a loss since the other player could then play in either column 1 or 4 and win. By playing in column 4, however, the player whose character is 'x' will win. Thus,

(game–report $^\triangledown$**((x – – –) (x o o x) (o x o x) (o o – –))** $^\triangledown$**x** $^\triangledown$**o)**

$\mapsto$ (lose full full win)

On the other hand, in the game position shown on the right above, the player whose character is 'x' may safely select any of columns 1, 2, and 3 (although none of these results immediately in a win), but will lose if column 4 is selected. Hence

(game–report $^\triangledown$**((o – – –) (o – – –) (x o – –) (x – – –))** $^\triangledown$**x** $^\triangledown$**o)**

$\mapsto$ (ok ok ok lose)

Complete the skeleton definition. (It involves the function **replace–nth** which you defined in Problem 8 of Problem Set 5.)

b) Evaluate each of the following functional expressions:

   (i) (game–report $^\nabla$((– – – –) (o – – –) (– – – –) (– – – –)) $^\nabla$x $^\nabla$o)

   (ii) (game–report $^\nabla$((– – – –) (o o – –) (x – – –) (– – – –)) $^\nabla$x $^\nabla$o)

   (iii) (game–report $^\nabla$((– – – –) (o o x –) (x o – –) (– – – –)) $^\nabla$x $^\nabla$o)

   (iv) (game–report $^\nabla$((– – – –) (o o x o) (x o x –) (– – – –)) $^\nabla$x $^\nabla$o)

   (v) (game–report $^\nabla$((o – – –) (o o x o) (x o x x) (– – – –)) $^\nabla$x $^\nabla$o)

6. Our next task is to devise a reasonable strategy for selecting a move on the basis of a given game report. Suppose, for example, that the game report is the list '(ok lose full win)'. Then it is clear that you should make your move in column 4. If the game report is the list '(full ok ok ok)', the choice is not so clear, although any one of columns 2 through 4 seems reasonable. Given the pessimistic game report '(lose lose lose lose)', however, the situation is bleak indeed; whichever column you pick, your opponent will be able to win. But you have to pick *some* column so that the game can reach its sad conclusion. In this case, therefore, columns 1 through 4 are all equally good (or bad!) choices.

Write a function **pick–move** of a game report containing at least one atom different from 'full' that returns a whole number n determined as follows:

- If the game report contains one or more occurrences of the atom 'win' then the function returns the position of the first such atom in the game report; otherwise,

- if the game report contains one or more occurrences of the atom 'ok', then the function returns the position of the first such atom in the game report; otherwise,

- if the game report contains only the atoms 'lose' and 'full' then the function returns the position of the first occurrence of the atom 'lose' in the game report.

– o O o –

8.5 Playing The Game

As we indicated at the beginning of the previous section, it is our intention to write a Scheme program that will enable the game of strategy we have been describing to be played between two players each of whom may be either human or machine. Specifically, each player will be an *object* having the following local state variables:

my–name the player's name.

my–char the game character used by the player.

your–char the game character used by the player's opponent.

won the number of games won by the player.

lost the number of games lost by the player.

Furthermore, each player must respond to certain messages as follows:

get-name returns the value of the variable '*my–name*'.

get-char returns the value of the variable '*my–char*'.

get-won returns the value of the variable '*won*'.

get-lost returns the value of the variable '*lost*'.

you-won increments the value of the variable '*won*' by 1.

you-lost increments the value of the variable '*lost*' by 1.

new-game returns a two-input function that inputs two game characters and assigns the first game character to the variable '*my–char*' and the second to the variable '*your–char*'.

get-move returns a one-input function that inputs a game position and returns the column number of the player's chosen move.

For the sake of convenience, we define a syntax-switching function for each of these messages. Here, for example, are the syntax-switching functions for the messages 'get-name' and 'new-game':

```
(define get-name
  (λ (player)
    (player ▽get-name)))

(define new-game
  (λ (player players-char opponents-char)
    ((player ▽new-game) players-char opponents-char)))
```

Exercise 165.

Write definitions for the syntax-switching functions for the messages 'get-char', 'get-won', 'get-lost', 'you-won', 'you-lost' and 'get-move'.

Next, we define the three-input function **play–game** of a game position and two players, the first of whom is to play next and the second of whom is his or her opponent. The definition begins as follows:

```
(define play-game
  (λ (game-pos next-player previous-player)
    (cond
      ⋮
```

It is possible that the game position is such that the game has finished. In that case, the winner is the player who has just made a move, that is, *previous-player*. So our definition continues as follows:

```
(define play-game
  (λ (game-pos next-player previous-player)
    (cond
      [(winner? game-pos (get-char previous-player))
       (game-over previous-player next-player)]
      ⋮
```

Exercise 166.

Write a definition for the function **game–over**. The function inputs two player-objects, the first of which has just won a game (which, of course, the second player-object has just lost). The function should 'inform' both players by appropriately incrementing the values of certain variables using the functions **you–won** and **you–lost**, it should display on the monitor the name of the winning player and the number of games won by each player, and it should return the atom 'done'. For example, if Fern beats Ernst, the following information might appear on the monitor:

```
(Fern won that game)
(Fern has won 12 games)
(Ernst has won 9 games)
done
```

If *previous–player* has *not* just won the game, then perhaps the game is a tie:

```
(define play–game
  (λ (game–pos next–player previous–player)
    (cond
      [(winner? game–pos (get–char previous–player))
       (game–over previous–player next–player)]
      [(tie? game–pos) ▽(The game is a tie)]
      ⋮
```

If the game has not already been won and it is not a tie, then we must determine *next–player*'s next move, make a new game position using this move, and recur on the new game position, remembering to switch the roles of *next–player* and *previous–player*:

```
(define play–game
  (λ (game–pos next–player previous–player)
    (cond
      [(winner? game–pos (get–char previous–player))
       (game–over previous–player next–player)]
      [(tie? game–pos) ▽(The game is a tie)]
      [else (let ((game–pos1 (play game–pos
                               (get–move next–player game–pos)
                               (get–char next–player))))
              (begin
                (display–game game–pos1)
                (play–game game–pos1
                        previous–player
                        next–player)))])))
```

The function **play–new–game** takes two player-objects and plays a game between them:

```
(define play–new–game
  (λ (player1 player2)
    (begin
      (new–game player1 ▽o ▽x)
      (new–game player2 ▽x ▽o)
      (play–game (make–grid) player1 player2))))
```

All player-objects of whatever type have the same local state variables, and they respond to the same messages in the same way in all cases except for the message 'get-move'. The nature of the response to this one message varies according to whether the player-object is human or machine. Obviously, computer player-objects will use the functions **pick–move** and **game–report** to make their moves. Human player-objects, on the other hand, have to be able to inform the computer which move they wish to make. To achieve this we use the primitive function **read**, which, when invoked as a thunk, has the side-effect of displaying a cursor on the computer monitor and waiting for the schemer to enter a data expression. The functional expression '(read)' then evaluates to whatever data expression is entered. The following short conversation shows the function **read** at work. (Note that the underlined data expressions are typed by the schemer; this is the only situation in which a schemer can type in red!)

```
⟹ (define s (read))
(a b c d e)
s
⟹ s
(a b c d e)
⟹ (cons 'Johnny (cons 'can (read)))
(speak Spanish)
(Johnny can speak Spanish)
⟹ _
```

The function **make–human–player** (whose definition is given on the next page) inputs the player's name and returns a human player-object.

```
(define make–human–player
  (λ (my–name)
    (let ((my–char #f) (your–char #f) (won 0) (lost 0))
      (λ (message)
        (cond
          [(eq? message ▽get–name) my–name]
          [(eq? message ▽get–char) my–char]
          [(eq? message ▽get–won) won]
          [(eq? message ▽get–lost) lost]
          [(eq? message ▽you–won)
           (begin (set! won (add1 won)) ▽done)]
          [(eq? message ▽you–lost)
           (begin (set! lost (add1 lost)) ▽done)]
          [(eq? message ▽new–game)
           (λ (ch1 ch2)
             (begin
               (set! my–char ch1)
               (set! your–char ch2)
               ▽done))]
          [(eq? message ▽get–move)
           (λ (game–pos)
             (begin
               (display (cons my–name
                              ▽(– Please type a number from 1 through 4)))
               (read)))])))))
```

Exercise 167.

Complete the skeleton definition given at the top of the next page for the one-input function **make–computer–player** that returns a computer player-object.

Exercise 168.

Suppose that **PlayerA** is defined as follows:

(define playerA (make–computer–player ▽Chip))

and that the functional expression '(new–game playerA ▽x ▽o)' is then evaluated. Evaluate the functional expression

(get–move playerA ▽((– – – –) (o x – –) (x o x –) (o o – –)))

```
(define make–computer–player
  (λ (my–name)
    (let ((my–char #f) (your–char #f) (won 0) (lost 0))
      (λ (message)
        (cond
          [(eq? message ▽get–name) _____ ]
          [(eq? message ▽get–char) _____ ]
          [(eq? message ▽get–won) _____ ]
          [(eq? message ▽get–lost) _____ ]
          [(eq? message ▽you–won)
           (begin (set! won (add1 won)) ▽done)]
          [(eq? message ▽you–lost)
           (begin ( _____ _____ ( _____ _____ )) ▽done)]
          [(eq? message ▽new–game)
           (λ (ch1 ch2)
             (begin
               (set! my–char ch1)
               ( _____ _____ _____ )
               ▽done))]
          [(eq? message ▽get–move)
           (λ (game–pos)
             ( _____
               ( _____ game–pos my–char your–char)))])))))
```

Exercise 169.

Suppose that **PlayerB** and **PlayerC** are defined as follows:

(define playerB (make–computer–player ▽Tick))

(define playerC (make–computer–player ▽Tock))

and that the functional expression

(play–new–game playerB playerC)

is then evaluated. Who wins the game?

One of the problems with computer players is that they play in a totally predictable way, never improving or getting any worse. In the next problem set we give computer players a strategy for *learning* about the game, so that the more they play the more skillful they become.

PROBLEM SET 15

1. When you completed the definition for the function **make–computer–player** you were probably made aware of the fact that, each time it is the computer player's turn to play, it calculates a game report for the current game position, even though it may have faced exactly the same game position in many previous games. This represents an entirely unnecessary duplication of effort which can be avoided if we introduce a new local state variable, '*knowledge*', for computer players whose value will be an association list in which the player keeps a record of all the game positions it has ever encountered. Each pair in the association list *knowledge* associates a game position with the corresponding game report. Then, when the player receives the message 'get-move', it returns a function which inputs a game position and behaves as follows:

   - If the game position is the first component of one of the pairs in the association list *knowledge*, then the corresponding game report is retrieved and the computer player picks its next move accordingly.

   - Otherwise, the player calculates the game report for the game position and adds a pair to the association list *knowledge* relating the game position to the game report before picking its next move in accordance with the newly-calculated game report.

   In order to carry out this intention, we add the new local state variable '*knowledge*' to the let-frame at the beginning of the definition for the function **make–computer–player** and bind it initially to the null list. In addition, we replace the clause that deals with the computer player's response to the message 'get-move' by a clause that causes its behavior to match our description above. The modified definition is given in Figure 8.6 on page 291. Notice that this modified definition involves the function **lookup** (which was defined on page 135) and a new function **extend–knowledge**, which inputs a game position, an association list, and two game characters, and returns an association list which is determined as explained on page 292.

```
(define make–computer–player
  (λ (my-name)
    (let ((knowledge ▽()) (my-char #f) (your-char #f)
          (won 0) (lost 0))
      (λ (message)
        (cond
          [(eq? message ▽get–name) my-name]
          [(eq? message ▽get–char) my-char]
          [(eq? message ▽get–won) won]
          [(eq? message ▽get–lost) lost]
          [(eq? message ▽you–won)
           (begin (set! won (add1 won)) ▽done)]
          [(eq? message ▽you–lost)
           (begin (set! lost (add1 lost)) ▽done)]
          [(eq? message ▽new–game)
           (λ (ch1 ch2)
             (begin
               (set! my-char ch1)
               (set! your-char ch2)
               ▽done))]
          [(eq? message ▽get–move)
           (λ (game-pos)
             (begin
               (set! knowledge
                     (extend-knowledge game-pos
                                       knowledge
                                       my-char
                                       your-char))
               (pick–move (lookup game-pos knowledge))))])))))
```

Figure 8.6: *A knowledgeable computer player (see Problem 1).*

- If there is a pair in the association list whose first data expression is the given game position, then **extend–knowledge** returns the input association list.

- Otherwise, **extend–knowledge** returns the input association list with one pair added whose first component is the game position and whose second component is the corresponding game report for the player using the *first* of the two game characters.

Using the function **assoc–f** (defined in Problem 13 of Problem Set 11 on page 218), write a definition for the function **extend–knowledge**.

2. The association list **knowledge** has one major flaw. Before it makes each move, a computer player checks to see if the current game position occurs as the first data expression in the association list **knowledge**. Of course, this involves a (possibly large) number of comparisons of lists—and the lists we are using to represent game positions are not exactly simple ones—which is a very time-consuming business. We can speed things up by *encoding* game positions, that is, by devising a system whereby each game position is assigned a code-word (called its '**position code**'), which is an atom chosen in such a way that different positions are assigned different code-words. Then, if we replace (the representation of) each game position in the association list **knowledge** by its position code, we will be able to check through the association list using the function **eq?** to compare atoms, and such comparisons produce results virtually instantaneously.

There are a number of encoding schemes that could be employed, but the following is perhaps among the simplest:

> 'Flatten' the list that represents the game position by removing all internal parentheses, and then create the desired code-word by 'pushing together' all the atoms in the resulting list. For example, the code-word for the game position
>
> ((o o x o) (o x – –) (– – – –) (x o x –))
>
> should be the atom 'ooxoox––––––xox–'.

a) Using the functions **accumulate**, **append**, and **implode**, write a definition for the function **pos–code** of a game position that returns the game position's code-word.

b) Rewrite the definition for the function **make–computer–player** given in Figure 8.6 and the definition you have just written in Problem 1 for the function **extend–knowledge** so that they manipulate the association list *knowledge* on the assumption that the first component of each pair in this list is a position code rather than a game position.

3. In this problem we give computer players the power to learn from their mistakes. The algorithm we use is as follows. In each game it plays, in addition to the information stored in the association list *knowledge*, the computer player keeps a record in another association list of each game position it meets together with the column that it selects. This second association list is bound to a new local state variable '*this–game*'. If the player subsequently wins the game, it takes no further action, but if it loses it *backtracks* through the game to discover at which stage it made its fatal error, and makes a note in the association list *knowledge* never to make that mistake again. To achieve this goal we redefine the function **make–computer–player** once more, as shown in Figure 8.7 on page 294.

You will notice that, in its response to the message 'you-lost', this new definition makes use of the function **backtrack**. Our purpose in this problem is to give you the task of writing a definition for this new function. Before you will be able to tackle such an assignment, however, you will need to become familiar with what the function is meant to achieve. So we now 'talk' our way through a typical game between **playerA**, a human player, and **playerB**, a computer player of this new type. This is how we start:

```
⟹ (define playerA (make–human–player 'Fern))
playerA
⟹ (define playerB (make–computer–player 'Chip))
playerB
⟹ (play–new–game playerA playerB)
⋮
```

On receiving the message 'new-game', **playerB** sets the value of the local state variable '*this–game*' to be the null list.[8] Then, **playerA** makes the first move:

---

[8] 'Initialization' of this type is always prudent because the values of local state variables may well have been changed during the course of previous games.

```
(define make-computer-player
  (λ (my-name)
    (let ((knowledge ▽()) (my-char #f) (your-char #f)
          (won 0) (lost 0) (this-game ▽()))
      (λ (message)
        (cond
          [(eq? message ▽get-name) my-name]
          [(eq? message ▽get-char) my-char]
          [(eq? message ▽get-won) won]
          [(eq? message ▽get-lost) lost]
          [(eq? message ▽you-won)
           (begin (set! won (add1 won)) ▽done)]
          [(eq? message ▽you-lost)
           (begin
             (set! lost (add1 lost))
             (set! knowledge (backtrack knowledge this-game))
             ▽done)]
          [(eq? message ▽new-game)
           (λ (ch1 ch2)
             (begin
               (set! my-char ch1) (set! your-char ch2)
               (set! this-game ▽()) ▽done))]
          [(eq? message ▽get-move)
           (λ (game-pos)
             (let ((this-pos-code (pos-code game-pos)))
               (begin
                 (set! knowledge
                       (extend-knowledge game-pos knowledge
                                         my-char your-char))
                 (let ((my-move (pick-move (lookup this-pos-code
                                                   knowledge))))
                   (begin
                     (set! this-game
                           (cons (pair this-pos-code my-move)
                                 this-game))
                     my-move)))))])))))
```

Figure 8.7: *A learning computer player (see Problem 3).*

```
(Fern - Please type a number from 1 through 4)2
(1 2 3 4)
(- - - -)
(- - - -)
(- - - -)
(- o - -)
  ⋮
```

The interpreter then requests **playerB** to make a move. Since this is the first game that this player has played, the value of the local state variable *knowledge* is currently the null list, so, in view of the fact that the position code for this game position is the atom '----o-----------', **playerB** updates the list *knowledge* to contain the pair

$$(\text{----o----------- (ok ok ok ok))}$$

and conses the pair '(----o----------- 1)' onto the (currently null) list *this–game* thereby producing the list '((----o----------- 1))' and recording the fact that it elects to move in column 1:

```
(1 2 3 4)
(- - - -)
(- - - -)
(- - - -)
(x o - -)
(Fern - Please type a number from 1 through 4)3
(1 2 3 4)
(- - - -)
(- - - -)
(- - - -)
(x o o -)
  ⋮
```

Now, this game position has position code 'x---o---o-------', so **playerB** changes the value of the lists *knowledge* and *this–game* as follows:

$$\textit{knowledge} : ((\text{x---o---o------- (lose lose lose ok))}$$
$$(\text{----o----------- (ok ok ok ok)))}$$
$$\textit{this–game} : ((\text{x---o---o------- 4) (----o----------- 1))}$$

The game then continues:

```
(1 2 3 4)
(- - - -)
(- - - -)
(- - - -)
(x o o x)
(Fern - Please type a number from 1 through 4)2
(1 2 3 4)
(- - - -)
(- - - -)
(- o - -)
(x o o x)
⋮
```

The code-word for this game position is 'x---oo--o---x---', so **playerB** updates the lists *knowledge* and *this−game* as follows:

knowledge : ((x---oo--o---x--- (lose ok lose lose))
              (x---o---o------- (lose lose lose ok))
              (----o---------- (ok ok ok ok)))
this−game : ((x---oo--o---x--- 2) (x---o---o------- 4)
               (----o---------- 1))

and the game goes on:

```
(1 2 3 4)
(- - - -)
(- x - -)
(- o - -)
(x o o x)
(Fern - Please type a number from 1 through 4)3
(1 2 3 4)
(- - - -)
(- x - -)
(- o o -)
(x o o x)
⋮
```

The code-word for this game position is 'x---oox-oo--x---', and the corresponding game report is the list '(lose lose lose lose)':

knowledge : ((x---oox-oo--x--- (lose lose lose lose))
 (x---oo--o---x--- (lose ok lose lose))
 (x---o---o------- (lose lose lose ok))
 (----o---------- (ok ok ok ok)))

this-game : ((x---oox-oo--x--- 1) (x---oo--o---x--- 2)
 (x---o---o------- 4) (----o---------- 1))

The game is then won by **playerA**:

```
(1 2 3 4)
(- - - -)
(- x - -)
(x o o -)
(x o o x)
(Fern - Please type a number from 1 through 4)4
(1 2 3 4)
(- - - -)
(- x - -)
(x o o o)
(x o o x)
(Fern won that game)
(Fern has won 1 games)
(Chip has won 0 games)
done
⟹ _
```

Let us now examine the bindings for the local state variables '*knowledge*' and '*this-game*' with a view to discovering what Chip's mistake was. The last move Chip made is recorded as the first data expression in the list *this-game*; it was to play in column 1 in response to the game position with code 'x---oox-oo--x---'. From the entry for this game position in the list *knowledge* we see that by the time this position had been reached, Chip had effectively already lost. It is certain, therefore, that Chip's next-to-last move was in effect a losing move. So Chip should update the list *knowledge* to indicate this fact by changing the atom 'ok' in the entry for the previous game position (that is, the one with code 'x---oo--o---x---') to 'lose'. As a result, this entry becomes the pair

```
(x---oo--o---x--- (lose lose lose lose))
```

and it follows that Chip's third-from-last move was also a losing move. His third-from-last move was to select column 4 in response to the position with code 'x---o---o-------', so we change the corresponding entry in the list **knowledge** from the atom 'ok' to the atom 'lose', thereby producing the pair

```
(x---o---o------- (lose lose lose lose))
```

Once again, we see that this is a no-win position for Chip, so it must have been his very first move that was effectively the losing move. His first move was to select column 1 in response to the position with code '----o-----------', so we change the corresponding entry in the list **knowledge** so that this position is now associated with the game report '(lose ok ok ok)'.

Thus, after completing the process of backtracking, Chip's local state variable '**knowledge**' will be bound to the list

```
((x---oox-oo--x--- (lose lose lose lose))
 (x---oo--o---x--- (lose lose lose lose))
 (x---o---o------- (lose lose lose lose))
 (----o----------- (lose ok ok ok)))
```

As you can see, by playing just this one game Chip has learned a considerable lesson about the game's strategy, namely, that the player who plays second must never select column 1 if the opponent makes his or her first move in column 2.

a) The predicate function **no–win–position?** inputs a position code **pcode** and an association list of pairs that associate position codes with game reports which is such that one of the pairs has **pcode** as its first component. It returns the boolean '#t' if and only if the game report associated with game position **pcode** contains neither the atom 'win' nor the atom 'ok'. Write a definition for the function **no–win–position?**.

b) Write a definition for the function **change–to–lose** of two inputs:

   • a pair **p** containing a position code **pcode** as its first component and a column number **col** as its second component, and

- an association list **knowledge** containing position code/game report pairs such that one of the pairs has game position **pcode** as its first component,

that returns the association list **knowledge** with the entry for column **col** in the game report associated with position **pcode** changed to the atom 'lose'. (You may find the function **remove** useful. See page 136.)

c) Let the function **backtrack–helper** be defined as follows:

```
(define backtrack–helper
  (λ (knowledge move no–win–f)
    (let ((new–knowledge (change–to–lose move knowledge)))
      (cond
        [(no–win–position? (first move) new–knowledge)
         (no–win–f new–knowledge)]
        [else new–knowledge ]))))
```

Complete the following definition for the function **backtrack**:

```
(define backtrack
  (λ (knowledge game)
    (cond
      [(null? game) knowledge]
      [else (backtrack–helper

             _____
             (_____ game)
             (λ (new–know)
                (_____ _____ (_____ game))))])))
```

$$- \mathrm{o\,O\,o} -$$

Having completed this problem set, we know how to create two (or more) computer objects that are capable of improving their playing abilities. The obvious next step is to define two such players and make them play a large number of games (a thousand, say). To facilitate this, the function **play–games** of a natural number n and two players will be useful:

```
(define play–games
  (λ (n player1 player2)
    (cond
      [(zero? n) ▽done)]
      [else (begin (play–new–game player1 player2)
                   (play–games (sub1 n) player1 player2))]))))
```

How long will it be before the computer player who plays first discovers a sure-fire winning strategy? We leave this for you to discover.

There are a number of ways in which the behavior of computer players can be improved further. First, an element of randomness can be introduced. The primitive function **random** inputs a natural number n and returns a whole number from 0 through $n-1$, chosen at random. For example, the functional expression '(**add1** (**random 4**))' selects a natural number from 1 through 4. You could use this function, if you like, to modify the definition for the function **pick–move**.

In addition, the definitions for the functions **pick–move** and **backtrack** can be improved so that the computer player takes account of the fact that a game position and its mirror image are very similar. (The following two game positions, for example, are mirror images of each other:

1	2	3	4
		x	o
	x	o	o

1	2	3	4
o	x		
o	o	x	

A strategy for winning one of these games immediately gives rise to a winning strategy for the other by 'reversing' all references to column numbers.) If Chip had been defined to have this ability then he would realize not only that he should not respond to an 'o' in column 2 by playing an 'x' in column 1 but also that he should not play in column 4 if his opponent starts the game by playing in column 3. This optimization not only saves space (by making it unnecessary for the list *knowledge* to contain entries for both a game position and its mirror image) but it also means that the computer player improves its skill at twice the usual rate.

If you (a human!) decide to play against the computer, then you will find it more interesting if you allow the computer player to move first. How

many games can you win before the computer finds a winning strategy? A
clever schemer will win many games by continually changing strategy, but
eventually the computer must surely triumph.

Having thoroughly investigated the game on a 4-by-4 grid, it is interesting
to generalize the program we have developed so that it plays games on an
n-by-n grid, where winning lines must contain m adjacent identical game
characters, and m and n are natural numbers such that $n \geq 4$ and $n \geq m \geq 3$.
The process of generalizing the program is not hard. You should start by
defining the following global variables:

(define *columns* 4)
(define *rows* 4)
(define *winning–line* 3)

and then rewriting all the definitions that rely on these quantities so that
they use these global variables. The only remaining difficulty is then to
generalize the algorithm for transforming game positions so that winning
rising diagonals become winning rows—but this is not hard. To test out your
generalized program, you could, for example, play a game in which to win
you must get four characters in a line on a 5-by-5 grid. Is there a winning
strategy for this game? Perhaps your computer can answer this question!

Then there's always the possibility of allowing more than two players to
participate in the game, or playing in three dimensions on a cubical lattice,
or ...

$- \mathrm{o} \, \mathrm{O} \, \mathrm{o} -$

Bibliography

Abelson, Harold, and Gerald Jay Sussman with Julie Sussman. 1985. *Structure and Interpretation of Computer Programs*. Cambridge, MA: MIT Press.

Dybvig, R. Kent. 1987. *The Scheme Programming Language*. Englewood Cliffs, NJ: Prentice–Hall.

Friedman, Daniel P., and Matthias Felleisen. 1988. *The Little LISPer*. Cambridge, MA: MIT Press.

McCarthy, John. 1978. The history of Lisp. In *Proceedings of the ACM SIGPLAN Conference on the History of Programming Languages*.

Smullyan, Raymond. 1985. *To Mock A Mockingbird*. New York, NY: Alfred A. Knopf.

Springer, George, and Daniel P. Friedman. 1989. *Scheme and the Art of Programming*. Cambridge, MA: MIT Press.

Selected Answers

Exercise 1 (page 3).

Parts (a), (d), and (f) are atoms. Parts (b), (c), and (e) are not atoms since (b) and (e) involve spaces, which are not characters, and (c) is not written in red.

Exercise 4 (page 8).

a) Three: 'heavens', '(to)', and '((Betsy))'.

c) One: '((( ) ( )))'.

Exercise 5 (page 10).

b) ((( )))   d) No output; the input is not a list.

Exercise 7 (page 12). b) Sentence (iv).

Exercise 10 (page 14).

b) No output; the **rest** machine cannot ingest atoms!

d) (five)

Exercise 15 (page 17).

b) Impossible. The second input is not a list. (As every elementary school child knows, two into one won't go!)

d) First input: hand; second input: ( )

f) First input: gift; second input: any non-null list containing exactly one data expression, the list '((for you))' for example.

Exercise 17 (pages 18–19).   a)   c)

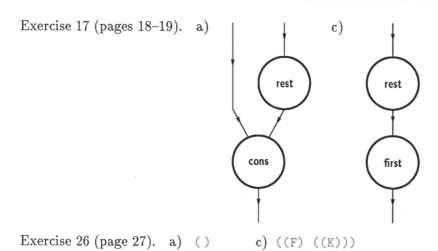

Exercise 26 (page 27).   a) ( )   c) ((F) ((K)))

PROBLEM SET 1
(pp. 28–30)

1.   c) The diagram on
       the right shows
       one possible so-
       lution. Other so-
       lutions have in-
       puts and outputs
       that are 'split'
       differently.

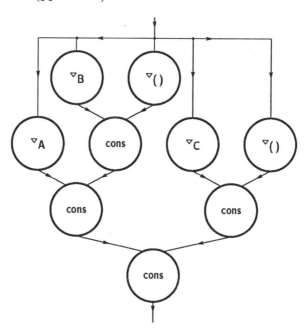

$- \text{o} \, \text{O} \, \text{o} -$

Exercise 32 (pages 38–39).

    b) Impossible. The replacement for '*a*' is not a non-null list.

    f) `#f`   j) `#f`

Exercise 33 (page 40). a) `C`

Exercise 36 (page 45). b) `#t`   d) `two`

PROBLEM SET 2
(page 47)

2. **(first (rest *s*))**. (Other solutions are possible.)

– o O o –

Exercise 37 (pages 51–52).

    a) **lambda (*a b*) (cons (first *a*) *b*))**

Exercise 48 (page 63).

a	*b*	(and2 *a b*)
`#t`	`#t`	`#t`
`#t`	`#f`	`#f`
`#f`	`#t`	`#f`
`#f`	`#f`	`#f`

The only situation in which the function **and2** returns the boolean '`#t`' is when both the first *and* the second inputs are the boolean '`#t`'.

Exercise 54 (page 69).

One possibility is as follows:

```
(define combine                     (define combine1
  (λ (a b)                            (λ (a b)
    (cond                               (cond
      [(bothatom? a b)                    [(bothlist? a b)
       (cons a (cons b ▽()))]              (cons b a)]
      [else (combine1 a b)]))))           [else (combine2 a b)]))))


(define bothatom?                   (define bothlist?
  (λ (a b)                            (λ (a b)
    (and2 (atom? a)                     (nor (atom? a)
          (atom? b))))                       (atom? b))))


                    (define combine2
                      (λ (a b)
                        (cond
                          [(atom? a) (cons a b)]
                          [else (cons b a)]))))
```

Exercise 55 (pages 74–75).

List (e) is a lat. Lists (a), (c), (f), and (h) are not lats, since enough of these lists is visible for us to be able to tell that they contain non-atoms, that is, lists. There is not enough information for us to judge lists (b), (d), and (g) one way or the other.

PROBLEM SET 3
(pp. 84–86)

7. (define equal?
```
   (λ (a b)
     (cond
       [(and2 (atom? a) (atom? b)) (eq? a b)]
       [(xor (atom? a) (atom? b)) #f]
       [(and2 (null? a) (null? b)) #t]
       [(xor (null? a) (null? b)) #f]
       [else (and2 (equal? (first a) (first b))
                   (equal? (rest a) (rest b)))]))))
```

Each occurrence of 'xor' may be replaced by 'inor' in this definition since each clause involving 'xor' is preceded by one involving 'and2', which 'removes' the one situation in which **xor** and **inor** disagree.

– o O o –

Exercise 65 (page 90).
    a) (define getfirsts
        (λ (*s*)
          (cond
            [(null? *s*) ▽()]
            [else (cons (first (first *s*)) (getfirsts (rest *s*)))]])))

PROBLEM SET 4
(pp. 90–94)

2. (define double
    (λ (*a s*)
      (cond
        [(null? *s*) ▽()]
        [(eq? (first *s*) *a*) (cons *a s*)]
        [else (cons (first *s*) (double *a* (rest *s*)))]])))

8.   b) If the problem is interpreted as demanding that the function **burrow** shall *only* accept lists, then a solution such as the one on the left below is required. On the other hand, if the broader interpretation is adopted that any function will do so long as it behaves as specified when the input is a list, then—strangely enough—a simpler definition is possible; for example, the one on the right below.

```
(define burrow                          (define burrow1
   (λ (s)                                  (λ (s)
      (cond                                   (cond
         [(null? s) ▽()]                          [(atomic? s) s]
         [(atomic? (first s)) (first s)]          [else (burrow1 (first s))]])))
         [else (burrow (first s))]])))
```

d) (define reverse
     (λ (s)
       (cond
         [(null? s) ▽()]
         [else (cons–to–end (first s) (reverse (rest s)))]])))

h) (define last   Alternatively:
     (λ (s)
       (cond   (define last
         [(null? (rest s)) (first s)]   (λ (s)
         [else (last (rest s))]])))   (first (reverse s))))

– o O o –

Exercise 68 (page 97).

a) (define zero?   b) (define add1   c) (define sub1
     (λ (n)   (λ (n)   (λ (n)
       (null? n)))   (cons n ▽())))   (first n)))

d) (define number?
     (λ (a)
       (cond
         [(atom? a) #f]
         [(null? a) #t]
         [(null? (rest a)) (number? (first a))]
         [else #f])))

PROBLEM SET 5
(pp. 104–111)

7. (define position
     (λ (a r)
       (cond
         [(equal? a (first r)) 1]
         [else (add1 (position a (rest r)))]])))

8. (define replace–nth
      (λ (*k* *a* *r*)
        (cond
          [(one? *k*) (cons *a* (rest *r*))]
          [else (cons (first *r*) (replace–nth (sub1 *k*) *a* (rest *r*)))])))

16. b) (define fib   (define fib–help
          (λ (*n*)   (λ (*n* *a* *b*)
            (fib–help (sub1 *n*) 0 1)))   (cond
                                                    [(zero? *n*) *b*]
                                                    [else (fib–help
                                                            (sub1 *n*)
                                                            b (+ *a* *b*))])))

– o O o –

PROBLEM SET 6
(pp. 117–118)

1.   c) (define pair   4. (define sumQ
          (λ (*a* *b*)   (λ (*r*)
            (cons   (cond
              a   [(null? *r*) $^\triangledown$(0 1)]
              (cons *b* $^\triangledown$()))))   [else (+Q (first *r*)
                                                            (sumQ (rest *r*)))])))

– o O o –

Exercise 84 (page 136).
   (define switch   (define rev–pair
      (λ (*alist*)   (λ (*pr*)
        (cond   (pair (second *pr*)
          [(null? *alist*) $^\triangledown$()]   (first *pr*))))
          [else (cons
                  (rev–pair (first *alist*))
                  (switch (rest *alist*)))])))

Alternatively, the function **reverse** could be used in the definition
for **switch** in place of **rev–pair**.

Exercise 88 (page 146). a) Dawson Birch.

Exercise 106 (page 195). a) (define vector?
                                 (λ (r)
                                     (list–checker? number? r)))

Exercise 107 (pages 195–196).
    c) (define all–divide–24?   (define div–of–24?
       (λ (vec)   (λ (a)
        (list–checker?   (divides? a 24)))
          div–of–24? vec)))

PROBLEM SET 7
(pages 199–201)

3. b) (i) (define append
              (λ (r s) (accumulate cons r s)))
       (ii) (define cons–to–end
              (λ (a r) (accumulate cons (cons a ▽()) r)))

– o O o –

Exercise 112 (page 204).
    a) (derived (s) (cons (quote (a b c d e)) s) ())
    b) ((a b c d e) Fred Jane Mary)

PROBLEM SET 11
(pages 213–218)

13. b) (define assoc
       (λ (r alist)
        (assoc–f r alist (λ (x) x) #f)))

– o O o –

Exercise 130 (pages 223–224).

    a) (2 3 5 7 11 13 17 19 23 29)

    b) The function **sieve** of a vector returns the vector, having removed all those numbers that are multiples of some preceding number(s) in the vector. In part (a), because the input vector begins with the smallest prime, **sieve** returns all the prime numbers less than or equal to 30.

Exercise 135 (page 227). (define M
                (λ (*m n*)
                  (accumulate + 0
                    (filter (λ (*x*) (prime? (add1 *x*)))
                    (interval *m n*)))))

Exercise 137 (page 232).

    a) #f   b) 1

    c) On the basis of our list-based description of function descriptors and the rules for evaluating lambda-expressions, and supposing that the function **tail** is defined as on page 232, the given functional expression should evaluate to

```
(2 derived ()
      (quote ())
      (() () ((s (1 derived ()
                   (cons
                    2
                    (lambda ()
                     (quote ())))) ())))))
```

    If, however, you are using the *EdScheme* interpreter and you take advantage of the fact that it provides **tail** as a primitive function, then the given functional expression evaluates to

```
(2 derived () (quote ()) (() ())))
```

Exercise 140 (page 236).   a) (define stream–nth
                      (λ (*k s*)
                      (cond
                        [(= *k* 1) (head *s*)]
                        [else (stream–nth (sub1 *k*) (tail *s*))])))

Exercise 159 (page 272).

d) (define play
   (λ (*game–pos n char*)
      (replace–nth *n*
         (play–in–column *char* (nth *n game–pos*))
         game–pos)))

   (define play–in–column
      (λ (*char col*)
         (cond
            [(eq? (first *col*) ▽–) (cons *char* (rest *col*))]
            [else (cons (first *col*)
                        (play–in–column *char* (rest *col*)))])))

(This procedure uses the function **replace–nth** which was defined in Problem 8 of Problem Set 5.)

Exercise 161 (pages 274–275).

a) (define transpose
   (λ (*s*)
      (cond
         [(null? *s*) ▽()]
         [else (cons (getfirsts *s*)
                     (transpose (cutfirsts *s*)))])))

PROBLEM SET 15
(pp. 290–299)

1. (define extend–knowledge
   (λ (*game–pos alist ch1 ch2*)
      (assoc–f
         game–pos
         alist
         (λ (*x*) *alist*)
         (λ (*x*) (cons (pair *x* (game–report *x ch1 ch2*)) *alist*)))))

3.   c) (define backtrack
       (λ (*knowledge game*)
         (cond
           [(null? *game*) *knowledge*]
           [else (backtrack–helper
                   knowledge
                   (first *game*)
                   (λ (*new–know*)
                     (backtrack *new-know* (rest *game*))))])))

– o O o –

Index

Numerals refer to page numbers in the text; a numeral followed by 'ex' refers to an exercise or problem on that page; a numeral followed by '*' refers to a footnote on that page.